VIOLETA PARRA

BY THE WHIM OF THE WIND

I sing the difference between truth and deceit.
Otherwise I don't sing.

Violeta Parra

KAREN KERSCHEN

VIOLETA PARRA

BY THE WHIM OF THE WIND

ABQ Press
Albuquerque, NM

Cover typography and design by Amanda Marie Campbell
Cover illustrations by Karen Kerschen
Author photo by Sandy D. Sommers
Drawings throughout by Karen Kerschen
Statuette on back cover and reproduction of copper plaque on subtitle page
were bought at street vendors from folk artisans in Chile.

Grateful acknowledgment is made to Isabel Parra and Ediciones Michay,
S.A. for permission to excerpt Violeta Parra prose and poetry in *El Libro Mayor de Violeta Parra*.
Grateful acknowledgment is made to Patricio Manns and Ediciones Jucar, for
permission to excerpt from *Violeta Parra: La Guitarra Indocile*.
Allen Ginsberg prose and poetry is used with permission of the Allen
Ginsberg Estate.
Reproductions of Violeta Parra's art provided by the Louvre archives.
For links to Violeta Parra resources, visit http://karenkerschen.com

www.abqpress.com

ABQ Press
Albuquerque, New Mexico
www.abqpress.com

ISBN 978-0-9843024-1-3

Contents

The Commandment

Puerto Montt quivers
with a deep festering rage;
what I am witnessing
is the End of the World.
In a bellowing voice
I beg of God, Answer me!
Why did You order this punishment?
He answers with eloquence:
He has lost patience with me
and it was time to clean house.

Above the trees bordering the plaza, gulls chattered loudly, while overhead, clouds moved inland off the salt sea bay, carried by a chilly ceaseless breeze. People hurried to and from the market for last-minute shopping. Tomorrow, the twenty-first of May, 1960, would be *La Fiesta de la República*, a Chilean national holiday commemorating Arturo Prat and the naval victory at Iquique, and all the shops would be closed.

The Post and Telegraph office stayed open later than was customary to accommodate the public before the holiday. Communication to other points in the country could be tenuous in Puerto Montt, a thousand kilometers south of the nation's capital, Santiago, and the last city of any size on the mainland. In the bay and beyond lie thousands of islands of an archipelago that comprises the southwestern edge of the continent.

Two women entered the telegraph office, still intent on a conversation begun outdoors as they queued up. While the postal clerk assisted the patrons ahead of them, the older woman wrote something on a slip of paper and showed it to her companion.

"What do you think of this?" Silvia laughed mirthlessly. When her turn came, the older woman handed the same paper to the clerk behind the counter.

"*Buenos días.* I want to send this cable," she said sweetly.

The girl straightened and proceeded to transcribe the message, but as she read it, her forehead creased into a startled frown. "*Señora,*" she said, "this is not possible."

"Why not? Isn't this the telegraph office?"

"Yes it is, but this is an impossible message." The woman glared at her.

"But *señora,* a message like this could cost me my job." The woman drummed her hand on the counter in a percussive rhythm and demanded to speak to the manager.

The girl disappeared into an office and soon returned, accompanied by a fellow with provincial features and an easy-going air.

He noted that the woman awaiting his attention was in her early forties, small and dressed plainly; her black hair draped the back of her wool shawl. Pockmarks scarred her olive complexion. Her dark eyes darted around the room and came to rest on him now, as he faced her across the counter with her slip of paper in his hands.

"Violeta Parra, I understand you're singing here later today?" He flashed his friendliest smile.

"Yes, tonight at the *Casa del Arte*." She gestured toward Silvia. "A whole group of us are performing. Will you be going?"

"But of course. I'm looking forward to it. I've seen the posters everywhere. How long are you staying here in town?"

"Just two or three days. We've already performed in Valdivia and Osorno. This is the last stop on our tour; the day after tomorrow we return to Santiago."

"Cultural tours like yours are a treat for us; this region is so isolated. We get to see artists like you only a couple of times a year. I happen to know that people from all over the province are coming to the concert."

She smiled appreciatively. "It takes real effort to get here. The halls are small. People prefer to go to the movies. Sometimes these ventures turn out to be a wretched loss of time and money for us."

There was silence. On guard for a change in tone, the man proceeded cautiously. "What is this about?" he asked, gesturing with the slip of paper.

"The cable? Well, we were walking from the square and when I noticed your office was still open, I decided to send a cable." His eyebrows furrowed with incredulity. In fact, the girl had not exaggerated; the woman was serious. He read aloud.

Listen, God. Won't you command an earthquake for me?
Violeta Parra

"All right, no problem at all," he said. "But I need your address. Write it down and I'll see that it's delivered."

"*Carpa de la Reina*," Violeta mumbled, identifying only the circus tent she occupied on parkland in a suburb of Santiago.

"Name of the street, *señora?*"

"No. There isn't any street or number. Just *Carpa de la Reina, Santiago de Chile.*"

"Perfect," said the man.

"How much is that?"

"Ah, don't worry. The addressee will pay for it."

"Good." She closed her purse and prepared to leave. "I hope that everybody will come tonight?"

"Don't worry, I'll be there with all my friends," the man promised.

Violeta and Silvia went outside, arranged to meet later, and parted company. Violeta crossed the plaza on a path paved with shards of clamshells. A row of trees shielded her from the wind. A clock sounded 1:00 p.m. She paused to inhale the briny air and listen to a *tonada* played by a blind organ grinder, who offered to tell her fortune. For a few coins, she watched as his squawking parrot withdrew a picture card from a deck. The man held the card very close to his face, considered it, and then predicted an unexpected visit. Satisfied, Violeta returned to her second-story room in a ramshackle hotel around the corner from the plaza.

The concert tour, commissioned by the University of Chile, consisted of Violeta Parra, her children, Ángel and Isabel Parra; Cuncumén, a seven-member folkloric group with whom Silvia Urbina sang; Ricardo Moller, the sound engineer; and Don Julio Alegría, the group's coordinator. The musicians had performed in Temuco on Friday night. Saturday, a mild earthquake signaled the possibility of further seismic activity, yet realizing they were unlikely to return soon to this remote locale, they decided to continue their tour. They gave a concert in Valdivia that night and on Sunday morning flew south to Puerto Montt. After registering at their respective hotels, several of them wired their families of their safe arrival.

Since it was still early, a majority opted to go sightseeing: a boat ride to the island of Tenglo for lunch of *paila marina*, a regional seafood stew; then back to the mainland for a bus ride north to scenic Lake Llanquihue, where they hoped to glimpse the Osorno volcano. Silvia wasn't feeling well and stayed behind to rest.

Violeta also chose to forego the sightseeing, because she wanted to mingle with the locals. Carrying a portable tape recorder, she joined the sightseers for the trolley ride to the docks at Ángelmo, but remained on the wharf to talk to the fishermen, woodsmen, and their wives, many of whom lived on the islands offshore. Choppy seas that have cut steep fjords, often rendering the islands inaccessible, lap the labyrinthine archipelago. The isolation has made for unique songs and customs.

As she had hoped, Violeta met a loquacious boatsman and recorded thirty minutes of conversation, which she promised to replay for him on a full-sized tape recorder back at her hotel room. She left the wharf at about three that afternoon and returned to her hotel for a late lunch. As she was being served dessert, seismic tremors began.

Violeta ran upstairs, two flights, to her room. In an instant, the tremors magnified into jolts. "I was thrown onto the bed, which was propelled across the room and against the door. I grabbed the doorknob. The door began to fan open and shut with me. I felt the floor begin to give way as a beam toppled over and a wall collapsed. I began to scream, 'Dear God, enough already,' repeating just those words, but increasing in intensity until I was howling. I was sure I was going to die."

An eternity passed. Everywhere, the hotel ripped apart yet remained upright though tilted. The stairway was pushed up and at a peculiar angle. By the time the quake ended, Violeta had become hollow as a shell. Disoriented, she went downstairs, wimpering.

She stood in the doorway for a long time, taking in the desolate picture of people pouring into the street. Women on their knees praying, men screaming. "Only in that moment did it occur to me to think of my companions. Then I heard a voice calling me from a distance. It was Silvia Urbina, of Cuncumen. We embraced, crying."

The quake transformed the city into a metropolis of Hell. Iron rails broke free of their spikes and writhed into serpentine tangles. Jagged fissures split open roadbeds. The force of stone against cobbled stone sent debris flying into ominous dustdevils. From the mountains came rumblings of boulders that plummeted and triggered landslides, mercilessly crushing entire villages of people and animals. With the earthquakes came volcanic eruptions. Dormant cindercones coughed tongues of blaze heavenward and spewed ashen rock. A deafening Apocalypse encompassed everything.

Then rainfall sent desperate, homeless victims darting around in panic through the streets of Puerto Montt looking for dry shelter. Violeta and Silvia took refuge with scores of others in the framework of a high school under construction. Silvia tried to distract Violeta from obsessing on her fear for her children, Isabel and Ángel.

After lunch, Isabel, Ángel, and their fellow sightseers were just returning from Tenglo Island by rowboat across a narrow channel when the quake hit. Suddenly the placid waters grew treacherous. Taller and taller swells rocked the boat, until it capsized and threw everyone into the water. Only Julio and Ricardo could swim. Quickly they righted the boat and helped the others grab hold. The currents carried the tiny vessel back to the island. Everyone survived.

It was 11:00 p.m. by the time Ángel, Isabel, Julio, and the others reached the mainland. On seeing the destruction of the hotel where Violeta was staying, they sought out the public shelter, and there located Violeta and Silvia by the sound of guitar music. Silvia spotted the drenched figures first. "Your children are here. They must have fallen overboard." Violeta gasped with relief and jumped to her feet to greet them.

Someone made a fire of debris on the cement floor for the newcomers to warm themselves, and everyone gathered around to hear their story. They reported loud whisking sounds made by gigantic needles of water that shot more than sixty feet high into the air. The water, they said, turned yellow and stank of sulfur. Published reports corroborated their account and told of a surging of such energy that in the shallower bays the water parted for instants to reveal enormous dark mounds of mud shaped like whales on the seabed floor. Worse, hours later, tidal waves clear across the Pacific to Japan leapt upon the most exposed coastal lowlands, snatching houses by their foundations, sinking ships, and drowning untold numbers of victims.

> *The little boat lists,*
> *so do I weep.*
> *By the whim of the wind,*
> *I take my leave.*

There was no concert that night at the *Casa del Arte*, but at the shelter the musicians sang late into the night. As time wore on, most set down their instruments to get some sleep, but not Violeta. Over the din of despairing sobs, she played her guitar and sang tender songs, as if to appease.

To help her relax, Silvia began to comb her friend's hair. The touch of the young woman's gentle stroke brought

Violeta's own fingers to a halt. She reached up, pressed her palm upon Silvia's wrist, and nuzzled her head against her friend's hand in a gesture of caress.

"How soft a young person's hands feel," she said.

The remark stayed with Silvia all her life – Violeta experiencing that simple affection as something precious. Violeta, so toughened by adversity, never saw herself as deserving of a gentle touch. Yet in that moment she took real pleasure in having her hair combed.

Destiny's Child

Cradling her newborn in her arms, Clarisa Sandoval noticed with alarm that Violeta already had two tiny teeth. The midwife reassured her, "Ah, she will be very intelligent!" Nicanor, the infant's father, raised his wineglass to toast the mother and child, then picked up his violin, and sang a song he remembered his parents singing.

> *San Jose gazed at María*
> *María gazed at Jose*
> *the two gazed at the baby*
> *who beamed at them with joy.*

Indeed, Violeta del Carmen Parra Sandoval grew into a lively girl with dimpled cheeks, bright black eyes, and curly tresses. And how she could talk!

Ñuble province is desolate country battered by prodigious rains and high winds that sweep the Andean foothills and pastures. Winter snows blanket its densely forested volcanic mountainsides; the snow line sometimes descends to Chillán, the provincial capital. Summer is by far briefer.

The Spanish never conquered the region's Mapuche Indians, but intermarried and shared the land in uneasy truce. A military presence remained constant, to battle for national sovereignty and then to bolster or quell political factions. In 1891, civil war against the Balmaceda presidency brought battalions of soldiers into Ñuble. Though Violeta's Mapuche grandmother was pregnant and close to her time, she ran away with her draft-dodging husband into the mountains. They were about to ford a river when they spied troops advancing across a field.

"Quick, get down here!" The husband pulled his wife out of sight under a wooden plank bridge. The two crouched scared as rabbits evading hunters. Suddenly fear triggered a change in her condition and there, hiding from the passing soldiers, she went into labor. The clops of horses' hooves drowned out her moans. Hours later, Clarisa was born.

The Sandovals, Clarisa's parents, were sharecroppers. Ricardo Sandoval Contreras was a handsome, blue-eyed, kindly man who worked a rich man's lands, grooming horses, cultivating vineyards and gardens in order to feed his own family of fifteen. Her grandmother, Audolia Navarrete Flores, was a traditional farm woman, who breastfed her babies, raised chickens and vegetables, knew about herbs, collected honey, drew water from the river for their daily needs.

Their daughter, Clarisa Sandoval Navarrete, grew into a robust woman, skilled with her hands, illiterate, temperamental. At seventeen, she married her first cousin, Juan de Dios Sandoval who died young and left her with two daughters, Marta and Olga. She bore nine more children by her second husband, a schoolteacher named Nicanor Parra Parra, Violeta's father.

A riverbank and the railroad tracks bounded the hamlet of Huape, nearly 900 kilometers south of Santiago. In 1910, news traveled without radio, by word of mouth. Acoustic music provided the sole entertainment. Local artisans crafted guitars and *guitarrones*, harps, woodwind flutes and *kultrunes*, snare drums and *tambores*. From the sheep's wool, women wove the *ponchos*, knitted the sweaters and socks, and crocheted the blankets to chase the winter's chill. Young girls learned to tat lace threads into intricate dress finery using methods little changed since the eighteenth century. Language too among these people retained a courtliness reminiscent of Spanish spoken a hundred years earlier. Extended families populated these communities; in Ñuble province, Sandovals and Parras were numerous.

In contrast to Ricardo Sandoval, Jose Calixto Parra Hernandez, Violeta's paternal grandfather, was an elegant, literate man who fought to defend the red, white, and blue Chilean flag in the War of the Pacific (1879-83), when Chile and Peru landlocked Bolivia and snatched the mining wealth of the Atacama Desert. He was a lawyer and property owner, and to Violeta, a most dashing gentleman.

Every year on the feast day of San José, his patron saint, don José threw a banquet. Eagerly she helped her grandmother, Rosario Parra Cansino, a plump, cheerful woman, prepare for the party. "Set out flowers, Violetita; yes, and the trays of salt, dear."

On an open fire grilled trout, chicken, and homemade sausages – accompanied by condiments of *pebre* and avocado, vegetables, bread, and fruit. Violeta's eyes grew wide as she watched the arrival of perfumed women with fans, men in dresscoats, and peasants who worked her grandfather's land all come to pay him homage. The guests sipped wine and sweet *mistela*, and later enjoyed a dessert of buns sticky with honeyed syrup.

As the men settled down to their cigars and mead and the women to their tea, Jose called out to Nicanor to start the music-making. Soon, the finely dressed couples glided on the tiled patio floor to the rhythms of waltz, mazurka, and quadrille.

Meanwhile, other musicians gathered under the stars to tune their instruments for the raucous exuberance of the *cueca*. Guitars established its syncopated two-beat rhythm, which drew couples to their feet –the man flicking his handkerchief overhead and at the hem of his woman, advancing his steps and gaze toward her; she concealing her face with her hanky, rustling her skirt to allure yet also evade, the two moving in a circular pattern reminiscent of a cock pecking at a pretty hen. The *cueca's* teasing playfulness with its percussive clapping and vocal outbursts became implanted in the young Violeta's heart as the essence of Life's perfection—a celebration of the virile *huaso* adoring his lovely *china* in a pastoral Eden. *¡Ay, si!*

Nicanor was a gregarious and restless man with a knack for playing just about any musical instrument that interested him—guitar, piano, mandolin, violin. When they were first married, the newlyweds left Clarisa's young daughters in their grandparents' care and set off by train for Santiago, where he hoped to grow famous by playing violin.

How astonishing the capital city must have been to them, with its indoor plumbing and electricity. Clarisa was easily hired as a seamstress at *La Casa Francesa*, a retailer of lace blouses whose clientele included first lady, Doña de Arturo Alessandri. But despite his best efforts, Nicanor failed to find work as a musician. Disheartened, he returned with his wife to the country. For a time, they lived in San Fabian de Alico, high in the Andean foothills, where their first son, Nicanor, was born. From there, they moved to the village of San Carlos, north of Chillán, where their union was blessed by eight more children—Hilda, Violeta, Eduardo, Roberto, Caupolicán, Elba, Lautaro, and Oscar René.

In 1919, Nicanor moved them again briefly to Santiago. They lived in a slum neighborhood so windy, gusts rattled the windows until they broke. He worked as a streetcar inspector, then a prison guard, and finally landed a post as a village schoolteacher in the rural south.

That year, 1920, an epidemic of smallpox swept across Chile. The disease terrified rich and poor alike by making corpses of healthy people barely a week after getting sick. Remote field hospitals were set up to treat the afflicted, but no one knew how to cure or even how to stop it from spreading. Those who survived smallpox were scarred for life.

As the train made its way south to Lautaro, where Nicanor would be teaching, three-year-old Violeta suddenly developed a soaring fever and her face, usually perky, swelled alarmingly. Clarisa wrapped her in a quilt and held her close, while Nicanor rounded up the other children, lest they draw attention to Violeta's illness and get them all thrown off. They arrived in Lautaro, found lodging, concealed Violeta at home, and nursed her until she recovered. But the disease left its unmistakable toll, for the pustules that covered her pretty face healed into ugly disfiguring pockmarks.

Yellow fever, then diphtheria followed smallpox. Chills, spells of delirium, a burning throat, and weak limbs became familiar sensations to the little girl. Clarisa nursed her through all her illnesses and grew uncommonly attached to her. *"El miedo es cosa viva,"* Fear has a life of its own, she would say to reassure her. This too will pass.

For weeks at a time, Violeta was bedridden, and then housebound. She grew moody, bored. While Clarisa sewed, Violeta would park herself under foot. *"¡Aquí mami!"* Any scraps of cloth her mother dropped Violeta would hand her like a prize. Clarisa began to teach Violeta to sew and to tat lace. Her mother's little discards became intricate patchworks and doll clothes. As she grew more adept, she helped her mother darn, baste seams, and sew on buttons. Her mother's clientele marveled over the youngster's ability to handle even silk with delicacy. As she sat still for hours plying the thread, Violeta sang to herself in a high-pitched voice, inventing lyric images that would be more fully realized years later in song and tapestry.

For his part, Nicanor was a gifted father who taught his children to sing. Listening to Hilda and Violeta sing his favorite tunes, he'd look into their eyes and coach them to let out their breath slowly, to reach the very last word. He regaled his children with tales of trained tigers and elephants, trapeze artists, and armies of clowns. "Let's make our own circus," he'd say. "I'll be the ringmaster and you'll be my stars." Then he'd doff a make-believe hat and bow to an invisible audience. The youngsters danced and pantomimed comedies of childish misadventures in which everyone had a role and inevitably someone got caught and punished with a mock spanking.

But outside the family's protective nest, Violeta grew keenly aware of her homeliness. Though quick to learn her schoolwork, she was often unruly, resentful of her teachers' pitying looks and other children's fear of her scars. Her siblings, usually close by, protected her from as much humiliation as they could, though frequently, the child went home crying from cruel taunts. "*¡Malhaya!* Cursed witch!" Violeta grew into a fairy-tale child, both damned and blessed, a keen observer.

From his father, Nicanor inherited a ramshackle house in the hilly countryside. The family spent summers there, breathing the fresh air and gazing upon the splendid vista and starry skies. Best of all for the children, the house was only four kilometers from Malloa, where their cousins, the Aguileras, lived. While the adults labored for the local farmers, the children roamed the footpaths and patchwork fields of vegetables, pasture, and vineyards.

One day, they found unlatched the gate to a garden in full bloom tended by Clarisa for a woman who sold bouquets outside the city cemetery. The garden's extravagant perfume inebriated the children. They grew giddy picking flowers and strewing petals in wild disarray. In no time, they stripped the garden bare of every living blossom.

When the owner discovered the shambles, she was outraged and humiliated the hapless Clarisa. The two women had the children return in flesh the income they had cost: Eighty lashes—ten for each rascal—a lesson they'd never forget!

Runoff from the Andean snowpack within view of the land created deep rivers and icy streams. The children splashed around in the sheltered inlets of the Cautín River. The entire clan frequented *El Saco*, a sandy beach sweet with the scents of pennyroyal and rosemary and ablaze in March with *copihue*, a red trumpet-flower in whose branches perched *picaflores*, giant hummingbirds. Nicanor, a studious youngster, never tired of collecting insects. Violeta adored watching her older brother subdue the fluttering wings or bodies of butterflies, dragonflies, and other insects.

At summer's end as the nights grew chillier and the sugar level set in the grapes, the Parras and Aguileras helped bring in the harvest. For long days, adults and children alike picked and boxed the grapes, then ate heartily and slept, to rise early for the next day's work. *Parra* in Spanish means grapevine, an image that once prompted the great Chilean poet Pablo Neruda to write of Violeta, "Parra you are, and sad wine you will become." But sadness would come later. Violeta was a happy and loved child, wandering amid the vines, nibbling the tiny grapes, collecting some in a basket to sell.

At the end of the day when the red glow of sunset filled the sky, a campfire blazed with the aroma of goat meat for the evening meal. As the meat cooked, don Nicanor prepared a spicy salad that Clarisa served to everyone who gathered. For dessert there was persimmon that grew nearby, lily-sweet and sticky. It was Violeta's favorite fruit, and she ate it with abandon.

Around the night's bonfire under the starlit sky, the adults sat drinking *aguardiente* and *pisco* and swapping tales of the ancient Araucanian warriors, Lautaro and Galvarino, of whippings and beheadings, of mythical monsters that lured man and beast into the rivers to drown, or magical beings whose presence might auger good fortune or signal tragedy.

Then came the music. The Aguilera daughters played guitar, rabel, *bandurria*, harp, and *vihuela*. Their stringed ensemble amplified when the men joined in on *guitarrón*, violin, percussion, and woodwinds.

After a harvest, songfests lasted for days under the cottonwood trees. Men were known to doze off with their guitars still nestled in their arms, and on awakening, pick up the beat of a never-ending song.

Unlike the Aguileras, Clarisa and Nicanor were ambivalent about encouraging their children's music interests. Although the father played several instruments and the mother's clear voice harmonized beautifully, both believed the trancelike intoxication of music perpetuated their poverty; Nicanor kept the guitar locked away from the children. There may well have been some truth to their concern, for with music came drink, and with drink, little else. The younger Nicanor once unstrung the guitar in a rage over one of his father's benders.

Violeta liked to imitate her mother's style of play by strumming the colored strings of her toy guitar with her fingers or patting a rhythmic beat on its wooden soundbox. But the flat sound never satisfied her. Then, during yet another convalescence, when no one else was home and she was rummaging around her mother's needlework, seven-year-old Violeta discovered the key to her father's guitar case hidden in the sewing machine. She retrieved the instrument, held it for the first time. It was heavy and unwieldy, but she supported it by sitting on the ground and resting it on her legs. Now she began to find the right places on the strings for her small fingers and a way to strum them as she sang slowly the songs that she had heard from the grownups.

No one heard her that first time. She watched her parents' hands when they made music, and found many opportunities to practice until, by chance, Clarisa walked in while Violeta was singing herself a lullaby and discovered her secret. The child's apprehension led to laughter at her mother's astonishment.

Autumn and winter festivals drew Nicanor and Clarisa's talents as storyteller and accompanist. Violeta's favorite was the *Cruz de Mayo*, a hybrid Christian and indigenous rite that assembled thousands of pilgrims to give thanks for the harvest and to pray for a safe winter. The devoted brought their animals to be blessed, while all along the village roads vendors sold goods and diversions of every conceivable nature—meats, *chicha* and fruit drinks, games run by barkers in gaudy costume, provisions, and palm reading. And the lights! Sparkling *luminarias* and bonfires lit the processional path for the venerated May Cross, which sat atop a platform festooned with fragrant wildflowers, draped in a necklace of red coral bells, candlelit and paraded through the village as a symbol of the Virgin's grace.

Time passed. The 1920s were desperate years when crop failures drove many peasants to the cities where hunger and unemployment fueled unrest and led to Chile's earliest labor unions. Four years of military rule coincided with the collapse of the nitrate industry in the northern desert. Colonel Carlos Ibañez del Campo called for the first of many US interventions, allowed the sale of Chile's national telephone system to ITT and copper mines to Anaconda and Kennecott, sparking bloody strikes.

Repression spread to the southern provinces. Military presence became so pervasive, children everywhere cowered like frightened birds avoiding a predatory hunter.

When Violeta's father, Nicanor, an outspoken member of the center-left Radical Party, complained at having his salary cut, he was fired. Pacing the floor of their tiny house, he tore at his hair, cursed Fate and politics.

Then, tragically, Caupolicán, the youngest Parra, caught pneumonia. Neither doctor's remedies nor poultices of semen could save him. Violeta watched in fascinated horror as her grief-stricken mother clutched his lifeless body in her arms, and keened ceaselessly for three days.

The loss of his job and his son destroyed Nicanor. He renounced even the pleasure of playing his violin. His entire body reeked of alcohol. Clarisa scolded, begged him to pull himself together, but pride blinded Nicanor to reason. So complete was Nicanor's undoing, he squandered even his father's land, allegedly signing over the deed while drunk. Nicanor abandoned his family, went to Chillán, and because he refused to work at anything but teaching, degenerated to living on the streets. Clarisa kept her brood intact by taking in endless piles of laundry, ironing, and sewing. Months passed.

Don Nicanor's desertion and subsequent news of his tuberculosis bewildered twelve-year-old Violeta. She went to see him, bringing his favorite foods. *"Papi,* won't you drink this milk and eat these wheat cakes? *Papi,* I brought you *yerba mate* for your teapot. Please *Papi,* mama sent you a piece of goose breast and I found you some shrimp. *Papi,* they're from the stream; you know the stream, it's so clear."

Soon thereafter he returned home to die a lingering death, his flesh gray, flaccid, musty with an odor no washing could scrub clean. When last attended by Clarisa he passed away; Violeta was standing watch in the doorway. Staring at her father's unseeing eyes and half-open mouth, she walked into the room and knelt down at his bedside, wanting desperately to kiss him good-bye. "*No, mi amor.*" Clarisa led Violeta away from his diseased remains.

Death was to become a seductive image for Violeta.

Violeta Parra, The Self-Absorbed Widower, canvas, 9.5" x 13.75". 1964.

The Circus Years

"*Jesús*, look at all those cars!" Hilda stopped combing her sister's hair when she saw the funeral procession headed through the iron gate. Thirteen-year-old Violeta jumped to her feet, tying her tresses into a quick bun. Their younger brothers, Eduardo and Roberto, came running from across the street.

Strains of somber classical music emanated from a victrola in the black limousine, along with a perfume of rose and magnolia blossoms from the funeral wreaths atop the hearse. The cortege stopped at an open mausoleum. As the mourners assembled, the Parra children inched closer.

Funerals presented opportunities for the children. On Sundays, they posted themselves on the paths near spigots, poised to haul water for people who brought bouquets to adorn the graves. Roberto and Eduardo scampered up the rungs of a rough-hewn wooden ladder to place handsful of flowers before the highest burial niches, or to wipe clean the facades of the granite resting places, which aggregate like crowded tenement apartments for the deceased masses.

Only the wealthy afforded burial deep in the earth. Just this morning, Roberto had washed the stone of a baby who had died a year ago that day; in his pocket jingled the coins the grieving mother had given him.

Now, the children stood at a respectful distance beneath a grove of holm oaks, to avoid being shooed away by the priest as the silver-trimmed casket was lowered into the burial chamber.

Once the coffin was interred and the wreaths deposited on the earthen mound within and outside the mausoleum, the mourners left. The Parra children snapped out of their reverie and set to work. The girls plucked flower petals from the wreaths and stuffed them into a paper bag. Later, they would boil them into toilet water to sell at market. Violeta believed with all her heart that she was rescuing blossoms destined to die for the deceased. Her hands turned them into fragrant garlands for their hair or into a bouquet for their mother.

At home, Clarisa's days had become a never-ending pile of laundry, her hands raw with bleach. At night she ironed and sewed on a treadle machine by candlelight. She barely slept.

The older daughters, Marta and Olga, had already left home, but Clarisa managed to keep Nicanor, her eldest son, in school as his father would have wanted. Indeed, later years Nicanor Parra would distinguish himself as a professor of mathematics and a poet.

The youngest tots were still at home under foot, but the others –Violeta, Hilda, Eduardo, Roberto – had grown willful, unmanageable. Clarisa gave up trying to discipline her brood. She had them quit school to work for their keep.

Hilda and Violeta cleaned houses and helped their mother with laundry. Briefly, Violeta lived with a couple, to care for their severely disabled infant son, Vicente, in exchange for room and board. Brothers, Eduardo, Roberto, and Lautaro roamed the streets of Chillán, like countless other ragamuffins who survived by grit and wits, playful hunters like the mangy kittens that prowled the cemetery stalking rodents and birds.

On market days, the Parra children earned coins by unloading the farmers' wagons of vegetables, grains, beans or small animals that weighed nearly as much as they did, then tending the horses. Then they parked themselves in the square and sang for food to carry home. By evening, they went home exhausted, hoarse, and hungry, but with a parcel of earnings.

Before their father's death, don Nicanor was always playing his guitar or his violin, or getting Clarisa to sing with him soothing or animated songs. Now, although Clarisa still sang while she worked, she was also apt to cry, or erupt in outbursts of frustrated anger. No one else played the violin, but the family guitar rose to paramount importance. Once Violeta taught herself to play, Hilda and Roberto followed suit – they had voices, why not hands? And if one of them spotted an idle guitar, they "borrowed" it for their very own.

The children often teamed up to see who could bring home the greater bounty. Brothers competed against sisters; or the children ventured out solo to garner more sympathy.

Violeta and Hilda usually worked together. They did well because they sang prettily and were quick to curry favor. If someone invited them into a house and offered them bread or cheese, one sister accepted politely, then the other would pipe up with, "But may we have some to take home for my little brothers too?" People were apt to be generous.

The children sang at train stations, and then boarded the trains and serenade the passengers for coins as they rode thirty or more kilometers from home. Sometimes they stayed away for days at a time, then returned with a basket laden with food–bits of cheese and bread, grapefruit, avocado, anything people were able to give. These were journeys of the innocent.

Clarisa's children were hardly alone in their wanderings. Landless peasants crisscrossed the countryside looking for work. Vacant pastures became encampments, the most flamboyant of which were ragtag circuses, which inevitably attracted the children. When one was nearby, they talked of little else but joining the circus life.

Finally one day, Violeta took Lautaro by the hand and led him to a nearby village where they had heard *El Circo Tolin* was performing. As they crossed plowed acreage littered with chaff that cut the soles of their bare feet, they tried to ignore the chill of the humid air, and their own apprehension and hunger.

"Surely once we find to the circus, they'll feed us and put us to work." Violeta urged her little brother along. Barking dogs announced their arrival in town. Local children showed them to the rickety circus truck, where they struck a deal with the manager to work in exchange for board. Lautaro went off to sell candy with other children and Violeta found herself being led away to a dressing room she would share with the clairvoyant.

Madame Rosa was an elderly, heavyset woman draped in a silk kimono, heavily made up, her face framed with abundant hair, her husky voice not unfriendly. Violeta watched her glide around on worn slippers; she surveyed the tiny room and her heart sank. Clothes hung to dry were strung across the cramped space; the only furnishings were a dressing-table sporting jars of greasepaint and a fragment of mirror, a carton used as both stool and valise, and a straw mattress. The woman drew on her cigarette with pursed, cherry-red lips.

"You're lucky. You won't have to perform tonight because the girl who sings couplets isn't leaving until tomorrow.

You'll get to see how the show is done." Violeta remembered one of her mother's favorite sayings: "One starving man thinks harder than a hundred smart alecks." She swallowed hard for courage and smiled.

That night, Violeta saw Madame Rosa spellbind her audience. Under the spotlight, the years melted from her person as she swayed to music. She peered into a crystal ball and prophesied in a stage whisper, "A sign. I see a sign for someone to inherit great good fortune." She looked up and stared into a hopeful face in the crowd. "An animal or child will bring one of you more than you might know." Everyone in the audience sighed with certainty or skepticism.

Later, as Violeta watched Madame Rosa remove her makeup, she found herself touching her own pockmarked face, imagining how it might look coated with pancake. "When I am costumed, women envy me and the men go mad, as it was when I was young," the elder woman remarked, wiping the perspiration from between her ample breasts. "But when the act ends, so does the magic."

Already, Violeta could see that the circus created an imperfect illusion–its lightness of spirit and its laughter were a momentary escape from monotony for the audience. But for those who lived its life, the circus meant a way to survive by banding together to entertain. The other Parra youngsters followed Violeta's example and joined the circus. They adapted easily, never shirking from labor; and in return, they were fed, housed, looked after.

The *Circo Tolín* was typical of the many makeshift shows the Parra children came to know, in claiming attractions far beyond what it could deliver. Thirty troupers, each an exotic foreigner, turned out to be six or eight people taking turns as acrobats and tumblers, jugglers, magicians, trapeze artists, clowns, dancers, and musicians. Its menagerie consisted of a single pony named *Pior es na'* ("Better than

Nothing"), who trotted in a circle and jumped low barriers, and a couple of dogs in funny hats who howled at the sound of a flute. The entire show was a makeshift hustle.

The circus caravan traveled from landed estate to town to landed estate, touring the region of Maule. *Señor* Tolín sold shows to the *patrones*, then staged them free of charge for the tenant farmers. If no *patrón* agreed to pay for a performance, the caravan parked in a field outside town or in the plaza, then drummed up an audience.

Even the most meager circus with its gaudy, flamboyant theatricality signaled a fiesta sure to charm the isolated peasants. Sometimes the staging so enchanted them, they returned day after day. In lieu of coins, they brought food and livestock, their naive generosity sometimes leading them to share more than they intended.

Circus people were known to be "telepathic"–a gift handy for spiriting away the occasional barnyard animal. During the day, the performers strutted around town in flowing capes, and when they eyed appetizing prey, one would say to the other, "Look at this chicken! It's in real trouble."

"What a pity; it's such a pretty little black hen."

Their remarks were sure to alarm its owner. "Can anything be done?"

"Oh *señora*, this chicken is clearly bedeviled! Just look at the evil spots in its feathers! If you don't get rid of the problem it'll bring you trouble." Once the woman was visibly worried, one of the fellows would pick up the bird and tell her to retrieve it from their encampment the next day, cured. But, when she came to claim her chicken, all they showed her were the charred remains of their dinner. "The fire destroyed it, *señora*. We couldn't save it."

Thirteen-year-old Violeta learned from circus people many lessons that served her throughout her life. She mastered the exaggerated stage movements and learned to project her voice and stay focused on her songs in the midst of slapstick, animals, and prop changes. She learned how to create a spectacle; how to exert herself yet make everything look easy; how to smile, sing, and dance to win that prized applause.

Violeta observed, too, the grim looks of peasants whose lives were circumscribed by a stratified social structure little changed since the Colonial era, when the Spaniards seized what had been communally held land. Sharecroppers now lived at the landlord's mercy, tending the grounds and voting as they were told, in exchange for a small parcel of land for home and garden, food, and firewood rations, and permission to graze animals in the common pasture. The landowners ruled with absolute authority, with coercive violence barely hidden.

Stories abounded and were repeated about the awful incidents taking place. In one, a *patrón* in Longaví hired a man to dress as a priest and hear confession. Anyone who confessed to storing extra crops or selling them at market for a better price got evicted. The dispossessed lost not only their home but their standing crops and any chance of finding nearby farm work. Vast numbers of desperate people roamed the countryside. As if through a scrim, Violeta watched such vignettes come into view and then dissolve into memory as she traveled with the circus. In poetry, she named the places she saw and the sensations they evoked. Humiliation in Serena, calamity in Recinto.

Homesick for their mother's attentions, coughing and sniffling with colds, the children occasionally returned home with their meager earnings to hugs, soup, and soap. Clarisa wished they would stay, but knew too that they were doing what was necessary to survive. Circus work sustained them and also had longer-term effects. Two of the brothers found their life's work in the circus: Lautaro organized the *Sindicato Circense*, a performers' labor union, and Oscar René became known as Canarito the clown, beloved throughout Chile.

In 1931, the *Circo Argentino* came to Maule. It was a substantial show whose owner, Juan Baez, was married to Marta, Violeta's half-sister. Don Juan had a large and well-mounted tent, a real band, and risers capable of seating 400 spectators. Although mostly it toured the small villages around Chillán, the troupe had taken its name from a mis-adventure in Argentina where they had been arrested for performing without the necessary papers.

On learning that her rambunctious siblings had been working the local circuses, Marta welcomed them into the troupe. Don Juan fascinated the fourteen-year-old Violeta. She marveled at how, as ringmaster, he beat a drum with his foot while blowing a trumpet to signal the clowns, who grabbed his trumpet and sounded it to call the next act.

Don Juan had a life-size ventriloquist's dummy named Don Cirilo to which Violeta grew very attached. Don Cirilo had the handsome face of a knave, and Don Juan animated it with a sharp tongue that answered him back while he played the straight man of the duo. To Violeta, the dummy was like a man who stood up to the fiercest affront and thus was worthy of her loyalty, which she expressed so affection-ately, one would think she were doting on a human being rather than a wooden doll.

Don Cirilo had to be dressed in trousers and a shirt with a bandanna for the show, a task Violeta relished. Between performances she packed him away fully clothed, but more often than not, when it was time to unpack and perform at the next locale, Violeta would find the puppet na-ked as a toothpick. She ran around frantically looking for his costume, and pity the poor fellow she caught wearing it.

"Take it off this second!" she hollered. "Don Cirilo can't go on stage like this!" Violeta's commanding voice inevitably cowed the guilty artist, whoever it was, to disrobe for the dummy.

On entering a new town, *Circo Argentino* drew attention with its truck top-heavy with gear, its performers singing and waving at everyone in sight. Once parked, they sprang into action hauling equipment, corralling the animals, raising the tent, setting up the ring, cooking nougats and *empanadas* to sell, posting flyers to advertise the spectacle. Everyone costumed and paraded through the streets, mindful of the growling dogs who menaced them. At every corner the artists danced a *cueca* or recited a couplet. Dressed in organdy, Violeta and her sister, Hilda, danced Argentine *rancheras* and tangos and sang in their childish voices. Before show time, the barkers lured the public to games of chance, while other troupers sold tickets to the big top. Marta managed behind the scenes to ensure that the tent was fastened properly, that the trampoline was taut, that there were sufficient seats and food, that everyone knew the order of the skits and any changes in the staging.

Joaquín, Don Juan's son, ran a popular boxing concession. One day, he was moving props with Roberto, a strapping fellow though barely thirteen. "It's a cinch I tell you. You're strong and fast; just duck the punches, play it for laughs, let the challenger win, and you'll do fine and make some money!" Roberto figured he had nothing to lose, so he agreed to be the circus' boxer. He didn't have any shorts, however, so he took Hilda's red panties and wore them into the ring.

All went well until Hilda spotted her brother. "*Ey chico,*" she screamed. "What are you doing wearing my bloomers?" The audience exploded in laughter. Hilda picked up an iron poker lying nearby, pushed her way through the crowd into the ring and whacked her brother hard on his arms and buttocks. Roberto howled and ran out of the ring as onlookers jeered.

Violeta came to know the circus as a world apart. Circus parents taught their children to trust their talents regardless of risk, though fate too played its hand. Once, Violeta watched horrified as an inebriated aerialist missed the hands outstretched to grab him as he flew from one swing to another. He fell, landed hard, and shattered bones because he worked without a net. Clowns brushed past Violeta from the sidelines to distract the audience as two men carried him away. The show went on.

After a show, the performers met in Don Juan's dressing room to review the evening and receive their portion of the gate. Without a fixed plan, no one ever knew if they'd make money, yet every artist banked on fame's potential. Their stage names–the Dolly Sisters, the Rajah, Hercules– suggested fantastical tales. A dog brought back from India, a scarf of pure fire, the only pig in the world able to tell fortunes! Those who'd traveled abroad, even if now they had barely enough to eat, bragged of the millions they'd once made. Violeta's desire for roving grew.

Meanwhile, Clarisa schemed with Marta to bring the youngsters home. A suspicious Violeta snooped around her sister's trailer until she found Marta's note telling her husband to withhold the children's pay to make them leave. Furious, Violeta altered the letter to ensure that they were paid their due, then led the children's mass desertion of *Circo Argentino*. They got work immediately with the biggest touring company in southern Chile. But shortly, Violeta argued with the owners, and Hilda convinced her to return home to their mother in Chillán.

By now, their oldest brother Nicanor had moved to Santiago to continue his studies. In secret, he'd written Violeta inviting her to Santiago. Brother and sister shared a psychic harmony throughout her life. His letter, awaiting her at home, gave Violeta new direction.

Early one morning, Violeta wrapped clothing in a blanket, slung her guitar over her shoulder and (taking care to not awaken Clarisa) roused Hilda. "Come take the train with me. I'm going on a little trip." The sisters traveled together a hundred kilometers, then Violeta kissed her sister good-bye and sent her home. She was headed for Santiago, having written to Nicanor that she was coming.

At fifteen, she was certain it was her Destiny to travel the world.

Adolescence in Santiago

As the train rolled into the *Estación Central*, Santiago's railroad terminus from the southern provinces, Violeta was overwhelmed.

Throughout the four hundred kilometer trip from Chillán, coal-fire smoke had showered her with soot that burned her eyes and throat and stuck to her clothes. A final belch of smoke dissipated overhead toward the distant canopy of glass and steel four or five stories above. A great screeching of metal wheels on tracks punctuated the train's halt. Passengers gathered up their valises and makeshift parcels and exited the train.

Pulling her shawl taut around her shoulders and taking her guitar and bundle of belongings in hand, Violeta stepped onto the station platform. The voluminous interior space dwarfed her. From all sides, hollow voices announced arrivals and departures, men shouted to clear way for moving cargo, whistles blasted, bells clanged. Strangers pushed past, hurrying to get on their way.

Violeta was lost. She shuffled along with the crowd through an immense steel portal, into the teeming market district. Never had she seen so many people or so much activity. Peddlers hawked clothing, trinkets, soap, candy from pushcarts, from wooden trays hung from the neck, out of hand, or laid out on the ground on blankets. Warehouse-men shouldered sacks of grains, canisters of cooking oil and kerosene, hauled produce and meats from trucks, wagons, or handcarts, goods to be sold in the stalls that lined the narrow alleyways in the streets beyond the station plaza. She was scared as a suckling pig about to be ripped apart by a wild-cat.

Violeta wandered into a covered market, drawn to the savory aromas that wafted from cook-pots simmering over kerosene fires; but she was so bewildered, she couldn't bring herself to buy an *empanada*. Shortly she would come to know this neighborhood, with its streets muddy in winter or swarming with gnats in the heat of summer. But now, she parked herself against a doorway, making herself appear very small, uncertain of where to go or what to do. An hour passed, then another. The bells of a clock sounded. Daylight faded to dusk. A young policeman approached and eyed her with a look of detached concern.

"Is everything all right?"

"My relatives don't know that I've arrived," Violeta answered.

"Why don't you come with me," he said in a pleasant manner, and led her to his precinct.

Public policy dictated that every evening vagrants be removed from the streets. Many were emigrants who arrived in the city late in the day and had no idea what to do next. As night fell, police swept through the market district, detained and questioned those who were obviously lost, to make sure they knew what they were getting themselves into. Violeta spent the night safely in a jail cell; in the morning jailers and detainees alike plied her with advice. She steeled her nerve and told them she would find work. At a nearby restaurant, she ordered coffee and a roll for breakfast. After paying the bill, she was penniless.

Seventeen-year-old Nicanor worked in a residence hall in exchange for room and board while attending a teachers' college. A serious young man who missed his family, he had written his sister encouraging her to come to Santiago to study too; but he had no idea that she would take him so literally. He was folding sheets in the laundry when a fellow student summoned, "Hey, Nicanor, there's a girl outside wanting to see you."

It was Violeta, guitar at her side, dressed in a long dark skirt, high-buttoned shirtwaist blouse, and shawl; her black wavy hair clipped back with bobby pins. It had been a year since Nicanor last saw his sister, and he had never seen her separate from their family. Her open face expressed complete trust. At fifteen she had grown into a young woman. His stunned stare betrayed his surprise at the unexpected encounter.

"Don't worry," she said. "I've got my guitar. I can take care of myself."

All at once, he realized what had brought her—his letter! He laughed and grabbed her in a bear hug so uncharacteristic in its affection that the other boys howled with good-natured jesting. From the moment Violeta arrived, Nicanor became a parent.

He took her to stay with their father's cousins, Matilde and Ramon Parra, who lived near the railroad station. He enrolled her in a nearby secondary school and with what little money he had, bought her a bed, a book-bag, and a school uniform—a mature undertaking for a young man. Their cousins were skeptical.

"Even properly dressed, you won't succeed in a city school. You don't have the upbringing," Matilde said. Violeta's eyes welled with tears. She fled, furious and scared that her cousin's assertion would prove true.

Nicanor rose in her defense. "My sister is aspiring to grow up!" His certitude stopped Mathilde short. Despite apologies offering encouragement for her school plans, Violeta couldn't stop crying.

Nicanor visited his sister frequently, but if two weeks passed without a visit, Violeta raged as though abandoned. He was her confidante, as much father as brother, and throughout her life her most potent muse. It was his advice that prompted her to write her thoughts in poetry. She wrote hundreds of verses, many of which captured a young woman's candor, a rural childhood, and coming of age in the midst of urban poverty.

Country rearing made Violeta independent. She was smart, knew what was expected of her, then conducted herself as she saw fit. She ingratiated herself by doing housework every morning first thing and by telling Mathilde and Ramon how much she valued their hospitality. The couple were young themselves, both in their mid twenties; after initial adjustment, they took their niece to their hearts as if she were their own daughter.

Violeta soon had an active circle of friends her own age and class, starting with Matilde's sisters, Nicanor, and their classmates. It was likely that at this time Violeta met Pablo de Rokha, a poet whose own bombastic eloquence appealed to her volatility; the two became lifelong friends. The group of young people frequented the neighborhood dance halls or gathered to play charades of characters featured on film posters. Violeta excelled at the game, reenacting the roles of fawning ingenue, jealous lover, and pious matron. Everyone in the group sang, but her singing was . . . well, different from what the others knew.

"Oh Violeta, no one sings like that here anymore!" "Are we in a barn? You're squealing, Violeta!" Little did anyone know that her "atrocious voice" and "corny songs" would later win acclaim. Among her peers, Violeta took the teasing in stride. Everything interested her. She never tired of exploring the city, with its throngs of colliding personalities and costumes. Her exuberance blossomed into refreshing charm.

As her relatives warned, however, Violeta was ill prepared for the difficult curriculum of a Santiago school. Socially she was conspicuously low-class among the chaperoned girl students, many of whom were strikingly pretty, with clear complexions and the carefree assuredness that comes from a more secure upbringing. Granted, Violeta made friends easily because she was defiant, but she never fit in. Eventually, faced with having to support herself, Violeta quit her formal studies.

After living with her cousins for two years, Violeta moved into the apartment Nicanor found for their mother and siblings, who had just arrived in Santiago. Nicanor graduated from the university, accepted a teaching job in Chillán, and left.

Santiago in 1932 reeled from the effects of the global Depression, with its widespread hunger and longstanding class animosities. On failing to find work as a maid, she vented her rage in bitter verse, describing how objectified she felt as she sought to earn her bread.

Eventually, she was hired as a barmaid in a seedy cantina near the railroad station. She dreaded the arrival of Carlina, an alcoholic whore, who would hand her whimpering infant to her pimp, then methodically proposition every man sitting alone at the bar, until one would nod assent and follow her to the toilet. Her disappearance inevitably amplified the baby's wails—one more barroom noise where Violeta was singing for tips.

One busy winter night, Violeta was drying beer steins when a sudden draft of chill air caught everyone's attention. A little boy stood at the door, propping it open with a guitar that dwarfed him.

"Can I come in to sing?" he asked. His spunk, both adorable and pathetic, prompted doña Berta to usher him in.

Right behind him followed a girl barely five years old. "This is my sister, Margarita, who is going to accompany me."

Without further hesitation, the boy struck a chord and the two children launched into a ballad whose bawdiness sparked the cantina like tinder that suddenly catches fire when laid over embers. En masse, couples got up from their barstools or chairs to dance, their bodies undulating to the erotic tune.

Suddenly self-conscious of lascivious men and the drink that diminished propriety, Violeta could not contain her horror at what she perceived as the children's degradation. She lunged toward them, screaming, "This is inhuman!" The boy returned a rosary of indecencies whose irreverence drove Violeta from the cantina. She returned the next night only reluctantly, as she was due to get paid for the week. "What an innocent *señorita* you are," doña Berta greeted her scornfully. "Those children you pity know more of the world than you'll ever know."

"But they're just babies and already they're living off garbage to survive. If that's the misery I have to bear, perhaps Life itself isn't worth living!"

Violeta was so upset, doña Berta let her sing that night for tips. But after work, the urchins were waiting for her. The boy tripped her and shouted insults while his sister pulled her hair until she screamed. Violeta fought them off, and ran away in tears. To banish despair, she went to church and lit a candle to San Jeremías, whom she was sure, was amused by her naïve distress.

Life at home was hardly less precarious—a dark tenement lacking privacy, a single bed for Clarisa and six children, barely enough food. It was Hilda who came up with the idea of inventing themselves as performers with an act.

"Why don't we sing together?" she proposed to Violeta, who was happy not to have to deal with the bars alone. They called themselves *Las Hermanas Parra* and soon were singing at taverns near the slaughterhouses; one bar in particular, *El Popular*, became their mainstay. Their brothers Roberto, Eduardo, and Lautaro often accompanied them. They sang a repertoire of popular songs—Mexican movie hits, Peruvian waltzes, Argentine tangos, and spirited gypsy *boleros*, which Violeta punctuated with the syncopated chatter of castanets. They also sang Chilean *tonadas* and *cuecas*, for those songs exposed submerged longings for the *campo's* Paradise Lost.

According to *El Popular's* owner, Violeta "didn't play very well at first, but she was very vivacious, loud, and able to carry over the din of conversation." Hilda, on the other hand, had a pretty voice and was more womanly in her mannerisms and style.

The women could spot trouble as soon as it walked through the door—foul-smelling men intent on drinking themselves drunk and picking fights. The police might drag a drunk from the counter as a yapping dog licked his puked-up wine. Sometimes a fight turned the entire saloon rowdy, sending the women fleeing to safety.

After a set or when the bar was getting rowdy, Hilda, whose body language was the more swaggering, carried her guitar like a hat through the audience, and bid the patrons to drop in money, and soon the girls were on their way.

One of the barflies was a beautiful young girl named Teresa whom many men coveted. She was a flirt with a sensual audacity that cut to a very animal place in men. Violeta was playing a polka when two men grabbed at Teresa, both wanting to dance with her. A knife blade glinted. Teresa screamed.

Violeta stopped playing and headed for the girl. "Where do you think you're going?" the bartender called and ordered her to "Get back there and sing." She did as she was told. The brawlers were thrown out of the bar, taking Teresa with them. The next day, newspaper headlines reported Teresa's rape and murder. Violeta denounced the crime in a poem extraordinary for its candor; by her society's standards, the very mention of rape was taboo.

> *The question of killing a bitch*
> *cuts short the triviality.*
> *Let there be fewer liquor permits;*
> *some pasture land to grow more beans . . .*

Her imagery had changed from the poetic idylls of her childhood to a stark measure of urban poverty.

Eventually, *El Popular*, where Violeta and Hilda performed most frequently, bought a jukebox, making the sisters' act unnecessary. The women took up at a beer hall popular with Santiago's railroad workers, and there Violeta met Luís Cereceda, the man who was to be her first husband.

Ten Years of Hell

The first time Luís caught Violeta's eye, he was cleaning the engineer's cabin of the locomotive on the Yungay-Santiago line. To call attention to himself, he rang the shiny bell–*talán talán talán*–long and loud. The cocksure flattery of his gallantry excited her.

Young people congregated in the *Estación Central*, strolling down the platforms in groups eyeing each other, discreetly hoping to be noticed as the trains arrived and departed. They exchanged furtive glances and messages on scraps of paper. "Meet me outside at six. I'll wait for you."

Like Violeta, Luís came from a village near Chillán. Other men of his family had worked for the railroad. It was customary for the womenfolk of railroad men to hire out to sing their voices raw at *velorios de angelitos*, the all-night vigils held when an infant or young child died. As children, Luís and Violeta might have met at one. Though they hadn't, Luís had seen Violeta years earlier when she rode the trains with her siblings long before either had moved to Santiago. Now, he was determined to know her. He sought her out at *El Tordo Azul*, invited her to his table between sets.

"What job do you do?" she asked him.

"I'm a machinist," he said, although he was only a custodian. Years later, Violeta told her friends she fell in love with a locomotive, rather than a man. Luís made no secret of his ardor. He followed her everywhere. "I'll have you with or without marriage," he vowed. She told him she wanted time to think, for having discovered the truth about his status, she was wary. Her independence was a bone of contention; he wanted her to put aside her music and start raising his family. Their impasse continued for quite some time with neither giving in.

Violeta's sister, Marta, asked her to stand in at her husband's circus, which was performing in Curacaví, about 50 kilometers from Santiago. Violeta, who loved to travel, even if only to vagabond the roads without any clear destination, jumped at the opportunity. Luís learned where she had gone and took off by bicycle the very next day, a Saturday.

On her arrival, Violeta found the circus atmosphere tense; she still resented her brother-in-law for trying to cheat her out of her pay. Luís arrived in the afternoon in time to watch his costumed lady perform. The contrast between being the center of his intense focus and being ignored by a chattering audience sent Violeta running from the ring into his arms. "Luís, will you take me back, right now, to Santiago?"

Chivalrously, he seated her on his bicycle. The couple must have looked a sight, Luís peddling with all the strength his legs could give, his body beaded with sweat and Violeta seated like a princess, her skirts tucked beneath her, her guitar strapped behind her back.

They married. For the first two years they lived in Santiago, where Violeta discovered what a jealous man she had wed. At first, he tried to tolerate her performing; but once he was promoted from custodian and earned what he considered a decent salary, Luís insisted that she stay home.

To please him, she obeyed but practiced every day for hours on end.

The birth in 1938 of Isabel drew the couple closer. But the confinement expected of a new mother irritated Violeta; soon she was bundling the infant, diapers, and baby blankets off to restaurants and bars to join Hilda (also mother of a young son) and sing for tips–this despite Luís's annoyance.

Riding the bus home from a club on the Gran Avenida late one night, Violeta dozed off. She sat in the first row, and as she slept, Isabel awoke in her lap. She squirmed down her mother's legs, a foot or two from the speeding bus' open front door and might have fallen out if Violeta had not awakened in the nick of time. The young mother swept her up into her arms and out of danger, unaware that someday another infant would slip away forever.

1938. Chilean politics felt the impact of the European war. The anti-fascist candidate, Pedro Aguirre Cerda, running on the *Frente Popular* coalition ticket, defeated Nazi sympathizer Gustavo Ross Santa Maria in a hotly contested race.

As a member of the Communist Party, part of the *Frente Popular* coalition, Luís was staunchly pro-workers. Fearful of violence, Violeta tried to stay detached, but Luís insisted that she accompany him to rallies. "If I go I want to sing," she argued.

Soon all the young Parras were entertaining at many such gatherings. All her life; nothing gave Violeta more pleasure than to sing as if amongst family, without the hassles of the bars, the tender folksongs of southern Chile.

January 24th, 1939, an earthquake toppled Chillán, the city nearest Violeta's birthplace, killing 15,000 and reducing great swaths of the city to debris during a hellish months-long period of seismic instability. Although international aid poured in on behalf of the *damnificados*, the quake victims, and Chile struggled to rebuild from the calamity, the right-wing opposition party virtually accused the *Frente Popular* of causing the quake. The wealthy hoarded food and staples, and withdrew their money from the banks in an effort to bring down the government. Prices rose. Food became scarce. The administration declared a state of siege and launched a food program to feed the hungry. Volunteers sold portions of beans and stew out of pick-up trucks that drove through the slums. To head off speculation by retailers, the government opened its warehouses and sold oil, rice, grains, and sugar to the public at wholesale prices. Violeta and Luís distributed bulk food out of their home.

Meanwhile, Violeta's sister, Hilda, leased a soda fountain in Puente Alto, a town not far from Santiago, and invited Violeta to operate it with her. Violeta convinced Luís to move to Puente Alto, so she could work with her sister. Then the railroad transferred Luís to the terminal at Valparaíso, sending Violeta to that Pacific ocean port.

By now, Violeta was pregnant with Ángel, who was born later that year in 1941. Despite her burgeoning state, Violeta performed in the sailors' bars, and it is said her voice grew stronger and more biting. Her fullness made her desirable and her extroversion infuriated Luís, who lashed out in fits of temper. Violeta gave in, and took to filling notebooks with verse after verse of poetry.

A local poetry contest caught Violeta's attention. When she told Luís she was going to submit a poem, he made no effort to stop her. To their surprise, she won an honorable mention and got to recite her poem at a special dinner.

Other than that sole highlight, Valparaíso was a dreadful year for the young mother, isolated from family and Santiago. The couple's fights grew violent, because, according to Luís, Violeta tried to "impose her ideas on me; she was domineering." Often, Luís left her bruised and stormed out of the house to join his friends at a bar.

The railroad transferred Luís again, this time inland to its hub north of Santiago in the mountainous Aconcagua province. Another stint in Valparaíso, and the family returned to Santiago for Luís's next assignment, where they remained for the duration of the marriage.

The family rented the first-floor apartment in a rambling old house with spacious rooms and a garden in the backyard. Luís's parents lived in the same building; his mother was "a sweet lady, very skinny and frail," married for the second time to a truck driver from whom Violeta would later record many colorful *cuecas*. Luís meanwhile was largely absent from the home, due to his irregular work schedule and habitual carousing. The family saw him late, scarcely, or not at all.

Children of their own might have satisfied most women of her class and age, but 26-year-old Violeta found domestic life boring. She occupied herself by sewing clothes, listening to phonograph records of Chopin, Beethoven, and tangos by Carlos Gardel on a victrola. When she could afford it, she took her children to the film-show matinees. She wrote poetry and showed it to her Nicanor. Violeta yearned to perform again. It was a tide the hapless Luís was unable to stem.

When Spain fell to the Fascists, many exiles fled to Chile and brought with them revolutionary songs and gypsy dance. A great surge of activity arose in solidarity with the Spanish people. In 1944, a flamenco dance contest caught Violeta's attention. She entered as *Violeta de Mayo*, the only Chilean contestant among twenty Spaniards. Having mastered the flamenco style, she sang the rousing music of the Spanish Civil War with the exuberance of a patriot and won first place. Success thrust the entire household into a Spanish cultural emersion. Violeta and her six-year-old daughter Isabel learned the Andalusian gypsy *zambra* and other colorful dances; even the toddler Ángel grew adept at *farrucas*, a cocky masculine dance style and the *pasodobles* march step of bullfights.

Before Luís realized what was happening, Violeta had joined an ensemble whose short, melodramatic plays for radio and live theatre catered to popular taste and drew large audiences. Violeta loved the commotion and wanted to do everything possible to give her children the chance to be on stage. She wrote a musical of her own about bullfighting and cast them as gypsy youngsters who danced to their mother's guitar. A supper club contracted a short run of the play. The success prompted Violeta to arrange other performances all over Santiago, even giving a children's matinee in the prestigious Opera Theatre. Later, she and Hilda recorded their first record of Spanish songs.

Everyone but Luís was having fun. Violeta ignored his complaints that she neglected the household, except to host rehearsals at home. The couple fought constantly

Another political crisis precipitated the couple's divorce. In 1946, Gabriel Gonzalez Videla was elected president of Chile, partly due to grassroots campaigning by centrist and leftist parties. With the onset of the Cold War in 1948, Gonzalez Videla issued a stunning order: The Communist Party must be purged from all union activities.

Nationwide, thousands of workers were fired, arrested and hauled off to concentration camps set up in the Northern desert, where they were brutalized, even executed. Because he recognized the power of popular culture, Videla targeted prominent artist activists, including Pablo Neruda, who fled into exile.

Memories of her family's dire straits during earlier political crises haunted Violeta, who despaired in poetry for the plight of the poor.

Luís saw the repression throw his entire life into crisis. People he knew were imperiled. He railed ineffectually. Violeta scorned his tirades, which fueled his fury. He insulted her, told her she was ugly, complained that the house was messy, that she was never home. He would get home late from work and find the children left with his parents. Why, a married woman ought to be home. That's what he believed. How dare she stray?

He turned to Nicanor, who agreed. "As a man, you should insist that your woman obey you."

An ugly fight ensued between husband and wife. "All you ever wanted was an employee, not a companion," she screamed. "I can't take it."

Luís gave up. "Okay, you follow your art; I'm leaving." He packed his belongings and moved out.

Nicanor invited Violeta and her children to share his flat in La Reina, an outlying township in the foothills where the fugitive Neruda had been known to be hiding. Violeta told anyone who asked, "My husband wanted a wife to clean and cook for him. I loved him, but he didn't appreciate my work."

When Nicanor won a fellowship for graduate study in England, Violeta chose to stay in La Reina and brave the onslaught of winter in a one-room shack without electricity or indoor plumbing. She greeted every morning ritualistically by singing. And just as her mother had done when she was growing up, Violeta sent her children, Isabel and Ángel, out to sing for alms.

Less Protection than the Color of Milk

When she saw the squalor in which her daughter and grandchildren were living, Clarisa insisted that they return home with her to Santiago. Though Luís had hurt her, Violeta was certain no other man would love her. Everyone tried to console her. "Where there's music and a guitar, there's no shortage of bread or friends," they said; though there was hardly enough bread to fill the bellies of her family.

Her sorrow inspired one of Violeta's most poignant songs, *La Jardinera* (The Gardener). In it, she spoke as one who took comfort in the language of flowers, as did her peasant *abuelitas* before her. To forget him, she imagined planting roses, dianthus, violets and daisies to soothe her heart.

Hilda, who was blessed with a sunnier disposition than her sister, suggested, "Let's team up again and perform as *Las Hermanas Parra.*" And so they sang at bars with evocative names–*No me Olvides* (Don't Forget Me), *Las Brisas* (The Breezes) on Gran Avenida, *La Nave* (The Ship), *Casanova*– that appealed to the peasant emigrants nostalgic for the terrain left behind.

Typically, the sisters started their day at *El Banco* (The Bank), a tavern frequented by butchers who worked graveyard shift in the slaughterhouses and unwound after work in the late morning. They were behemoths who smelled of meat and blood and lumbered through the smoke-filled saloon. But if anyone dared challenge them when they laid down their pesos on the counter for a beer, enormous knives and meathooks would flash, sending bystanders retreating out of harm's way. Violeta and Hilda's repertoire of serenades and comical songs averted more than one fight. Hilda's alto was the more honeyed voice, Violeta's, higher pitched.

The owner of *Las Brisas* let the sisters perform nightly (whereas at some bars they entertained only on weekends) and even let them nap on a bed in the back room between sets. When they rose to perform again, *Las Hermanas Parra* came trooping out showing broad smiles, their hair freshly combed, ready to light up the crowd with a rousing waltz or soulful ballad. The sisters were well regarded in these establishments; the clientele saw them as kin–modest young women strumming their guitars to support themselves. When their brothers joined them on stage, the group dynamic grew more audacious. Lautaro missed no chance for laughs, and Roberto knew bawdy *cuecas* from the brothels.

The sisters had their first commercial breaks: RCA Victor recorded them, which led to their appearance on a variety show called *Fiesta Linda* and at higher-class bars, such as *El Ensayo* (The Rehearsal), set in a flower garden, and *Patio Andaluz* on the Plaza de Armas, frequented by tourists with cameras. Violeta herself recorded two songs, *Casamiento de Negros*, based on a popular toast to newlyweds that Violeta set to music, and *Que Pena Siente el Alma*, a folkloric waltz. The record became a hit.

The glamour and sexualized innuendos of the media world alarmed Violeta. She heard one deejay tell a young hopeful that refusing his advances might loosen the screws of her microphone. "It costs something to climb the ladder if one shuns love," he whispered as the girl walked on-stage for her debut before a live audience.

Chilean radio in the 1950s played an ecclectic mix of foreign sounds—Cuban *rumba* and *bolero*, Brazilian *samba*, Columbian *cumbia*, Mexican *ranchera* and *corrido*, Argentine *tango*, as well as the Big Band sounds of Benny Goodman and Tommy Dorsey. Violeta resented the absence of Chilean music. "What's wrong with the *cueca* and *tonada* that they're relegated to national holidays alone?" she argued.

Hers and Hilda's appearance was anachronistic. They traipsed through the streets in gypsy skirts and lisle stockings, their tresses drawn back in barrettes. Although Hilda rouged her cheeks and lips, Violeta was too self-conscious of her pockmarks to wear makeup.

To dress presentably for stage, the women shopped at a thrift store filled with the discards of wealthy women. They passed over the sheaths or flared skirts worn by Santiago fashionistas, and chose simple, dark dresses that did not distract from their hands and their instruments.

Doña Amelita Arce, the shopkeeper, had a son named Luís, who worked as an upholsterer. A happy-go-lucky fellow, he saw past Violeta's imperfect complexion and modest attire and lost no time insinuating himself into her life. Soon, the pain of losing her railroad man made way for the lighthearted affection Violeta felt for this affable man who appreciated her as she was. The couple settled into a comfortable if chaotic intimacy as husband and wife in 1949 in doña Amelita's house. When Carmen Luisa was born in 1950, they took an apartment upstairs from a grocery store, which Violeta attempted to manage. But Violeta put Isabel, then ten, and Ángel, age six, in charge of running it. They ate the jam, give away the vegetables, closed and went to the movies. The business failed.

In this marriage, Violeta's desire to perform was applauded by her husband. Luís, who had a good tenor voice
that complemented hers. Violeta also earned money by sewing, not finery like her mother, but larger items (backdrops,
house curtains) required by theatres. With friends and family they organized as a theatre troupe and got government
sponsorship to tour the north as a variety show. Violeta's
cousin, a priest in Antofagasta, booked their engagements in
nitrate-field encampments in the Atacama desert. Rigid
class distinctions dictated even the seating arrangements in
these mining camps: laborers sat in the front, white-color
workers sat behind them, management sat in the rear; and if
better seats were available, no one of a higher social standing would move up to occupy them.

The show featured slapstick comedy, magic tricks,
dance and song numbers. Everyone played multiple roles
and changed costume frequently. Even the youngsters had
bit parts, which sometimes they bungled by forgetting they
were supposed to be acting. Violeta and Hilda performed
their Santiago repertoire and brought the *mambo,* which was
all the rage in the city, into the hinterlands.

After one of her more tender rustic songs, someone in
the audience called out to Violeta, "You have such a special
voice, you ought to sing solo!" He planted a seed.

Like many theatre groups, the troupe suffered compet-
ing egos, and eventually deteriorated over contention for top
billing and pay. Then, Hilda was invited to perform solo at
a Santiago agricultural fair. It seemed reasonable enough to
her–an opportunity to make a little extra money–but Violeta
flew into a jealous rage.

"Hilda, either they contract the two of us or that's the
end of our duo!"

Hilda didn't take her sister's warning seriously, and
went off to play accordion at the fair. So ended the joint ca-

reer of *Las Hermanas Parra.* The sisters remained close, amiable, still attended each other's performances, and sometimes even sang together, but they never reconstituted their duo on an ongoing basis.

The argument upset Violeta; her own loss of self-control frightened her. She withdrew into a silent state as if to atone, played her guitar and allowed it to transport her. After the break with Hilda, Violeta turned for advice to Nicanor, the brother who always encouraged her. "Musically, she's traveling a different road than I want to follow," she told him.

"What path draws you?" he asked.

Her face took on a dreamy look. "The one whose lyrics we heard when we were children. I miss those songs."

"Then why not sing and perform them alone?" Nicanor suggested. He helped her assess her repertoire (she had twenty-five authentic songs that she liked to sing) and urged her on to a solo career.

Nightclub trends dictated that folkloric music be staged with great melodramatic sentimentality: a *caballero* in poncho and spurs declaring eternal love to his peasant sweetheart. The style had a following, but detractors as well. Musicians and folklorists condemned it as a travesty that patronized the peasantry, trivialized their misery, and glossed over the animosity between tenant and *patrón*. Musicians themselves fared little better than the subjects of their songs; countless artistic properties lost copyright to promoters who contracted talent but never paid.

Striking out alone, Violeta sought out venues where she performed on her own terms. She had her first success at a neighborhood cultural center run cooperatively by its artists, where she sang *tonadas* and *cuecas*, or plucked long instrumental interludes on her guitar, enveloping the atmosphere in melancholy or cheer, depending on her whim.

Something new was also growing. Violeta began to use a folkloric style to convey contemporary experience, such as the insidious pressure men so often exerted over women.

Nicanor applauded her originality, but was quick to note, "You might launch yourself on the street, but remember that you have yet to confront the giant, Margot Loyola," one of the foremost folklorists of their day. The two women met, when Margot Loyola walked into the community center where Violeta was entertaining children with a song she had written about a dog. She had gotten everyone to bark; the entire room sounded like a pound at feeding time.

The song's simplicity so charmed Margot that she asked, "Señora, where did you collect that *tonada*?"

Violeta glared back, "Señora, don't you know my music yet?"

"No. But you should be proud I mistook your creation for something traditional."

With that, they became friends. Margot's was undeniably the richer, more pleasing voice, but she was always respectful of Violeta's extraordinary musicianship. Neither woman lacked completely the other's strengths, but Margot lived with privilege never accorded Violeta, and their differences of social station colored their interactions. There was a photograph published in which a self-possessed Margot is looking right into the camera while the diminutive Violeta gazed at her with undisguised admiration.

Nevertheless, the women shared confidences and songs they had collected. Margot became the godmother of Violeta's last child and egged her on to expand her repertoire.

"You have no idea what wealth of emotions, especially sorrow, I am discovering is expressed in lyrics," she told Nicanor during one of their visits. She wasn't sure she could interpret for others what she understood intuitively, but Nicanor never doubted her storytelling abilities. He challenged her to collect songs systematically.

Nicanor's directive became Violeta's life's work. She explored the stories underlying lyrics, the reasons people sang, the choices they made. Her innate curiosity reprieved her from her own pent-up anguish. Violeta often credited her brother's prompting for her success. She believed, "If it weren't for Nicanor, there wouldn't be a Violeta Parra."

Las Hermanas Parra

Song To a Little Angel

Peasant squatters from the south settled Barrancas, a flat fertile plain near Santiago, hoping to homestead the land with shacks of scavenged wood and tin. The region was only minimally served by electricity and running water; people used kerosene for fire and heat and drew water from a public faucet. When the rains came, vegetation turned chartreuse; the unpaved streets, huts, and patios, mud red.

Clarisa moved there in 1952 and opened a storefront restaurant. Her eyesight failing, she enlisted Violeta's help to grill the frybread *sopaipillas* and cook the lentils and noodles, whose aromas wafted into the street. Violeta scurried around in the kitchen, humming her own tunes while keeping an eye on three-year-old Carmen Luisa, who was prone to wander.

Across the road, doña Rosa was washing clothes in a basin under some plum trees, and as she washed, she sang to herself.

> *A gardener of love*
> *plants a seedling and leaves,*
> *another waters and enjoys her,*
> *of the two whose is she?*
> *… after plucking the flower,*

you knew her and you left her,
what does it mean to be loved?

Violeta had stepped outside, and at hearing the unfamiliar song, went over to listen. Out came her notebook and pencil and soon she'd jotted down most of the lyrics in her own shorthand. Rosa continued singing, and when the song ended broke from her distant gaze and smiled directly at Violeta.

Shyly, the younger woman asked, "Have you ever been married?"

"Oh yes!" She laughed. "I had twenty-one children and more than a hundred grandchildren. And when they come to visit, my house is as noisy as a chicken coop!"

Rosa was a midwife; for years she'd delivered most of the babies born locally. "When I first came to Barrancas from the South, I worked as a milkmaid, but I didn't like the work, so I took up sewing, and then finally worked as a midwife."

"Then how did you learn midwifery?"

"By watching my mother and grandmother," she said. "They were *curanderas*, healers in a hacienda near San Fernando. But when my mother took ill and couldn't go out, people would come to cry at our doorstep, and I had to help," even when she was very young. "Sometimes, I'd get home and find two *gorditas* ready to pop, and I'd be taking care of one when the other would start screaming. And I'd be doing this alone."

She was rightly proud of her ability to deliver women of their babies despite numerous complications. "I've delivered babies presenting with buttocks first, face first, even partially transverse. But when a baby is completely transverse, ah, ... those I had to take to Santiago by ambulance." She shut her eyes. "I worked too hard. I'm 78, nearly 79.

Three years ago, my heart started giving out." Then she looked hard at Violeta. "But I'm stubborn and I intend to be around for a while."

Her washing finished, Rosa piled the wet clothes into her basket. Violeta followed her to a line where she hung them out to dry.

"Once I healed a baby so full of worms that the doctor didn't believe he could be cured. And a lot of people brought me children who were cast an evil eye." That hard stare again. "Some people have such strong blood, all they have to do is look at a youngster with malice toward its parents and the child will get so sick, his gall bladder might even burst, and he'll die. But if the parents catch it in time, they call me and with three blessings of the cross they'd be healthy.

"Another time a snake wrapped itself around a child's legs—what a fright! The child had fallen out of bed, asleep, and landed on the snake, which coiled instinctively. After that, the child didn't want to eat—he was rigid with terror and surely would have died of fright. Parents have brought me children who were practically dead—their bodies writhing, their bones creaking as though they'd break, their eyes staring vacantly, with saliva drooling from their mouths. I prayed for them and laid hands on them, and presently, they were stretching out and falling asleep. Take them home, I'd tell the mother, and let them get some rest. And by the next day the children were out in the street playing."

Rosa knew remedies for treating shock and curing spasms. How to massage the body and use medicinal herbs to treat stomach aches and liver problems with poultices and infusions prepared from meadow or woodland plants. Often when Violeta saw Rosa, she would ask her to sing something new, and Rosa often complied; but when asked reveal her *curandera*'s secrets—what she'd say to chase bad luck from a house, how to make the Devil flee, how to cure infertility, Rosa guarded her knowledge jealously. She also dodged any questions about songs that dealt with human emotions. Those, she insisted, were sacrilegious. "The old man who taught them to me was related to the Devil."

"But Rosita, you know some that aren't profane" (Violeta had heard her singing devotional songs) "and I'll bet you even play them on the guitar." Clarisa had told Violeta that Rosa kept a guitar in her room.

"Oh, but I couldn't do that. I used to be a goldmine of songs, but the wind and the rain have washed them away. My memory's not what it used to be."

"But how can you not know them?" Violeta persisted.

"Look, by ransacking my memory the songs might get out, but they'll sting like a wasp!"

Violeta handed Rosa her own guitar, which was leaned up against the table. She took it reluctantly muttering that this would be a waste of time; but her gnarled fingers found chords that she started to play. Violeta hummed along, urging her on. "What you don't remember isn't important. Your playing is fine." The encouragement released from Rosa songs she had not sung in years.

> *The sun is born in San Pedro*
> *and the moon in Santa Clara,*
> *the portals of glory*
> *are never dark.*

By now, 1953, Violeta felt determined to keep alive the collective memory of poetic songs that link the culture to its ancient past.

Violeta had begun formulating her own ideas about the transformative quality of rustic music, particularly in its two variants—religious songs (*canto a lo divino*) that evoke higher spiritual powers and secular songs (*canto a lo humano*) about people's daily lives with all their foibles. She collected, studied, and sang the songs, and taught them to children.

The absoluteness of life and death pervades the rural landscape and the rugged lives of its inhabitants. Customs echo the harsh, plain facts. One tradition unique to the south Chilean countryside is the *velorio del angelito*, the funeral wake held when an infant has died. Roman Catholics believe an unchristened baby's soul cannot enter the kingdom of Heaven, but lingers in Limbo. Indigenous belief mitigates the sentence: a newborn's innocence alone entitles it to divine pardon and imbues it with the power to intercede for the living. To prepare for its heavenly afterlife, the deceased is accorded an all-night ceremony of departure, sung as *cantos a lo divino*.

Violeta had attended *velorios* with her mother and relatives, but growing up in the city, her husband, Luis Arce, had never witnessed the impressive vigil. How everyone drew close. How emotion filled the candlelit darkness. How sincerely Violeta joined in. Though first and foremost a singer, Violeta became one more mourner. The poignancy of the music meant to suppress weeping (for no one is supposed to cry at a *velorio del angelito*) clouded every eye with tears.

> *Already, the dear little angel*
> *has gone to Heaven*
> *to pray for his grandparents,*
> *for his parents, and little brothers.*

In poetry, Violeta recalled the death of a severely disabled boy named Vicente, who lingered for three years; and when he died, his death came as a solemn relief. Violeta shuddered to recall his mother's screams as she gazed at her lifeless son, slumped on the ground. The child was carried inside by the village women who gathered to comfort her and prepare for the *velorio*.

"Rosa, how do they perform *velorio del angelito* in your region?"

"Huy! Violeta, Beautifully! First we fixed up the dining room, and surrounded the baby with a heavenly scene." Vicente's inanimate remains too were set on a table transformed into an altar with silvery paper stars that glistened in candlelight. "This was the custom in the old days, Violetita. And songs! What a time it was to sing and drink *gloria'o*." Violeta nodded vigorously. "How beautifully they all sing! Yet how can these songs be so exquisite, when the mother is overcome by a sorrow unlike any other."

Atop his flower-strewn altar, Vicente too lay as if asleep in a garden amid the cherubs and seraphim. To commemorate his death, Violeta wrote a song cycle that addressed the *velorio*'s four phases of grief. As the *velorio* begins, verses of *saludos* acknowledge the sacred passage.

> *I greet the happy day*
> *God carried you to Heaven*
> *to have you in the bosom*
> *of the land of blue skies.*
> *Already, your roots are severed*
> *Santa Ana awaits you*
> *with resounding of bells....*

Songs of sufferance, inspired by the agonies of Christ, filled the hours from midnight to three in the morning. Of all the songs Rosa knew, these were the most haunting and the ones Violeta asked Rosa to sing.

They carry him to Calvary
burdened with a cross, . . .
the humble Virgin weeps
with eyes closed tight;
she is consumed by her affliction
on seeing this reality.

As night progressed toward dawn, the singers sang
verses of wisdom inspired by the Scriptures, to acknowledge
the teachings of Moses and Solomon, to honor God's creation of the world, to accept the Last Judgment, and a personal sentence of Fate.

Mercifully they call to ring
the bells of oblivion;
yet how is it possible to douse
the flames of burning love?

Once the skies have lightened, the men left to dig the
grave and the women prepared the deceased for burial.

"With the coming of daybreak, Violetita, we cut out a
little white shroud from new cloth. Everything–the scissors,
the thread, the needle–everything must be new. Then we
dress the infant in a little seat of straw, with a crown and
some toys in its little hands. And on its back, Violetita, we
put wings, so that the infant seems alive and looks as though
it were going to fly away." Vicente's robe was white too, but
its sleeves were tattered into shreds. He lay with a little
crown on his head, holding a garland of flowers.

At dawn, the mourners' songs turn to the final departure of the dead child from the world of the living. Violeta
spoke in Vicente's voice.

Mother of mine, don't cry for me
because I am leaving this world.
... Don't wet my little wings any longer
... You only delay the entry into Heaven
of your little white dove.

Violeta collected many such *cantos a lo divino.* Later personal tragedy inspired one of her greatest poetic songs.

When did her brightness dim,
and where did her sweetness go?
Why did her body fall like a ripened fruit?
When the flesh dies, the spirit searches the heights
for the reason its life was cut short so prematurely.
the reason for her death, imprisoned in a tomb;
When the flesh dies, the spirit is left in darkness.

The Songs of Elders

Rosa was reminiscing one day over a cup of tea. "They play the harp where I come from, as well as guitar." Violeta too recalled the sweet strains of that intricate instrument, which is almost exclusively the domain of women. "Yes, we used to sing for weeks on end. We'd be out hunting birds. There'd be plenty of food. One guy spent a week singing here, another week there. They'd come looking for him, even fight over him–that's how good his voice was and how many songs he knew. And the man died singing, he did, with his guitar right in his hands!

"Once, when I was out walking in the countryside, I joined up with a bunch of people from the south, and we all went to the mountains. We camped in a grove of hawthorns and drank wine and danced *cuecas*. You can imagine what a lively time that was!" She broke into a mischievous song,

> *In Arauco a young girl*
> *very curious and without feeling*
> *murdered her father and her mother*
> *to run away with her lover.*

This evil youngster
went straight to Hell
and to Lucifer she promised
eternal affection.
Let the Devil take her,
said Saint Peter.

Violeta leaned across the table. "Rosa, you know, there must be so many singers out here right in our midst, in the villages around Santiago."

"Yes, that's true."

"Why not introduce me to the musicians you know right around here in Barrancas?"

"Ay, Violeta, that would be an adventure like what I might have done as a girl! What a fine idea!"

At Ramon Reyes's house, Rosa didn't bother with formalities. "Don Ramon, Don Ramon! Wake up!" The old man was sitting beneath an arbor in a drunken doze.

"Huh? Go away."

"Just a little song," Violeta pleaded. He mumbled something to himself and fished up his guitar. Mid-tuning, he dozed off. Then, with a shudder, grew more alert and started to play. As he warmed to his singing, he fell into a trance. At the end of the song, he lay back and fell asleep.

Violeta's initial forays to meet the elderly singers lasted no more than a day. She'd get up by seven, dispatch her household chores and was showered and ready to go in an hour or two. Leaving breakfast ready, she took her guitar and didn't return until dark, brimming with stories of people she had met reminiscent of those she'd known growing up.

Having a sense of purpose made her audacious. Once she tried to talk the widow Mercedes Guzman de Sanchez into tuning her harp. "These are old fingers," the eighty-year-old woman complained when she refused, but to appease her, she plucked a few chords on her guitar and sang a melodic verse. Violeta copied down the words hastily, asking permission only afterward.

"Who could stop you?" doña Meche chided. Then, having warmed to her visitor, she launched into a rousing song, "Because it's what makes the dancers show off!" And Violeta absorbed it greedily, certain she was capturing the soul of the singer.

> *Long live the pretty whore*
> *I'd wanted to embrace her*
> *but here I am, far away*
> *singing her a serenade.*

When Violeta's children noticed that whenever their mother put up extra food and did all the laundry, it was just a matter of time before they would hear, "*Adiós*, I'm going to see my elders." And off she went. Her son, Ángel, who was still a young boy, recalled, "There were times we wouldn't see her for days on end, and then suddenly she'd wake us up at 4:00 a.m. Come eat, kids! She always brought home something delicious."

Violeta, now 36, walked, hitchhiked, rode by horseback, train, or bus over dirt roads throughout central Chile in any weather. If she arrived drenched at the homes of strangers, she'd rely on them to give her dry clothing and make a bed for her. She went to live with the peasants, never doubting their hospitality.

Violeta never knew beforehand what she was looking for or what she might find; any clue to traditional daily life intrigued her—songs, legends, musical forms, sayings, recipes —virtually anything authentic. If subjects were shy or reluctant to reveal what they knew, Violeta won them over by addressing them as a child does a grandparent, with simple affection.

Someone might say, "in such-and-such a place there's an old man who . . . ," and according to Luís, who often accompanied her, "people had scarcely given us directions before we were knocking on the door to someone else's house."

"My name is Violeta Parra and I've come to sing with you." She knew that they all sang.

"Yes, but you sing first, Violeta. Then we'll sing."

"Very well, we'll each sing a song."

Veterans of the country began to seek her out too, and Violeta welcomed them all into her home. She was always cooking and bartered food for song. If there wasn't enough food, she busied herself so that no one would notice she wasn't eating. Songs or stories became commodities to her, which she had to earn, buy, feed, beguile, trade to get. Her family tolerated her generosity without question. Once the entire family ate nothing but beans every day until they finished a sack she had bought to get a song.

En route to a remote village, the bus Violeta and Luis were riding developed a flat tire. Waiting for the tire to be repaired meant delaying their journey by hours, so Violeta insisted they hitchhike. They walked down the road to the next shade tree and soon a police car approached from the distance. The officers stopped and listened without much enthusiasm to Violeta's concerns, which she punctuated with guitar strums brandished like a gun. They agreed to drive the couple to the next crossroads.

As Violeta and Luís got out at their stop, one of the policemen turned to her.

"Let me ask a favor of you now, Violeta."

"What do you want from me?" she asked disconcerted, until he withdrew his own guitar from the trunk and handed it to her.

"Will you tune it for me?" The three men then waited in the middle of the road, while Violeta tuned the policeman's guitar.

If no one would join her, she went alone to the villages carrying booty to share – a flask of liquor, candy, or trinkets. After drinking together, no one denied her. They'd sing for her and then suggest another house, "over there, there's a woman who knows a lot of songs."

Nicanor, Violeta's brother, accompanied her when she met don Antonio Suárez, a centenarian who lived his whole life as a tenant farmer. He still enjoyed good health, though he'd spent his life hauling water from a well, cultivating crops, and harvesting honey from the hives without getting stung. "The bosses have no complaints about me," he told them.

He had a jovial banter; but when Nicanor asked him what he thought of Violeta's work, he dismissed it. "Whatever I sing is just going to end up buried in a pile of papers."

They would've left empty-handed, but for don Antonio's quips.

La plata se gana al sol y se consume a la sombra, money is made by light of day and spent in the shadows.

Del formal se espera mucho, much is expected of you if you're a serious person.

When caught stretching the truth, he offered *el hablantín vive a tropezones*, someone who gossips is bound to slip up.

Violeta visited don Antonio so often, she won him over as an ally. Then one day he showed up at her house in Santiago with a gift. "I have a *guitarrón* for you Violeta, but you'll have to find someone else to teach you to play it. The *guitarrón*, a bass guitar brought to Chile from imperial Spain, was unknown in the city, though in the countryside, a few *campesinos* still played their twenty-five strings. Violeta was thrilled.

Although don Antonio sang well, his efforts to play the nearly forgotten instrument were frustrating to hear. If you come visit me this Sunday, I'll introduce you to *El Profeta Ángulo*. He plays the instrument as it was meant to be played."

That was how Violeta met Isaías Ángulo. The sixty-eight-year-old man astonished Violeta with his nimble virtuosity. She praised him for the intricacy by which he teased the melody out of the strings, then toyed with him to watch his reaction. "They tell me there are a lot of good singers in these parts."

"I wouldn't know, Violetita, but I do know that I can leave any other musician in the dust! The mark of a true singer is his arrogance, for the moans he can elicit with his instrument." She giggled. Don Isaías was a kindred spirit. They visited frequently; each time, she learned new songs or verses to ones she already knew, both religious and secular, such as *La Ciudad Deleitosa*, which depicted the Paradise of peasant lore:

> *There is a faraway city*
> *Where the poor go*
> *The walls are made of bread*
> *And pillars of cheese . . .*
> *No one goes hungry*
> *Not even if they wanted to . . . .*

Of all the elders he met, it was don Isaías whom Ángel called *abuelo*, grandfather. Violeta decided her son should live the peasant life instead of going to school, so she arranged for him to stay with don Isaías for over a year. The elder gave Ángel a *guitarrón* carved with daggers.

"Where this *guitarrón* came from, any singer who bothered its player might come to harm and whoever mastered it was someone to be reckoned with." Ángel became an excellent *guitarrón* player.

Don Isaías also gave Violeta an antique, finely crafted *guitarrón* from the region north of Santiago, which bore a silver inscription, *Familia Cortes de Monroy, Copiapo, 1808.* Because of its enormous size and weight, the *guitarrón* is played traditionally by men, its sound echoing the deep male vocal range. But Violeta played it proudly, heedless of its masculine associations.

The more Violeta heard of the folkloric music of the elders, the more determined she grew to broadcast it over the radio. Like doña Rosa, don Isaías bragged about the fabulous music he and his friends made when they gathered for a song circle.

"How about holding one right here for all of Chile to hear?" When he realized that she was serious, don Isaías agreed to do just that. It took time to win his friends to the idea.

On the day the song circle was to be taped, a few musicians promised to show up, but others refused. Their resistance annoyed don Isaías. He took off with Violeta to find out why they were staying away.

"What's wrong with Violeta's putting this on the radio?" don Isaias thundered at one old man. "Are you going to take your verses to the grave?" The man stood his ground. It was noon. He had just picked a melon from his garden. There seemed no prospect of resolution to the stand-off until Violeta realized that someone else was involved: his *senora.*

"God lent us music as a temptation," he said. "I promised my sweetheart I'd stop bingeing on music and drink." Violeta appealed to his *senora*, who not only acquiesced, but joined the party.

A frail tenant farmer came to the song circle, but refused to sing or play his guitar for Violeta. When pressed, the eighty five-year-old don Juan straightened up stiffly. Suddenly the music stopped.

"I swore I'd never sing again, ever in my life."

"But why not?"

He hesitated. "Because God took my sweetheart, my little granddaughter. The night I sang at her *velorio*, . . ." Already he was choked up.

"Chile needs your songs," Violeta insisted.

Reluctantly, don Juan took up his guitar, tuned it, and began to sing an elegy in a hoarse voice; he had indeed damaged his vocal chords by singing to exhaustion. Once Violeta gleaned the guitar accompaniment, she joined in. Afterward, don Juan gave her an old notebook with all the verses of the song written down.

Another younger man joined the song circle to contribute a song. He apologized for his lack of talent, which Violeta wouldn't hear of. But don Isaías could barely contain himself. "For the love of God, how can you bring yourself to sing, when you're so out of tune?" But the fellow didn't miss a beat and sang ten verses before he was satisfied he'd contributed enough.

The party was well underway when don Emilio, the local chairmaker, arrived and Violeta learned of his special ability: divining the location of mines. Violeta stared with amazement.

"Yes," he whispered, "I have found twelve of them!"

"But they could make you rich," she said.

"Of course, if I were to work them, I could be rich. But I only like to find them. I stumble on them when I go off to hunt rabbits in the mountains." He was reluctant to sing for Violeta, for he was toothless beneath his thick mustache. Finally after coaxing and a pipeful of tobacco, he relented. Even despite his gummed elocution, Violeta described his voice as sweeter than all the others.

The elders' song circle grew rowdy, with plenty of drinking and laughter, as the men strove to outdo each other with the originality and eloquence of songs improvised or remembered, on a given theme and musical style. "Let's sing a song of possibility," someone suggested, and with that, he started singing about a pumpkin that weighed a hundred kilos. Someone else picked up with a tale about magical black beans. And then another about an invisible lover. They postulated impossibilities, such as a horseman riding from France to Mexico—they had no idea where these places really were or that those lands were separated by an ocean.

Even in Violeta's day, few minstrels remained who could improvise—a talent largely lost. Much as she loved the game, Violeta herself did not have the improvisatory knack. She was a singer and composer of written lyrics, who learned a great deal from the elderly peasants of Puente Alto and other communities near Santiago. Later, she extended her research to the south and north of Chile, harvesting musical heritage for fifteen years and yielding over three thousand songs.

Así Canta Violeta Parra

To Chilean sophisticates of the 1950s, foreign culture epitomized glamour, wealth, and prestige. They listened to European and Yankee music, read translations of English-language best sellers, watched dubbed Hollywood movies, and aspired to the life style of "Oklahoma!" and Main Street. Classical musicians looked abroad for their voice.

But some viewed the resultant adopting of foreign styles as mental colonialism.

Against this backdrop, Violeta fought to make a living with her music. Feisty, she argued her way into studio offices –almost violent in her rectitude–and frequently was turned away. But her ability to make people listen to her won respect. Producers may have resented her, but they recognized talent and its potential to generate profit.

Violeta debuted on a radio show called *Aún tenemos la música chilena!* –"Do we ever have music, *Chilenos!*" She was introduced as "a singer-songwriter who has traveled through cities and puddles, beaches, deserts, mountains and plains to bring us the authentic peasant woman."

Her unadorned delivery compelled anyone who listened to acknowledge something undeniably familiar.

Her prestige grew; reviewers in both entertainment and folkloric worlds began to take her more seriously. But her limited commercial experience caused her to accept unfavorable conditions as well, such as a studio accompanist whose extraneous guitar flourishes threw off her rhythm.

Then one lucky day, an iconoclastic station manager gave Violeta the freedom to shape a program more closely to her own intentions than ever before. He told his crew, "She'll sing and teach you the meaning of each song, and from that you'll put together a professional radio program."

At her first work session, everyone in the control room gathered around to hear her. Some were amazed, even frightened, but others were more courteous and even admiring. Violeta demonstrated encyclopedic knowledge of her material, something appreciated by jazz and classical music devotees, who perceived Violeta's music much as they might the exotic music of other continents. Her vibrant, introspective repertoire was virtually unknown to city dwellers, who assumed rustic life to be nothing but drudgery.

The pilot show was an unqualified success and won Violeta a contract to host a short series of half-hour programs.

After just a few shows, *Así Canta Violeta Parra* went to regular broadcasts, once a week on Fridays at 8:00 p.m. and rebroadcast on Sundays over repeaters the length of Chile. By 1955, Violeta received a regular salary for three half-hour programs a week, requiring a programmed script, which she cowrote.

Regrettably, few of the transcripts and none of the program tapes were saved–a shame because they contained unique recordings of Violeta's elderly friends. Nevertheless, her radio experience gave Violeta a chance to learn the mechanics of radio production in a fully realized form.

Typically, her shows were built around a vignette that unfolded in semi-documentary style. Violeta gathered and organized the raw information and then gave it to her director to script and pace with recordings. In one show, Violeta depicted community planting as it was practiced by people in her uncle's village. As she told the tale, she accompanied herself on the guitar.

"It was called *mingaco*, and it always reminded me that man isn't worth anything all alone. But when they get together to accomplish something, then they have the right to call themselves men! Let me tell you a little story. It might have started when the old Domingo Aguilera sat pensively in his hut looking at the tools lying on the floor."

She plucked on her guitar a melodic phrase reminiscent of her elderly uncle. "When he was young, Don Domingo thought it was so easy to plow through the earth and smell the odor of the soil, ready to receive the seed. But with the passage of years, his plow's cutting edge had worn out. His sons had grown and married, and the women at home couldn't help him with the plowing, which took tremendous strength. Then he remembered his neighbors from down the hill. Surely, they could conduct a *mingaco* and help him plant the lentils among the vines."

Another musical interlude, this time upbeat. Violeta launched into a lively quatrain about the *campesino*'s topsy-turvy world.

Violeta had a knack for developing a program from ordinary events by showing its extraordinary details. To tape a show about the wine harvest, she insisted on capturing the squishing sounds of people crushing the grapes by bringing a bucket of grapes onto the sound-stage and having her children crush them with their feet.

She staged a model *velorio del angelito*, an infant wake, right in the studio, complete with a shroud, and insisted that everything be bought in the shops where the *campesinos* would go. When Violeta set up the tableau, everyone fell mute. While they were designing the sound, the producer realized he wanted a church bell ringing the death knell. Working at Violeta's house, they went to ask the parish priest if he might ring the bells. He looked at Violeta dubiously, then said, "You know what we can do? Wait a little longer, because nearby there's a man who is gravely ill." Sure enough, an hour later the bell began to ring.

Violeta was living again in La Reina, in the crisp air of the foothills above Santiago. The opportunity to buy land meant going into debt, which startled her family; but Violeta seized the chance to have her own place, and drafted able bodies to construct a modest hut with a dirt floor. Working shoulder to shoulder with the men, she dug singlemindedly a hole for a septic well. They carried water from a faucet a block away and stole electricity from the public lighting cables. Until the roof was finished, they slept under the stars.

Whenever the radio crew came to La Reina for taping, an improvisational theater ensued. People greeted them in the street, children shouted into the mikes, and the crew recorded the happening live, complete with dogs barking and other ambient sounds. Amidst of this spontaneous narrative, they inserted the songs. For a show recreating the *Cruz de Mayo*, a pagan religious festival, they lit bonfires in the street.

Once they had the taped portions, they'd convene at Violeta's house. But before settling down to work, Violeta served traditional refreshments, such as a Chilean summer drink of nectarine juice and limed corn. Then they listened to the recordings, and resolved the production details.

Violeta spoke often of her friend, doña Rosa Lorca and her wealth of rustic wisdom. Yet doña Rosa resisted being recorded for radio. This made Violeta even more determined to do so. Finally, she found her chance. She invited doña Rosa into Clarisa's for a beer, directed her friend to a table by the wall, and while they waited for their malt liquors, fussed with something out of sight.

"Rosita," she said, "sing me a *cueca*." Rosa didn't hesitate. She picked up the guitar and sang a lively song, then having warmed up, segued into a waltz. Singing together, the two women were giddy by the time doña Clarisa came to the table.

"Why not stay for lunch?" she suggested.

"Oh no! I have to go." But as she stood up from her chair, Violeta took some money from her purse and handed it to her. "What is this for?" Violeta and Clarisa were looking so pleased with themselves, Rosa's puzzlement turned to indignation. Violeta stooped beneath the table again, and arose holding her tape recorder. "Why you've taped everything I've said!"

Violeta nodded. "And sung."

Rosa laughed. "You know, this is really good. My nephew's been angry with me for telling you so much. '*Tía*, don't you see that she's making money off you? She'll get rich, and what about you?' I said to him, 'Why should you care? It's my business!' Now I can show him how things work out."

When Violeta next showed up with her handsome young radio crew, doña Rosa put up no resistance. They sat on a low step of the porch and Rosa talked easily about growing up in the south, a conversation much like any she and Violeta had had many times before. She spoke of her girlhood, sang songs, recited sayings, described being a midwife.

The men recorded the conversation on one, then two reels of tape, all the while encouraging her to tell them more. They returned sometime later to play the edited tape for Rosa.

By now, doña Rosa was eager to help. Violeta needed to record animal sounds. Clarisa kept geese and chickens, a pig and a ewe out behind the restaurant, and Violeta first tried to get them to squawk by feeding them, but soon discovered they didn't make noise when they were eating. "Rosita," she asked, "How can we make the animals squawk?"

"I have it! Get ready!" Rosa grabbed the tail of the pig and twisted it. And the pig let out a squeal that went right onto the tape for a radio show.

Violeta tried in vain to irritate the other animals, but they were all absorbed in their feed. Then Rosa said, "Stop scattering the corn, but call to them as if you were, and when they approach, throw the feed all around, differently, to confuse them." Violeta did so, and sure enough, the geese honked and the chickens clucked.

There was still the ewe to record. "Rosita, how are we going to make her *baa*?" Without hesitating, Rosa picked up a bottle of red wine sitting on a nearby table, grabbed the sheep's head, and poured some down its throat. The ewe bleated and Violeta got her sound-print.

Violeta introduced that program by paying tribute to Rosa. "I've always imagined Chile to be the best book of folklore ever written. When I met doña Rosa Lorca, I felt like I was opening that book."

Groups groups gathered to listen together on Sundays, reverently. The show was acclaimed in the press, even editorialized in *El Mercurio*, Chile's newspaper of record. Key to the show's success was Violeta's superb rapport with her subjects, which made the show very warm and human. And when asked how she perceived the public, Violeta answered, "I see no difference between the artist and the public: I sing for them, not for myself. It is the miracle of contact." The ideal guided Violeta throughout her professional life. She saw the public and herself as one people who sang out to be heard.

Soon, the quantity of fan mail arriving at the radio station exceeded anyone's expectations. Thousands of letters arrived. Lacking furniture, the Parra's rooms were filled with emotional letters, from both elderly, nearly illiterate peasants and sophisticated urban intellectuals, expressing gratitude for the music and stories they hadn't heard since childhood.

To answer even some of her mail, Violeta needed pencils, paper, and envelopes. Every letter required a stamp. Some people asked for photos.

Ángel went on the air and asked people to send his mother stationery and stamps, because they couldn't afford to buy them. And sure enough, people started supplying her, so that she could answer some of her fan mail, and also heat her *rancho* through the cold winter and light the wood that heated the oil in which Violeta fried the *sopaipillas*.

Así Canta Violeta Parra was broadcast for more than a year, until the radio station itself went off the air due to internal problems. Yet its tenure marked a milestone for Violeta–critical exposure during which she found her public personality.

Every year, the national media guild awarded prizes for excellence in the performing arts–the Chilean Oscars. Violeta's husband Luís insisted that they attend the awards ceremony, though they had barely enough money for the tickets. "Violeta, I'll bet you're going to win! She didn't believe me, but I convinced her to go." They sat in the balcony as ordinary spectators, when suddenly, a celebrity announcer called Violeta's name and summoned her on stage to receive the *Premio Caupolicán*, the Caupolicán Prize, an award given every year for excellence in folklore. Violeta took the statuette in her hands, cradled it to her bosom, and caressed it as though it were a precious living thing. She was pregnant, glowing with life, and tears of joy sparkled in her eyes.

Violeta and Luís didn't get home until five that morning, and when they did, carrying a ham and bottles of wine, they woke up the children to celebrate. This was a very important occasion!

That day, Luís took Violeta to the Plaza Baquedano, a favorite site for photographers with their tripods and box cameras, to pose for a picture with her little statuette.

Rosita Clara

Rosa Clara Arce Parra was born in early Spring, on September 22, 1954, when the first roses were budding. Violeta hardly paused to give birth. After being awarded the Caupolicán Prize, she was honored by the *Sociedad de Autores y Compositores*. To supplement her radio income, she taught guitar, *cueca*, and *flamenco*. She was also writing new songs.

Violeta's house bustled with the sounds of instruments being tuned, live and recorded music, the comings and goings of people. Somehow everything, including the new baby, got taken care of whether she did it herself or others pitched in. It didn't matter. The music, the folklore–those things were important.

One rainy June afternoon, Violeta took Rosa out for a walk. She sang her a lullaby with fatalistic lyrics like those that rock-a-bye babies everywhere. Though prone to colic, Rosa was cooing in a melodious voice, just like her siblings did when they were babies, for their mother was always singing.

Near the Franciscan convent on the Alameda, some musicians approached them jubilantly. "Violeta, guess what!

They've chosen us–you too!–to go to Poland and sing at the World Youth Festival."

Violeta couldn't believe it. A European Communist party was inviting her to Europe to sing at a gala event. Everyone chattered at once about travel and passports. The two-week festival was less than a month away, in July. Violeta had never been out of the country; suddenly she had the chance to travel.

The baby wriggled in her arms, hoping to regain her mother's undivided attention. What was she going to do with Rosa Clara? Violeta puzzled over the predicament, excited but also resentful. How could she possibly go? Should she take the baby? Rosita, a small child, was eight months old and still nursing. Did she dare leave her home with Luís and his mother? They could take care of her. It was only two months, after all. The festival will be fabulous. Things will work out. Somehow, she had to come up with the money.

Leaving Rosita behind was an odd and unacceptable thing to do. Violeta told very few people of her plan or her agonizing ambivalence. A jealous Luís barely understood, though usually he indulged her whims. "No other mother would leave her baby," he said more perplexed than angry. Violeta's attitude hardened. There was no time for deliberation.

Drawing on every resource, the family raised the equivalent of one hundred eighty U.S. dollars in Chilean currency for her trip. Everyone was thrown into confusion. Four-year-old Carmen Luisa went to live with a family friend. Ángel, aged eleven, stayed home with his grandmother, dad, and baby sister. Isabel was now living with a young man. The children accepted their mother's motives: She was doing this for Chile, for folklore, for the workers and for their music.

Though she herself initiated the separation, Violeta had misgivings on the eve of her departure. Dread overcame her as Violeta surrendered the whimpering Rosa to Luís' arms.

She boarded the plane for Buenos Aires and prayed "to Jesus to dim the light of her motherly love." By the time the plane landed, Violeta's breasts were engorged, for she had abruptly ended nursing the baby. Her body tense with pain, Violeta went straight to a hospital and asked for help. They gave her an infant to feed so she could express her milk and an injection to suppress her mammaries. Violeta cried inconsolably, missing her infant, and was certain Rosita too was wailing in her crib, blameless, missing that sacred food.

Violeta's depression worsened when she boarded the ship for Genoa four days later. Her shipmates tried to cheer her up, by turns cajoling her and threatening to spank her if she didn't lighten her spirit.

Wandering near the dock of Rio de Janeiro, where they'd stopped to take on passengers and cargo, Violeta met a Negro woman carrying an infant in her arms. Violeta's heartbeat quickened to see the baby, pink-cheeked, dressed in a gown fashioned of ribbon. "Oh, please let me hold your golden angel," she asked. The negress handed the baby to Violeta, who addressed her as though she were her own Rosita Clara. The infant laughed at Violeta's oddly acid voice. The mother grew apprehensive the stranger was lingering too long.

When Violeta climbed the gangplank to the ship, she confronted an angry captain, for she had delayed their departure time. The sky overhead turned rose-colored as the ship set sail, but once in open sea, it became for Violeta a prison surrounded by great depths. It was a difficult crossing. She got seasick. The monotony of the ocean voyage ruffled tempers on board. Fights broke out, and in one, Violeta was almost hurt.

Even among the artists of the South American delegation, Violeta cut a unique figure. She was constantly singing and was never separated from her guitar. The women who shared her stateroom disparaged her for being *una rota,* a peasant without prestige.

She affected irritating mannerisms, spoke of herself in third person. "Here is Violeta Parra! Violeta Parra has arrived!" Though she struggled to cope with her misery, everyone saw her sitting head in hands, bemoaning how much she missed her family. By the time of docking in Las Palmas, Canary Islands, Violeta had alienated herself from virtually everyone on board.

Her vivacity returned, however, when the ship finally docked in Genoa. African delegates met their South American brethren on the wharf and everyone traveled en masse by train to Warsaw, Poland.

By the time they arrived, all the delegates were united as one voice chanting, "The poor have been trapped in Hell for too long!" Sloganeering, cheering throngs greeted the performers as they joined in a citywide extravaganza. A sleepless whirlwind of recitals, interviews, concerts, and rallies ensued on stages erected in neighborhoods, plazas, markets, union halls, theatres, and stadiums. Each country presented its very best performers before enthusiastic crowds.

Violeta gave a two-hour, open-air recital. The public was unfamiliar with her music, but they listened to the songs, not so much with enthusiasm as interest. Her disheveled appearance called attention to itself, but her magnetic showmanship won audience acclaim. Even her detractors came to appreciate her virtuosity on guitar and her ability to communicate with her audience.

That evening, Violeta went strolling with friends through old Warsaw, when some Poles who had heard her perform that day spotted her. They threw flowers to her. Violeta delighted in her triumph and in being part of creating the festival's vision of world harmony. In poetry, she extolled "the nappy hair of the African," "the whiteness of the Roman's skin," "the grace of the Japanese," "the gentleness of the Hindu." What mattered were "the blood ties between Black and Mongol, Canadian and Spaniard, Tibetan and Andean that bind the world's people like a global vein of love."

In early August, the festival ended, the streets were swept clean of debris, and everyone scattered. Some Chileans returned home, others traveled around Europe. Everything happened so abruptly, Violeta was caught unprepared. She walked the streets of Warsaw aimlessly, yet could not mobilize to leave Europe. Someone invited her to Prague. She declined, dreaming that "Mother Russia beckoned," and traveled instead to the Carpathian mountains, where she marveled at an alpine landscape reminiscent of Chile.

Before leaving home, Violeta had written to the Chilean ambassadors of all the European capitals she hoped to visit. It was a curious document, imbued with her unique sense of mission: "Violeta Parra, Chilean folklorist, advises the Ambassador that she is arriving on such a date and wishes to be received." She brought her Caupolicán statuette to indicate her importance.

She took a train to Vienna, but en route was pickpocketed. She pawned a brooch that Luís had given her as a gift and was disappointed to receive only two dollars. Violeta headed for the Chilean embassy and asked to see the ambassador, who was not impressed. "Why don't you ply your talents in France, my dear. You'll be better received there."

An indignant Violeta went to the train station and demanded a ticket to Paris. She slept as the train crossed Austria and Switzerland; by dawn, she was in France but by the time she disembarked in Paris night had fallen. She had thirty-four dollars, a valise, and a guitar. A taxi driver drove her to the Saint Michel hotel.

The next morning, Violeta called at the Chilean Embassy. She must have made quite a sight–a peasant woman in that most elegant of surroundings. No one knew anything about her letter. She was asked to leave, but refused. Someone said dismissively. "I'm not expected to cater to every itinerant musician or painter who comes calling. Why, there are hundreds of you, all wanting to perform in Paris. You'll find the network easily enough." To Violeta, the man's demeanor was as arrogant as the *huemul* stag of the Andes that graced the Chilean emblem and he needed a reminder of the nation he was representing. It was nearly September, Chile's patriotic month. Violeta began to sing the Chilean national anthem. She was bodily evicted, but two people followed her outside and told her where she might find other Chileans.

Violeta wandered the streets of Paris. Then by a fluke of luck, a *compatriota* spotted her and took her to his room. He and his roommates cordoned off a tiny space for her and let her stay with them for four days. Violeta rested, laundered her clothes, and at night went from bar to bar asking to sing Chilean music to a Parisian public.

One of her new Chilean friends told her about a fellow who might team up with her to sing at the *L'Escale*, a night club in the Latin Quarter. When they met, the man was visibly disappointed by her homeliness. Violeta said,

"What did you expect, someone to fall in love with? I can sing. That's the point, isn't it?"

When she auditioned, Violeta felt as if she were facing the guillotine; she was doomed if they didn't like her. Her most ingratiating smile greeted the audience; she hid her frayed nerves, her tearing eyes. She sang and was astonished by the chorus of bravos that rewarded her. Paris had opened its doors to her. *L'Escale* hired her to sing there nightly and paid her enough money for her to rent a room of her own in a nearby residential hotel on Rue Monsieur le Prince.

Everything seemed to be working out. She had a job, somewhere to stay, and soon would save enough money to get home. Then, Violeta picked up a letter at *Poste Restante* that was to change her life irrevocably: Twenty-eight days after Violeta left Chile, on July 27, 1955 at 10:30 am, Rosa Clara died of bronchial pneumonia.

Little Jasmine Flower

Sobbing, Violeta ran upstairs to her room clutching Isabel's letter, lunged onto the unmade bed, and allowed the news to consume her. Grief suffocated her with the finality of the granite stone that sealed the baby's cemetery niche during a funeral Violeta did not attend. She wept in convulsive screams. She condemned herself with self-loathing. Her reality slit as if by a dagger into shame and severed maternity.

She might never admit it to others, perhaps not even to herself, but her commitment to folkloric was stronger than her capacity to nurture. She had not been particularly protective of any of her children. But only Rosita Clara had sickened and died as an *angelita*, a guardian angel fated to watch over her kin.

Violeta vented her rage on Luís, sending him venomous postcards. She blamed herself, but also him for having betrayed her trust by letting the baby die. Luís' mother had taken care of the sickly baby, but failed to heal Rosita when she took ill. Luís told Violeta he missed her and loved her. But "after a child dies, many other things die also. And she didn't stay away for two months, as she'd said, but rather two years. And when she didn't return, I thought, 'Every-

one's got to follow their own path.'" The couple never reconciled.

Unable to face her family, Violeta stayed in Paris to
mourn her daughter's death. Rosa Clara's passing haunted
her as much for the loss of her own innocence as for her
memory of the tiny child who never grew. Alone, she sang
the songs of reverence, sorrow, acknowledgement, and departure of the *velorio del angelito.*

> *If you departed on high*
> *I ask God in Heaven*
> *to grant me consolation*
> *for the grief of your departure.*

Alone, she mourned Rosita's journey to the spirit's
mysteries. She judged herself unworthy of forgiveness. She
toughened herself to humiliation. In her new awareness of
herself, she was damned.

Adrift in self-imposed exile, Violeta dedicated herself
entirely to artistic labor; music prodded her Satan's pitch-
fork. Having lost any other hope, she entertained audiences
from the depths of her heart.

L'Escale, the nightclub where Violeta worked for most
of her two years in Paris, was a dingy jungle, near Jean-Paul
Sartre's *Cafe Fleur.* Its décor delighted tourists and French
youth with its audacity–chairs anchored to the ceiling,
brassieres and jockstraps dangling overhead, a piranha
swimming in a fishtank. Amber lights illuminated curls of
cigarette smoke that filled the air. Couples came to *L'Escale*
to rendezvous and flaunt their licentiousness. Breathy sighs,
wandering fingers, scents of sex. The music, purely Latin
American.

Violeta alternated with other performers in one-hour shifts until three in the morning. Some nights, the moods of her music harmonized in fantasy environment; other nights she struggled against an unruly house. When ignored or drowned out, she'd stop singing abruptly to command attention. Once, she hurled a shoe at an oblivious pair, much as one might assault a cat to make it stop howling.

As Violeta's musicianship became known in the Latin Quarter, she got work filling in for other musicians, usually playing percussion. Besides guitar, she played castanets and accordion. Gradually, she developed a routine.

And as in Chile, she began to extend more of herself to others, through food and hospitality. Having little money, she would ask the butcher for dog bones, then stew them with parsley and corn and prepare delicious *cazuelas*, which she would serve with frybread *sopaipillas*. Chileans traveling in Europe sought her out. Fernando Alegría recalled her table set with sprigs of rosemary to fill the air with a scent reminiscent of home. "That was how she expressed her tenderness toward people she loved." As she darted around cooking, chatting, listening, his eyes followed her legs, which were shapely.

Despite lacking physical beauty, Violeta's vivacity suggested a much younger woman. At thirty-eight, her graceful frame was vigorous and her long black hair still shone. Gradually, the veil of her mourning lifted, and she renewed interest in men. Both her husbands had been younger than she; her subsequent lovers, younger still.

Her relationship with a handsome, fine-featured Spaniard lasted months, until she could no longer accept the intensity of his love. Violeta had grown detached. When she turned him aside, the young man collapsed in a chair, his eyes swollen from crying. Violeta watched him weep, as though enduring yet another humiliation.

Homesick, she wrote home to Nicanor for mementos to remind her of their childhood in Chillán. Would he send her some clay miniatures from the marketplace? Would he be her eyes and ears? She needed his vision to make peace with her estrangement.

Folklorist Margot Loyola came to Paris and roomed nearby. The two women saw each other constantly. Violeta now projected greater self-assurance. A year spent abroad had expanded her intellect well beyond that of a rustic musician. The fugitive nature of things obsessed her. Everywhere she saw transformations. She grappled with questions of love, displacement, powerless, injustice. Margot frequented *L'Escale* to hear Violeta perform, but one night Violeta asked her to substitute for her. She'd had a painful, allergic reaction to a facial peeling. Margot filled in for her friend's sets, but discovered she lacked Violeta's stamina.

By the time she returned home, Violeta had made Europe aware of her culture. When she performed in a crowded lecture theatre of the Sorbonne, her solo voice brought the cavernous hall to silence. In 1956, she recorded folkloric songs for the *Musée de l'Homme* and the UNESCO archives, as well as *Chants du Monde*, a commercial record company dedicated to world music, which issued an album entitled *Violeta Parra–Cantos de Chile*–her first LP as Violeta Parra, folklorist. She traveled to England, a trip notable because the Chilean embassy in London received her warmly and arranged recitals and an interview for the BBC's American Service.

Still, Violeta found the English reserve impenetrable. She complained bitterly to Margot that the Parisians were a cold public, unlike the Hispanics, whose warmth she understood, but "in London, it's even worse, much worse. What are we doing here?"

Yet Violeta did understand what had brought and kept her in Europe. She was there to sing the Chilean song. She saw herself as an emissary bound to challenge the European misconception that since Latin Americans were people from economically underdeveloped countries, they were also culturally disadvantaged. When her audiences applauded, it wasn't she whom they were honoring, but her country.

During her first Paris stay Violeta began writing *Décimas,* her autobiography in verse, "using a pencil and no particular order in mind." She might have recounted first the circumstances of her trip to Europe and how fate played its hand. She expressed gratitude for the strangers who were kind to her, but she also told of many who were cruel. Violeta never lost faith, but hers was the humility of a wanderer who trod the earth with eyes cast down. The world was her theatre, under whose klieg lights she uttered her say in verse and later in tapestry.

Violeta Parra blamed herself for Rosa Clara's death and she wrote to examine its imprint on her psyche. The tragedy stained forever Violeta's self-worth. The deceased infant took poetic form as a white dove, a butterfly, and then as a flower stripped of leaves, leaving only the spirit.

In November 1956, a year and three months after Rosa Clara's death, a Santiago magazine ran a brief announcement of Violeta Parra's return home by boat. Her brother Nicanor and her former radio producer, José Maria Palacios, met her flight from Buenos Aires. To José María, she had written, "I hope that my contract will be waiting for me at *Radio Chilena.*"

Now, burying her face in the bough of *copihues* that José Maria presented, Violeta's eyes flooded with tears that wet the red bellflowers like the rains of the Chilean south where they had grown. En route to Nicanor's house where the entire family was gathered, Violeta talked and questioned — how was her mother and Hilda and her brothers and the children and her house? She brought new songs and lovely gifts.

Love showered Violeta in the poignant family reunion. Six-year-old Carmen Luisa hugged her mother as if she'd never let her go. Isabel and Ángel watched her patiently. As though seeing the dove of Rosa Clara fly through the portals of Heaven, Violeta broke down and wept. The infant was never more present than by her absence.

Over dinner, Violeta regaled them with stories of her trip and plans to continue her work. She sang an entirely new repertoire of songs. Her compositions were more purely original, though always based on folklore. Violeta was allowing the possibility of joy back into her heart.

Hours later, exhausted, huddled close with her family in one bed as though docked in harbor after a storm, Violeta hummed a new melody. "I found this music in the color of the sea," she said, "one day when I felt close to Chile. It was grey like the ocean's turbulence in quiet, but threatening waves. In the color of the sea that day, and in the death of my daughter, Rosa Clara, and in the bed of Rosa Clara's grave."

Isabel's healthy *guagua*, Cristina, born while Violeta was abroad, brought Violeta unexpected solace. Photographs show Violeta adoring her grandchild, who was quick to display her own musicality and was performing with the Parras by the time she was six.

Paths

Outside the cottage, Violeta surveyed her yard. She walked to the spot where she had planted a sapling years ago, expecting to find a shady spot but instead finding only weeds and bare earth. A butterfly flitted by. Birds chirped. Where was the tree? Some Devil dug it up and transplanted it to his own patio. Everyone said it was her sister-in-law.

Crickets laid claim to her vacant house during her absence; spiders cobwebbed the corners and a family of mice nested in a basket of fabric scraps. As she wandered from ramshackle room to room, she remembered being a wife and holding Rosa in her arms. She saw things more simply then, was able to take more for granted. Absentmindedly, she picked up a glass, a piece of lace, handled them, put them down. Memories returned. She struggled against panicky sadness. Where were her rosewood buttons, her bobbins for tatting lace? It was useless to ask; only the insects answered. She set to work cleaning, to reclaim the space as her own.

There was other work to do. She now grasped how educated people viewed folklore; her European experience had made her more objective, serious and introspective. Now in familiar surroundings, she knew she had to integrate past and present. Her writings suggest that people left her alone, realizing she needed solitude to heal, strip away illusions that had helped bring her home. It was hoped she'd remesh into family life, which also suffered from her absence.

Although she had mourned the infant's death from afar, now she grieved again. The pain set her apart in sacred space. Her personality grew more intense. Peace did not come easily.

> *The week that my roses*
> *came into bloom*
> *I was in such a bad mood*
> *I saw only their thorns.*

The day she went to the cemetery to lay a wreath at the baby's grave, she began to be haunted by a recurring dream, which she committed to poetry. Every night, she was awakened by a corpse that was yet alive and awake. Would the skeleton ever be laid to rest? Insomnia turned Violeta suspicious, fearful. She wondered whether that cunning corpse "wanted to be mine but could not." The last verse may be construed as Violeta's first literary allusion to suicide.

> *. . . To its death I draw closer*
> *with expectation and faith,*
> *but I do not know what to do.*
> *Or if I do know,*
> *I cannot muster the courage.*

In another verse, two years after Rosa's death, Violeta visualized meeting an animal whose howls had penetrated to the bones of her marrow. It let her go, its aloof posture suggestive of the husband who now wanted little to do with her. She was ashamed of her sins but never asked for absolution by a priest. Instead, she resolved to "dance to the sound of the wind through the plain" and feel its breeze.

Everyone who heard her new repertoire was impressed by how much Violeta had matured artistically. Yet on- and off-stage, her personality also displayed a marked chill.

Jose Maria secured her new radio contract. She recorded her first LP for the Odeon label's *Folklore de Chile* series, *"Violeta Parra Canto y Guitarra"*, and sold a song, *Casamiento de Negros*, to RCA Victor, for which she received a lump sum payment but lost copyright.

Anxious to resume her fieldwork, Violeta applied for academic funding, but was rejected. Undaunted, Violeta drafted her scrawny thirteen-year-old son, Ángel, into service to lug a cumbersome, European tape recorder on excursions into the countryside. Sometimes her brother, Nicanor, joined her. Two members of the radio crew also joined her. Photographer Sergio Larraín was eager to capture her subjects on film. Luís Gastón Soublette, a musicologist and the station's record librarian, recognized her unprecedented work: No one else of peasant origins had ever collected the largely hidden music of Chile's central heartland.

Nothing frightened Violeta. She never dreamed anyone would threaten her, and so she went everywhere, freely, to collect material. Larraín accompanied her to a Santiago tavern where she had performed as a young girl. It was early evening, and the atmosphere was so rowdy and aggressive, he was hesitant to take pictures.

"Don't be scared," Violeta whispered and smiled to give him courage. She tapped a rhythm on the table, calmly calling attention to herself as she sang in a low voice. Little by little, men joined, and soon everyone was vocalizing. To Larraín's astonishment, they sang beautifully. Years later, he observed that "these were people who were very deprived had such wealth of music! When I saw that, I decided she was capable of investigating every realm of folklore and revealing what most Chileans were completely ignorant of."

Gaston Soublette volunteered to transcribe the music Violeta collected. It was a skill she lacked, although she had invented her own way of notating score and memorizing the melodies. She valued Soublette's ability, but because she also saw it as privileged training denied to her, she resented it.

Once after spending an entire day together collecting *cuecas*, Soublette and Violeta returned to her house. She was tired, impatient at having to repeat herself for him. "You can't follow this because it has nothing to do with you. You're involved in this project strictly for the songs, and nothing else!" This touched off an argument so ugly, Soublette picked up everything he had written that day, tore it up, and stormed out.

Another day, after researching poetic songs, Violeta invited Soublette to her mother's house to notate their material. They had worked about an hour and a half, when she instructed Ángel, "Go get the glasses and help us prepare some *vino con harina tostada*, wine with toasted flour, would you, son?"

Ángel returned with enough glasses for everyone–Ángel, Isabel, Carmen Luisa, her mother, Violeta, and Soublette. But Violeta prepared only five beverages.

Ángel said to her, "But *mamá*, aren't you going to give some to don Gastón?"

"No, that *pituco 'e mierda* wouldn't drink *vino con harina tostada!*" and she shot a defiant glance to Soublette

Soublette recalled later, "Since I was a *pituco*, an educated snob, Violeta didn't think I could enjoy the rustic beverage."

Remarkably, Soublette saw past Violeta's antagonism to her frustration over how little her intuitive research was respected. He saw a troubled woman, overwhelmed by the enormity of insights that were hers alone and accomplished without sponsorship. The two achieved a productive working partnership; though sadly, their efforts were not published in Chile until after Violeta's death.

Violeta Parra, La Cueca, embroidered on jute. 51" x 32". 1962.

Concepción

In 1957, the University of Concepción invited forty-year-old Violeta to be an artist-in-residence and teach summer-school workshops in the *cueca*, the national dance. Thrilled, she took Ángel and Carmen Luisa and moved the five hundred kilometers south to the cultural mecca of Concepción. For the first time since she left the countryside at fifteen, Violeta had access to the region of her childhood as a working folklorist supported by a progressive university.

Violeta's work centered in the Visual and Performance Arts Department, housed in a two-story colonial mansion facing a wooded green at the foot of a hillside. The facility was a beehive of classes held in studios and outdoor spaces, an environment that fostered informality between students and the artists who were their teachers.

Everyone teaching that summer lived in ground-floor rooms that surrounded a tiled patio where Violeta taught dance. She and her seven-year-old daughter, Carmen Luisa shared a single room, while fourteen-year-old Ángel boarded with other boys his own age at a secondary school across the street, although he visited every day. Violeta found herself surrounded by artists, musicians, writers, and actors. She was as much student as teacher. The time spent in Concepción became her university education.

Of all the summer's activities, what most enchanted Carmen Luisa were the rehearsals of an original new comedy called *Dos más dos son cinco* (Two plus two are five). At any time, a student actor might sweep past her, living his role. She watched choreographer and director blocking out the cast's movements through a scene, or the stage crew assembling backdrops with the same fascination as her mother had had with the circus. The ensemble soon adopted Carmen Luisa as their mascot. Her memory was flawless–during rehearsals she spoke up to prompt an actor with a forgotten line. And one day, Carmen Luisa gave a solo rendition of the entire play, imitating all the parts in distinct voices. To the amazement of all, she had memorized everyone's roles!

Violeta had never taught and her evaluations were mixed. Without question, she was a demanding teacher. She had no patience for students slow or ambivalent to learn. But when she she perceived someone who connected with the dance and what it meant to her, Violeta was inspired.

"The *cueca* is a dance your grandparents and their grandparents knew. It's how they flirted, and how people in the country still dance to have fun," she said. "To dance it successfully, you have to understand its structure," and she explained its sequence of steps, unchanged for hundreds of years. "Once you learn it correctly, it will free you to dance personally, with your own flourishes." She strummed an elaborate *cueca* heard at parties.

> *In Santiago a rooster crowed*
> *and they heard him in La Serena.*
> *Folks in Copiapo asked as well*
> *'Did you hear that crowing rooster?'*

"You've got to feel the rhythm in your body." She started clapping: *one-two-pause one-two-pause*. "Everybody, join in." When the sound grew large with the beat—*one-two-pause one-two-pause*—she perked it up with her guitar and sang out a verse while stepping lightly through the dance movements.

"The dancers are flirting, but coyly. They turn, the male advances and the female avoids him. But remember, you're on a farm. So men, you're dancing as if you're a rooster; and women, you're the sexy little hen.

"Yes, you know how that is–the cock pecks at her and she's having none of it, at first. She rustles her feathers to shoo him away. The man flicks a white handkerchief at the woman's skirts. She steps back, yet rustles her skirt to entice him."

To Violeta, the *cueca* epitomized what was authentically Chilean. Everyone danced to exhaustion during her classes. At the end of the summer term, she organized a fiesta in a public park where her students danced the *cueca* with every conceivable flourish. She rewarded her protégés with mouthwatering *empanadas* and thirst-quenching *mistela*.

Pleased with her efforts, the university rector, David Stichkin, extended her contract for a year to teach music and dance. As soon as the contract was renewed, she had Gastón Soublette hired as a resident musicologist and soon he was joining her on excursions.

Since her arrival in Concepción, Violeta had been venturing out alone on weekends with her tape recorder to the tiny villages. If any students asked to come along, she apologized that she preferred to travel by herself, so as to have the best chance of establishing rapport with her peasant informants. Sometimes, she simply got off a bus or train to follow a path she had seen someone walk. Farmers gave her rides on their mules to haciendas so remote in the wooded inland hillsides that the language, attire, and manners of the people were still reminiscent of colonial times.

Violeta also convinced the university to let her establish the region's first museum of folklore and set about gathering the artifacts of rural life—handmade kitchen utensils and farm implements, pottery, embroidered broadcloth and lace, ponchos and shawls, tooled leather and spurs—while collecting regional music. She assembled musical instruments—the bass *guitarrón*, an indigenous drum called a *kultrún*, a rattle made of goat hooves. The museum would honor and give dignity to the countryside's hidden culture.

Violeta was rightly proud of her ability to uncover living history. Together with Soublette, she compiled over one hundred *cuecas* and many *tonadas*, ballads in a minor key sung by women about passion.

One elderly woman called the *cueca* "jealousy-makers." Noting their surprise by the term, she repeated. "*Amartelás*, jealousy-makers. *Cuecas* can be very provocative. Don't you see, the words can carry innuendoes that provoke anger."

In numerous instances of musical evolution, Violeta ferreted out innuendoes that suggested underlying stories. A song that began *a lo divino* might take on a secular twist, become ironic. A verse one singer might have remembered might complement another's fragment; when singers forgot a verse, they improvised or borrowed from another song. A poetical *décima* sung by men in the mid-nineteenth century might change in meaning or connotation when women sang a variant.

Although the associations were obscure, Violeta sleuthed village by village, *rancho* by *rancho* for missing fragments with which to reconstruct songs hundreds of years old. And she was surprisingly successful, as with the legend of *Blanca Flor y Filumena*, which has been traced to the thirteenth-century Spanish troubadours and found its way into Chilean folklore.

> *A dance was held*
> *of war and peace*
> *for a man's lovely daughters,*
> *Blanca Flor and Filumena.*

Violeta's half-sister, Olga, lived in Concepción and introduced Violeta to relatives nearby, including a blind herbalist named *doña* Francisca Martinez, called *La Panchita*, said to be 100 years old. Violeta pursued, flattered, and cajoled the woman, hungry for her knowledge of ancient songs, until finally she acquiesed. "Okay, Violetita, let's go talk and sing whenever you want." Convinced she had overcome the elder's reluctance, Violeta prepared her a magnificent lunch of shrimp, *pan amasado*, and homemade *pebre*, served with wine *pipeño* bought from a fortuneteller.

At the end of the meal, Violeta said, "Okay, Panchita, sing to me something you heard as a child." Then something delightful happened. Tapping her fragile fingertips on the table and intoning a commercial melody from the radio, Panchita added a verse of her own,

> *By the whore, whore,*
> *the whore of your mother*
> *who gave birth to you.*

She repeated this several times, giggling with child-like glee, then picked up her basket of herbs, and left everyone present flabbergasted by her audacity.

A cultural salon took place in those days at the home of a prominent Chilean writer, Daniel Belmar. Daniel was a generous man who kept his larder filled with turkey, lamb, and fresh-water fish, any of which Violeta was happy to cook into sumptuous regional dishes.

There, Violeta met Enrique Bello, whose avant-garde magazine, *Pro-Arte*, published a wide range of arts, criticism, essays by thinkers of world prominence, such as Solzhenitsyn, Le Corbusier, and Ionesco. Bello attended the gatherings, as did Pablo de Rokha, Violeta's long-time friend. Beneath his formal manner, Pablo was an expansive and entertaining raconteur whose perspectives spurred lively banter.

Recent remarks about the *cueca*'s provocative nature led Violeta to air the topic at Daniel's. Everyone, including Violeta, knew that the *cueca* encompassed many more moods than was danced in student workshops. Pablo de Rokha regaled his friends with an erotic vignette.

"Picture a rodeo, or maybe the ranchhands have finished castrating the calves for fattening on the lands of the *patron*. After dreary winter months, the apple trees have come into flower and the thrushes trill their flute-like songs. By the eighteenth of September, Independence Day, when Olga bows the strings of her *vihuela*, young people get restless. A *macho* strums his guitar with the fervor of a suitor to some damsel who makes his blood boil. 'The sausage grows enormous,' like wine surging through the loins of a colt. He may be in love with the charms of Carmela, but eh, if he can have the enormous eyes of Luchita when she smiles with hot peppers, well . . . ."

"Carmela will dance to lead him on, as a lady would," said Violeta.

"Yes, of course, but the *cueca* is a gift washed down with wine and *chicha*. Virility and femininity, as the literary asses say, stomped on the grave of an idolized woman."

"They danced *cueca* in colonial houses noisy with soldiers' homecoming, to obliterate the memory of gunfire."

"Ah, yes. Coarse ferocity makes the dance colossal. Men dance with liquor bruised by sorrow or horror, like a bull in the *bodegas*, with plenty of blood.   The *cueca* is to Chile what the bullfight is to Spain."

"Let's not forget the *cueca* danced in the dresscoats of the rich, tipsy with champagne, contemptuous or comical, danced as if by a clown."

"Heh, but best of all is the *cueca* of the brothels," Pablo offered. "The couples may dance broke, crying over a last cup of wine, but their hips are writhing suggestively, their lithe hard bodies advancing toward the intensity, leering into the eye of a hurricane."

The laughter of the men spoke volumes about the houses of pleasure and the *cueca*'s lustier side–knowledge unavailable to respectable women. Violeta's brothers had often told her about how lasciviously the whores danced, lifting their skirts to reveal more than ankle and taunting their clientele to arousal. Violeta wanted to see this for herself, and the bawdier the conversation grew, the more she wanted to witness this. As a woman, her desire was not unique, but her determination was. As she saw it, she had ventured with her tape recorder to bars, docks, timber mills, and mining camps; and regardless of how coarse the people were whom she encountered, she had put them at ease and had gotten them to reveal themselves to her. Why not the brothels too?

Apparently, her argument was convincing, for her friends took Violeta out for a mischievous, indulgent night of abandon to dance and drink at the local brothels. She regarded the excursion as valid research, and made no secret of its fact, for she was not ashamed, nor did she feel she had done anything wrong.

Soon, tongues wagged at her audacious behavior. Rumors circulated that not only had she taken license with propriety, she may have actually sold her honor. Violeta Parra had not prostituted herself, this or any other time, of course. She savored brothel life as a folklorist, to experience its music and dance. Yet, that she'd crossed the boundaries of a woman's proper place created scandal.

In the art department's bohemian atmosphere, Violeta loved to watch the artists paint and draw and she had no inhibitions about posing for them.

Her affair with painter Julio Escámez began while he was painting a mural in a pharmacy. It covered three walls and depicted the curative arts: early medicine and native pharmacopia, present and future. In the panel showing a public clinic, he incorporated portraits of his friends, including Violeta, whom he rendered from a girlhood photograph she supplied, dressed in purple and holding a spray of baby's breath. Julio was eight years her junior; his attentions flattered her. Their liaison ephemeral. A matter of days.

Julio was in love with a woman his own age, an *indigena* reminiscent of all the mysteries of the southern forest where he grew up. Perhaps he needed the fling to take stock of whether to marry the girl or to have the dalliance as a way to avoid commitment. In any case, Julio incited both women to jealousy.

As she watched the mural take shape, Violeta attempted to impose her will and get Julio to remove the young girl's several likenesses. "I must insist you erase that Indian from the mural."

Julio only sneered and warned Violeta that their sensuality might linger longer if she did not sour it herself. "That Indian, as you call her, is very beautiful."

When the girl used her feminine wiles to win back her boyfriend, Violeta stalked them. One night, she hid behind them in a movie theatre and whispered curses. Two days later, she went to Julio's studio. When Julio spurned her, Violeta flew into a rage. She grabbed a utility mat knife and slashed every canvas bearing the image of her rival. The incident so terrified the painter, he fled abroad at the end of the school year, reportedly settling for a time in Costa Rica. He never married the girl.

Both the tumultuous affair and the brothel uproar called unflattering attention to Violeta, beyond the pale of the university's code of conduct. Officials charged that her comportment as a university employee disgraced the university's image and undermined its authority. She was asked to leave.

Controversy erupted. She brought the trouble on herself, men were likely to say. Women chastised her wayward behavior, and said she deserved to be fired. A minority of individuals were impressed by her independence, despite its cost. Many more agreed privately that the episodes precipitating her dismissal arose because she was a woman and therefore, was held to a different standard than men. To justify the firing, some officials even stooped to insinuate that Violeta had not written a song for which she was most famous, *La Jardinera*. Violeta endured the humiliation as she prepared to return to Santiago with Ángel and Carmen Luisa.

Plans for the folkloric museum to which Violeta had devoted copious time and effort were suspended. Violeta wanted the university to safeguard her archive, so she brought all fifty-five audio tapes that she had recorded while in Concepción to the office that housed scholarly material. The tapes were accepted only reluctantly and later erased. Likewise, her collection of rustic pottery, paintings, and musical instruments was shelved, but allowed to fall into private hands. More refined art objects replaced those that Violeta had displayed. The museum did not survive.

Despite her inauspicious departure, Violeta's period in Concepción was among the most fruitful of her life. She broadcast radio programs. Her research with Gastón Soublette was later published as *Poésie Populaire des Andes*, in a bilingual edition in Paris, and as *Cantos Folklóricos Chilenos*, posthumously in Chile. Both recreate Violeta's conversations with the rural minstrels who revealed their lives and songs. Violeta cut two new records of folklore for the Odeón label. Both albums featured cover art by local artists, Nemesio Antúnez and Julio Escámez.

She completed her autobiographical *Décimas*, which she had begun in Paris. It chronicled in direct, colloquial language a poverty-striken childhood, marital troubles, a baby's death. Years later, when the Alerce record company released a posthumous recording of excerpts, not even patrician Chileans, "who sounded like they wore a clothespin on their noses when they spoke of The People," could ignore her unique contribution, though they had ridiculed her self-taught style plenty behind her back while she was alive.

Violeta's teaching experience taught her techniques for holding a concert audience's attention. Her intelligence and prolific output won her the esteem of many artists and writers. Musically, she matured. She began composing what she called a "Great Folkloric Symphony," an auditory patch-work of song and melody.

Before leaving Concepción, Violeta gave two memor-able concerts. She had composed a musical homage to artist Nemesio Antúnez, which she and soprano Olga Muñoz per-formed as a work for guitar and soprano in a matinee recital. And in an open-air forum on a clear summer night, Violeta sang before an audience of thousands. Her hair pulled up into a simple bun, she talked about her experiences compil-ing music and folklore, about the elders who shared their customs and language and demonstrated an array of native Chilean instruments—*guitarrón*, *kultrún*, bells, reed recorders, rattles.

The concert capped an era lived intensely, in which her passions translated into some of her most vibrant songs. Social commentary now featured in Violeta's repertoire. In an ode to the city of Chillán, *Yo canto la diferencia*, she voiced pride in being a provincial woman of integrity and honest roots.

> *I sing in the style of Chillán*
> *if I have something to say*
> *and I don't pick up the guitar*
> *just to get applause.*
> *I sing the distinction*
> *between what's true and what's phony.*
> *Anything else, I will not sing.*

After the concert, Violeta convened a feast for her friends on a lagoon, near the mouth of the river Bío-Bío. In an abandoned one-room shack of rough-hewn logs, she set up a kitchen. Around a bonfire, she sang all night long, her voice insistent, her eyes more brilliant than ever. As the sun rose and the ducks were slashing their wings in chilly water, Violeta sang,

> *The star cannot hurt me anymore*
> *the moon cannot embitter me*
> *Life is a fortune –*
> *flashy, flourishing, noble.*

A tender sentiment, though one that could not sustain her. Violeta may have recognized the virtue of self-protection, but neither then nor later was she able to control her will.

By the Whim of the Wind

Back in Santiago in early 1958, Violeta sublet a room in a painter's studio, but proved such a raucous tenant, the landlady asked her to leave. She rented an apartment on Ejército Street. The elderly doña Rosa Lorca lived with her briefly, but soon left for the *campo* because she missed its humidity and hated being unable see the moon from any of the apartment's windows.

The intellectual ambience of downtown Café Sao Paulo reminded Violeta of Concepción; soon, she was one of its habitues opining on literature, art, music, film, history, and current events. Was Chile being swallowed up by Yankee culture? What was it about Santiago that distinguished it from other Latin American capitals? She was writing poetry and setting her own and the poetry of friends to music.

One afternoon, a spare young woman introduced herself. Gabriela Pizarro had studied folklore with Margot Loyola and now wanted to learn from Violeta. By asserting that *"campesinos* bear most authentically the culture that makes us Chilean," she endeared herself to the Violeta, who took her on as a protégé, and gradually revealed everything she could about insinuating herself into the reclusive rustic world. The two women were of different generations, but they became genuine friends.

While at an open poetry reading in that cafe Violeta learned of a contest. She put Gabriela to work typing her verses. Gabriela's boyfriend, Héctor Pavez, another promising young folklorist, was supporting himself at the time by transcribing class notes at the medical school. Soon, quantities of paper, carbon paper, typewriter ribbons, and pens disappeared from the school supply closet to prepare Violeta's contest submission. She won no prize, but reasserted herself in local circles.

A flamboyant young troubadour sought her out. Victor Jara sang with Cuncumén, an ensemble of teachers who performed folk music at neighborhood gatherings. His virtuoso guitar-work and a biting wit distinguished his original songs. When he and Violeta played duet, their twenty-year age difference evaporated. His candor influenced Violeta's subsequent lyrics, which grew more outspoken.

Seventeen-year-old Ángel usually scorned the would-be folklorists who fawned after his mother, but not Victor, who matched him quip for quip. Like another son, Victor followed Violeta's regimen for strengthening his lungs by lying on his back and singing with a brick on his chest. The young men became lifelong friends. Their shared affinity for Argentine music, particularly the evocative *milongas* of Atahualpa Yupanqui, infuriated Violeta, who saw this digression from Chilean music as disloyalty.

Already, Violeta agonized over her children's growing artistic autonomy. She largely determined Isabel's musical direction, which Victor helped broaden. Isabel's talent had yet to fully emerge, though already she was a married woman of twenty, had recorded several of her mother's songs and was poised on stage. Though Violeta tried hard to influence the direction of her children's music, her unconditional maternal love was undeniable. She is remembered for taking their hands into her own and caressing their long slender fingers, which she characterized as being perfect for piano.

Brother and sister volunteered at the university film school's Channel Nine, one of Chile's fledgling television stations. Its production studio attracted many bright young people eager to learn stagecraft. One of its chief programs was a live talk show featuring colorful personalities. Naturally, Violeta was invited on as a guest.

The first time Violeta attended a rehearsal, she discovered that what the audience saw as a televised conversation between two people involved much more preparation than for radio. The tedium exasperated her. Once the program host had spoken his flowery introduction and the camera was finally focused on her, she departed from the script with an outburst. "What am I doing here with all these cables around my feet? I should be at home playing guitar instead of answering all these fool questions!" And with that, she broke into song and stole the show.

Once accustomed to the production routine, Violeta committed herself to it and added stipulations of her own. Props had to be absolutely realistic. She brought from home her own tables, chairs, and a teapot in which to brew *yerba mate*. She insisted that coals in the brazier must actually be lit; no colored lights simulated fire on her set. No one dared argue. Violeta's fame grew. She appeared regularly on televised folkloric programs as a figure who stimulated debate between native culture and foreign influence. While mainstream Chilean media aped the glitzy Hollywood star system, her authenticity was refreshing.

She was not alone. Sergio Bravo founded Chile Films as a center for documentary cinema, where students could train and develop their own filmic language. He based his short, *Casamiento de Negros*, on the song Violeta had sold to

RCA Victor, and the two became lovers. Violeta added music to several of his documentaries, including one about a weaver of wicker, and another about threshing. Reportedly, Sergio's infatuation was the stronger; Violeta saw the pairing as an affirmation of her talent. The day she learned that Sergio had asked a classical pianist to compose the score for a new film, she ended the affair.

Windfall proceeds in 1958 from Violeta's sale of *Casamiento de Negros* enabled her to add indoor plumbing to her tiny bungalow in La Reina. That winter, the University of Antofagasta asked Violeta to teach workshops on *cueca* and folklore of the southern heartland, so different physically and culturally from their own. She invited Isabel along for company to this northern port city in the stark pink mineral-rich Atacama desert, and to help demonstrate the dance from a young person's perspective. Mother and daughter, hugely successful, "left some two hundred people there dancing the *cueca*." At the end of their stay, Violeta gave a concert in an immense regional soccer stadium.

Isabel remembered her mother's generosity. Before returning home, Violeta splurged and spent nearly everything she earned on feminine niceties (cosmetics, nylon stockings, cashmere sweaters, soaps and creams) and family treats.

Their trip north coincided with a religious festival held in mid-July on the desolate Andean *Altiplano*. Once a year, Indians and Christian pilgrims pay homage to *la Virgen del Carmen*, Violeta's namesake, by enacting a pre-Columbian pageant about the death of a beautiful, despotic woman called *La Tirana*, who once controlled the oasis and its life-giving water. Ritual and Catholicism merged into a ceremonial dialogue of good and evil, life and death.

For an entire day, Violeta sat on a bridge near the plaza, solitary amidst the crowd, taking it all in. The procession of the Virgin icon to chanting prayers and aromatic incense, the demonic figures wielding whips to torment Christian supplicants, the unwary, the misbehaving. Fraternal societies sponsor the flamboyant masked punishers, making for an odd détente with the archdiocese in this enactment of myth and judgment.

She taped music (later used in a film documentary) and learned the rudiments of the indigenous woodwind *quena*, panpipe *sampoya*, and guitarlike *charango*. Andean music was to grow in meaning for her.

Once home, Violeta began experimenting with a new art form: maskmaking. By wetting cardboard supplied by her brother-in-law who worked at a paper mill, she formed a dough-like mass, which she shaped into recognizable images. Enormous cardboard bas-reliefs of human and animal figures began to fill the house.

For millennia, Chiloé Island, monarch of the archipelago that rims the southwest edge of South America, remained isolated from the mainland, due to formidable atmospheric conditions that caused tricky currents, squalls, and fog that often shrouds the region. Until 1958, ferries crossed the rough seas between the mainland and Chiloé only once a week. News that ferry service was being increased to a daily basis piqued Violeta's curiosity; never had she visited this remote province. She decided to travel there to meet its people and learn their customs before modernization suppressed what was innately unique about their character. In 1959, Violeta spent two months traversing the gravel roads of this rainy terrain. She discovered a hilly landscape crevassed with streams rich in catfish and trout;

carpeted in ferns, fuschia, and dense vines; canopied by laurel trees, avocado, cinnamon, hazelnut, and persimmon; a jungle sanctuary to wild cats, deer, and fox.

None of Violeta's diaries or letters from Chiloé have been published, but one song reveals the depth of her compassion for the islanders and their traditional lives. *Según el favor del Viento*, "By the Whim of the Wind," is based on the native *sirilla* dance rhythm. When she sang it, Violeta's voice had an aspirated tone suggestive of the everpresent dread of storm. The lyrics tell of a man and woman who harvest the *pellín*, the gnarled live-oak heartwood that grows on the northern slopes of the islands, and must brave the sea to bring it to market. Their rickety launch groans as it leaves a sheltered port for the deep channel; *yerba mate* tea gives meager comfort. The woman peels potatoes, ignorant of "another world of satin and velvet."

> *By the whim of the wind*
> *The woodsman goes to sea* . . . .
> *Traveling south or north,*
> *The little boat lists,*
> *so do I weep.*
> *By the whim of the wind,*
> *I take my leave.*

Violeta traveled by launch, cart, bus, and on foot to the settlements that dotted the coast. She visited the remote Indians living in straw *rucas* on the beach or in the forest. Everywhere people welcomed her—"Good afternoon! Come in and warm yourself by the stove"—and invited her to hear their songs and stories and learn their crafts and customs. She trekked the wool road from Castro to Dalcahue, past flocks of brown and white sheep, meeting the women who carded and spun, wove and knitted the wool. From them, she learned to sew an *arpillera*, a pictorial tapestry quite unlike the style she knew from the mainland and Isla Negra. Instead of the patchwork of fabrics and the little cloth figurines sewn into place, the island women's two-dimensional tableaux featured flat masses of color created by juxtaposing long stitches of wool over coarse burlap. It was a technique Violeta was to make her own.

Of the two musical threads that Violeta heard in Chiloé, she considered sentimental songs dating from the nineteenth century the less important than the more ancestral songs linked to indigenous roots. She encountered unfamiliar instruments—the three-stringed rabel of Moorish origin, a bowed *charango* fashioned of a board and two glass bottles, a free-standing *tormento*, which is hammered. She learned new dance rhythms—*pericona, chocolate, sirilla, costillar, pavo*, others derived from indigenous, Spanish, or German origins, and found that the ubiquitous *cueca* was danced by islanders more slowly than on the mainland and with different foot-stomping.

Music chased the melancholy that set in when the maritime weather invoked terrors believed to be supernatural. Violeta composed a song based on the legend of the phantom ship that lured sailors to their deaths in the treacherous coastal waters. She might have crossed Cucao Lake by ferry; in Charles Darwin's day, the lake crossing took eight hours by rowboat.

Violeta returned to Santiago, brimming over with fabulous tales unfamiliar to her friends; after hearing them, Gabriela Pizarro and Héctor Pavez decided to travel there too. When the couple returned, the three gave a major recital. By now, Héctor had fallen in love with Gabriela, but was as yet reluctant to commit to the relationship. His ambivalence caused Gabriela no end of tears, many shed in Violeta's company as they huddled close to the heat of a brazier, sipping tea. Finally, fed up with Héctor's insincerity, Violeta chased him down and gave him a sound thrashing, after which he proposed matrimony to his *novia*.

Violeta took seriously her role as Gabriela and Héctor's "wedding godmother." She attended the nuptials dressed as a mischievous sprite, wearing a raccoon coat and colored stockings. Isabel was incredulous.

"Mama, what's gotten in to you?"

"Never you mind!"

At the church, she fastened a yellow garter around her leg. Later during the party when the garter slipped and brought down her stocking, Violeta teased the newlyweds suggestively about all that would slip away that night. Then she proceeded to break dishes. This enraged Gabriela's mother, who tried to get Héctor to stop her, not realizing that Violeta was enacting a peasant tradition to ensure the newlyweds' happiness.

A man began to recite a romantic poem, but Violeta made farce of its sentimentality.

"My love, …."

"You aren't my love."

"Do you hear me?"

"No, not at all!"

"Wait for me, my love!"

"No. I think I'll go!"

By now people were dying of laughter, and the man was so offended by Violeta's mockery, he left the party.

Héctor and Gabriela spent their wedding night in Violeta's house, while Violeta serenaded them all night long.

Patriotic displays held on September 18th, Chile's independence day, made all of Chile sentimental about *cueca* and the folkloric life. Inspired by the public merriment she saw at

La Tirana and Chiloé and always alert for new ways to make money, Violeta decided to host her own independence day celebration. She built a *ramada*, a thatched open-air shelter on a vacant lot and moved her entire family into it as their temporary home. In that setting adorned with paper Chilean flags, balloons, and boughs of leaves, she staged a tableau of rustic life. The Parras welcomed anyone who wished to celebrate with them and sold hundreds of homemade *empanadas* and traditional drink. The spectacle attracted throngs of spectators.

When everyone had eaten and quenched their thirst, Violeta shifted from hostess to emcee. "Well, ladies and gentlemen, shall we make a little music?"

Without waiting for an answer, she played on her guitar a simple repetitive melody that enchanted her audience. Her infectious energy kept the pulse of the music and dance alive for three days and nights. Other singers pitched in; Sergio Bravo showed his documentaries.

To Violeta, folklore was not something to be confined to a museum, archive, or single holiday, but lived and sustained. Her capacity for merging rural customs into urban experience brought her fame and later, the loving memory of her people. After the success of that first gathering, Violeta arranged to celebrate what she called *dieciocho chicos*, "little September 18ths," throughout Santiago. Isabel remembered this direct contact with the public as exhausting work, but something for which Violeta is widely, fondly remembered.

She devoted herself to performance–live in concert, on radio and on television. By now, she had seven record albums, produced in Chile, Argentina, and France; her latest, *Toda Violeta Parra*, introduced new songs she had collected and had written. Her knowledge of indigenous cultures reinforced her inclusive vision of Chilean heritage. Yet Violeta did not publicize all the songs she learned. She collected but did not record the traditional songs of the indigenous Mapuche of southern Chile. And when someone taught her music from Easter Island, despite it being some of the first of that genre heard in continental Chile, Violeta made little attempt to interpret it herself.

Instead, Violeta could be counted on for a rousing production based on her own rustic roots. In concert at the University of Chile, Violeta presented an organ grinder and circus band. She introduced someone who played melodies on the kind of *charango* she found in Chiloé, an instrument constructed of a board and two liquor bottles held taut with strands of wire. Highbrow critics may have disparaged her coarseness, but audiences loved her for it. In thunderous ovations at the end of a concert, they were known to have saluted her in distinctly Chilean style—on their feet, by jumping in place.

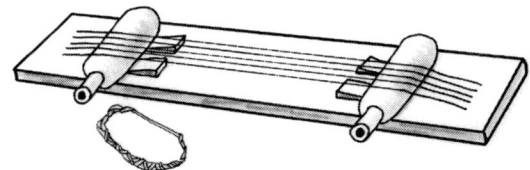

Outbursts

Pablo Neruda invited Violeta Parra to sing at one of his frequent salons in his Bellavista home, *La Chascona*. Violeta set to music two of his poems—a populist verse, *El Pueblo*, "The People," and the passionate *No te quiero sino porque te quiero*, "I do not love you only because I love you." Years later, Neruda honored her in cubist verse.

Violeta Parrón entered,
Violeting the guitar,
Guitaring the guitarrón,
Violeta Parra entered.

Violeta steered clear of animosities rife among her fellow artists. Her lifelong friend, Pablo de Rokha, lambasted Neruda for insincerity on behalf of "the people" from whom de Rokha was convinced Neruda had distanced himself. Neruda countered by labeling de Rokha "Joe Blow" for the grandiosity of his prose. The two men, blind to their similarities, sparred publicly. Yet Violeta managed to both men's affections, and they in turn accepted her on her own terms.

In 1959, the Santiago Museum of Modern Art inaugurated an open-air art fair in the *Parque Forestal* on the banks of the Mapocho River. The event, which was to resemble the district of art vendors' stalls along the Seine in Paris, has since become a Springtime tradition. Naturally, Violeta applied to exhibit her handbuilt figurines in clay and masks, but was rejected by curators who viewed her efforts as too naive. Nevertheless, Violeta persisted and won.

It was her first art exhibit. She set up a studio right in her stall and modeled her figurines before the public or serenaded visitors to capture their attention. This antagonized other exhibitors, who petitioned the authorities to stop her from "making noise" but she responded as a "lioness poised to fight, shut down, small, her bun askew, hair uncombed, assuming the world revolved around her." Tempers flared, and the situation prompted Nicanor Parra, her poet brother, to comment in a lengthy ode entitled *Defensa de Violeta Parra*:

> *Nobody better complain when you sing your heart out*
> *or scream as though they were cutting your throat,*
> *Volcanic Viola!*
> *The listener must keep a religious silence*
> *Because your song knows where it is going.*
> *Perfectly.*

The *Club de la Unión*, a fashionable Santiago business club, hired Violeta to sing in a dining hall furnished in colonial antiques, its walls adorned with oil paintings lit by crystal chandeliers. Patrons seated in plush chairs ate their lunches and ignored her. She was background music, nothing more. Dessert was being served by the time she had finished her set.

"Why don't you go into the kitchen and have something to eat?" a gentleman suggested between puffs on his cigar. Maybe he was tired of listening to her, or was simply addressing Violeta as the rich do the poor–politely, but dismissively. Whatever it was, he offended her. She pulled off a shoe and hurled it at him.

"Why you ungrateful bitch!" He rose from his chair and chased her around the table. Violeta gripped her guitar ready to defend her life. Two men subdued her and escorted her out. She went home famished; the Club never paid her a cent.

1960. Inspired by the Cuban revolution, the University of Concepción organized a conference to discuss contemporary Latin American culture and to host a forum of hemispheric unity against U.S. imperialism. Two North American beat poets, Allen Ginsberg and Lawrence Ferlinghetti, attended. Nicanor encouraged his sister to attend; likely, it was her first return to the University after being fired, but she swallowed her pride to contribute her song and her delectable cooking to the event.

When the conference ended, Nicanor invited Allen Ginsberg to Santiago. Ginsberg recorded in his diary impressions of that Sunday visit:

> *Catherine, daughter with guagua (baby) is visiting, sitting on front porch, Violeta Parra is touching the guitar and singing, the kitten stretching under her foot … Nicanor relaxing with eyes closed, on sun chair. A boy of 12 half naked in bathing suit with smooth brown skin, twists around the porch post and listens, I in easychair inside the open door, relax and watch with morphine. The wind is rustling through the trees in Chile.*

Of the interior, Ginsberg noted:

> *Chile, March 15, 1960–the fading page–lamp-light, an old picture of the virgin on the wall–in easy chair–an antique phonograph playing Chilean Tangos recorded 25 years ago–the*

ancient violins now crumbled to dust, the voices cracked, or mute
—a butterfly soprano waltzing in the back streets—Parra, sad in
his Professor's suit, remembering a melody his father touched on
the violin nearly thirty years ago—

The two poets collaborated; Parra helped Ginsberg translate "Kaddish Hymn" to Spanish. And Ginsberg recorded "arguing with Parra last nite and many times before over Marxism …. Made me feel bad." The picture of an argumentative family crops up again in a poem Ginsberg wrote about an eclipse seen March 12, 1960.

Parra spits,
   eclipse,
he sneezes
the family argues
in the back
   room
about a red spot
   in the
   penumbra.

In May, 1960, natural disaster cut short Violeta's concert tour of the South and took its toll on her health. A month-long swarm of nine earthquakes with magnitudes averaging 7.25 on the Richter scale devastated 400,000 square kilometers of Chile (fully one third of the nation) and killed 10,000 people. At its epicenter, scientists measured intensities of up to 11 on the Mercalli scale. Eleven—more intense than any ever recorded!

Temblors toppled Concepción. Jolts echoing through Valparaíso's populous canyonland sent people screaming in terror. The first 82-foot high wave of three tsunami that crossed the Pacific pulverized Valdivia's ocean port. Water spouts shot skyward, exposed earth in one instant, then crashed down to flood the land and sweep entire villages out to sea with the oceanbound surge. The mainland coast-line altered permanently. Rain saturated mountain hillsides that collapsed and buried everything in their path. Avalanches obstructed the outlet of Lake Riñihue; as the water level rose, volunteers with tractors and pickaxes labored for 64 days at their own peril to clear the blockage, aware that the waters might burst through and drown them.

Mapuche Indians bludgeoned to death a six-year-old boy, cut out his heart, and offered it to the sea to placate the gods whom they believed responsible for the seismic Apocalypse.

News of the unparalleled devastation stunned the nation. First reports of the plight of the *damnificados* by telegraph and radio from regions of exquisite remoteness were met with disbelief. The Interior Department ordered news censored. As had happened years before, the conservative president, Jorge Alessandri, berated a journalist for melodramatizing coverage of the calamity on *Radio Minería*.

"Excuse me Mr. President," the man replied, "but in my opinion the sensationalism and alarm are being caused by the earthquakes and tidal waves, not by the reporting."

Violeta returned home from the aborted concert tour hysterical, her nerves raw from the tragedy she had witnessed. Exhaustion was diagnosed as hepatitis, mandating months of bed rest, a course of treatment reminiscent of her childhood.

Now again confined indoors, Violeta withdrew to the intricacy of needlework. The *arpilleras* she had seen in Chiloé inspired her to stitch in the Chilote style, using wool as a coarse thread. She embroidered every piece of cloth she could find, despite leaving curtainless windows or a bed stripped of sheets. When friends visited during her convalescence, Violeta had them unravel old wool sweaters and roll them into skeins of rainbow colors.

Embroidery gave Violeta the chance to observe people unobtrusively. She noticed gentleness, the tilt of a skeptic's head, the torso of one receptive or resistant to attention. All the while, her fingers stitched in coarse yarn her visions of people, birds and animals. Occasions of trance-like daydreams, *nubecitas*, she called them, enveloped her. She emerged fed with poetry, color, and texture.

Her pictorial tapestries depicted garlands of flowers on a tree of life, mask-like faces, stars moving across a textured sky, threads running across a weave as the waves cross an ocean surface. Her images combined in unexpected ways. The art that came out of these convalescent beginnings would receive great acclaim several years later.

Violeta Parra, Party at Violeta's house, canvas, 9.5" x 13.75", 1964.

What Things Life Holds, Zambitay!

Gilbert Favre was a conservatory-trained clarinetist who enjoyed a broad range of good music from jazz to folk, including the Violeta Parra songs he'd heard on the radio. During the four months he had spent in Chile, Gilbert had seen little but the sand, vases, and mummies of an archeological dig in the Atacama desert. His colleagues encouraged him to go to Santiago to unwind and hear some music.

"Why don't you look up Violeta Parra when you're in Santiago," someone suggested. Gilbert decided to do just that.

On the university campus, he bumped (literally) into Adela Gallo, sending the camera dangling from her shoulder swinging precipitously. When he introduced himself as a musician and said wanted to meet Violeta Parra, Adela laughed and told him he'd have his chance—today, October 4, 1960, was Violeta's forty-third birthday. She'd take him to her party!

Music and friends emanated from the two-room house in La Reina. Adela led Gilbert inside and barged right into Violeta's bedroom. The convalescing Violeta sat propped up against some pillows in bed, flirting with a man perched on the edge of her mattress. At being interrupted, Violeta screamed, "You bitch, leave me alone. Can't you see I'm busy?"

But Adela cut her short. "Shut up, Violeta. I've brought you a *gringo.*"

And with that, Adela nudged Gilbert forward to introduce himself. He was twenty-four years old, with prematurely greying hair. His taut body bronzed by the sun roused her to longing. Not five minutes passed before Violeta ousted the other fellow.

When his hands caressed her face, she surrendered to his physicality. He drank her *tinto*, her luscious red wine. The man who gave her pleasure that birthday night was to become the love of her life.

After their initial encounter, Gilbert returned to his archeological dig and they did not correspond.

Violeta applied to exhibit her *arpilleras* at the annual *Parque Forestal* art fair, and this time the selection committee objected to her vivid color. Nonetheless, Violeta did get to display a series she called *Nacimientos* (Births) and garnered her first critical praise for her painterly weavings. The favorable review led to two shows in Brazil (the prestigious *Bienal de Sao Paulo* and one at the Museum of Modern Art in Río de Janeiro)–much to the astonishment of many.

Meanwhile, Gilbert quit the archeological project, returned to Santiago, and sought her out. Though he didn't remember where she lived, he recalled that her children worked at Channel Nine, so he went to see them.

Isabel was amused by his efforts to communicate "with the couple of words of Spanish that he spoke." She drew him a map, told him which bus to take, and sent him on his way. By the time Isabel got home that evening, Violeta and Gilbert's intimate party was well underway. Violeta put on no airs for him, but set him at ease in her simple cottage where she lived her country ways. They lived together for several months.

In early 1961, she heard that her brother Lalo was drunk and destitute in Buenos Aires. She made immediate plans to go fetch him and send him home. Once there, however, she decided to take advantage of her trip and promote herself as "a voice of Chile." She missed Gilbert – his tenderness and "nasty hands." He wrote back asking her to come home. She replied by inviting him to Argentina.

> *My little boy,*
>
> *I love it when you write to me in French. . . . Only when there's a difficult word do you translate it in parentheses. I understood today's letter perfectly both literally and spiritually. . . . My heart aches over my slow progress in this filthy city, but I cannot let it destroy me. If you can come, . . . we will be the happiest couple on earth.*
>
> *Yes, Gilbert, I am made of tough steel and an unbreakable will. . . . I didn't come here to show off. I want to sing and teach a truth . . . . I am a little bird who can light on the shoulder of every human being, and sing and warble close, very close, to his soul. How can I leave without at least having tried ? . . .*
>
> *Millions of fiery needles pierce my skin. I am skinny and cunning, . . . also comfort-loving like a cat. You have awakened me, like one who wakes up at midnight to eat a sweet, fresh peach. ¡Qué barbaridad!*
>
> *Yesterday my money ran out, and then along came an actress and bought my mask of Pablo. She paid me 4,000 pesos, which is enough money for ten days. . . .*
>
> *¡Ay! I'm so angry, Gilbert, because things don't happen fast enough. . . . I kiss you passionately.*
>
> > *Violeta*

Violeta grew surly, caring only about how her acquaintances might advance her career. In fact, she was getting some breaks. Someone got her a record contract and attempted to get her a concert. A fellow singer helped her publish a songbook. An Argentine painter gave her some canvases and brushes, and she went looking for a gallery to hang her work. She was sewing *arpilleras* that she was pleased with. Yet she suffered without Gilbert.

> *Tuesday I start recording my music. . . . Ay, my darling,*
> *what a pain! At least when I write you it consoles me a little bit.*
> *Don't think that I am misbehaving, please. . . .*

In solitude, Violeta's composition advanced appreciably. She was not devout, but expressed herself with many songs *a lo divino* that she had collected and that manifested religious faith. The germinating lyrics grew political: Witness the plight of the poor. Her song, *Porque los Pobres no Tienen*, Because the Poor have Nothing, issued an indictment of the Church.

> *Because the poor have*
> *no hope in this world,*
> *they seek shelter in Heaven*
> *as a just balance.*
> *For this reason, the processions,*
> *the candles, and songs of praises, little dove.*
> *What things life holds, zambitay!*

> *From time immemorial*
> *Hell was invented*
> *to frighten the poor*
> *with its eternal punishments.*
> *And the poor, who are innocent,*

in their innocence believe, little dove.
What things life holds, zambitay!

. . . To perpetuate the lie
Their confessor calls to them;
he tells them God does not want
any revolution at all,
Nor demands, nor unions
That offend his heart, little dove.
What things life holds, zambitay!

Its first recording appeared on the album Violeta cut for the Odeon label in Buenos Aires, but when the song was aired on the radio, its lyrics were labeled sacrilegious. With stunning speed, the Catholic diocese forced the album out of circulation. The incident became news and brought her publicity. Concert plans jelled.

Now if only her children could join her on stage, Violeta was sure their show would be a fabulous success. She appealed to Gilbert to convince her family to come, describing a large theatre for several recitals, her newest art work hanging in the corridors and lobby.

Nicanor, Isabel, and Ángel declined to join her, but Violeta convinced Odeon to underwrite Gilbert's expenses for him to transport her props. Gilbert resisted committing himself to an arrival date.

Come soon, my darling. . . . I have great news: two
programs on Channel 13—one on April third and the other on the
tenth. . . . I'll be doing two shows in a theatre. First half,
color slides with my paintings and the background music (Anti-
cuecas). Second half, a recital of Chilean music. The exhibit
will take place in a very important gallery; the person in charge
has already seen my works and he liked them.

Bring the tapestries without the stretcher frames, the same thing for the paintings, and declare them at the border. I have a friend at Customs, a Mr. Arteaga. He likes me very much. . . . You should take him a record of mine (the latest) and he will let all of my works pass through. . . . Ay, Gilbert, this separation pains me.

. . . Tell me everything, everything, don't hold back about anything, anything. . . . Last night I couldn't sleep. . . . Hugs for everyone. Tell them all to write me. I need to see you and embrace you. . . . Yours alone,

Violeta

Violeta told everyone at the hotel that Gilbert was coming; but as the concert date approached, some must have wondered whether he'd show up.

The very day of the concert Gilbert arrived in Buenos Aires, bringing the clothing, canvases, and props Violeta requested. She gave a brilliant concert, moving entranced through the evening. In frenzied lust the lovers celebrated her success.

A few days later, Violeta developed an uncomfortable burning sensation, and when she sought treatment, learned Gilbert had given her a venereal disease.

Confronted by her outrage, he admitted that he'd been partying with friends and they went a whorehouse– "the first and only time in my life!" She flew at him with fists and nails, knocked him down, pummeled him sore, then threw him out.

Gilbert took another room in the same hotel, but they saw little of one another for nearly a year.

In June 1961, Isabel and Ángel Parra were invited to perform at an international youth festival in Helsinki. They invited Violeta along and she accepted.

Absent Dove

Violeta rested little aboard ship, as she sailed to Hamburg, Germany. She kept busy embroidering tapestries that she planned to exhibit at a cultural center during the music festival, and she conducted a workshop throughout the Atlantic crossing so that every Chilean aboard could dance the *cueca* with flair. Enlisting her six-year-old granddaughter, Tita, to keep rhythm on a *bombo* recently bought in Buenos Aires, she improvised an ensemble. Without an intimate life partner, however, Violeta grew demanding; family relations strained.

At the festival, the Parras won top honors. Violeta's tapestries drew an appreciative audience for their colorful glimpse of a distant country's handicraft. The family traveled from Helsinki, Finland, to Genoa, Italy, to meet Ángel's bride, Marta, whom he'd wed shortly before the trip, while Violeta was in Argentina. Marta's arrival reunited the newlyweds, but the reunion turned sour.

"Where's my Carmen Luisa?" Violeta expected her daughter to have accompanied Marta.

"She didn't come. She didn't want to leave her friends."

Violeta grew hostile. "How could you be so stupid as to leave her behind? Why didn't you make her come?"

"Her father let her stay. Her *abuela* said she'd take care of her. She didn't want to go." Marta backed away, but Violeta lunged at her with fists flailing. Ángel rushed to Marta's protection, but Violeta struck everyone who neared until finally she exhausted herself. Marta was caught between her new sister-in-law, Carmen Luisa, who wanted a break from her mother, and her formidable mother-in-law. Accusations and recriminations poisoned the air, already humid with tears.

Violeta, isolated by the intensity of her emotions, headed for Paris, determined to earn the money to send for her daughter. In the Latin Quarter, she rented the cheapest room she could find–a wretched windowless hole in the *Hotel de la Candelaria*, where many people who worked in the bistros lived.

Violeta returned to a routine of cabaret shows from late afternoon to early morning. Violeta performed more confidently than ever, accompanying herself on an array of native instruments, including a drum rigged with a foot petal to provide a bass beat. Her performance style suited the club's showy atmosphere. Besides lively dances, her repertoire included serenades and *tonadas*, and songs that argued against the status quo.

> *Look how those presidents laugh*
> *when they make promises to the innocent. . . .*
> *Look at how the police shine*
> *to deliver a prize to the workers.*
> *Just watch the captain and sergeant*
> *staining the pavement red. . . .*
> *Look at how the month of Mary blanches*
> *and the daylight of the poor blackens.*

Isabel and Ángel and their families followed Violeta to Paris, and were soon performing at *La Candelaria*, where they worked for the next three years. Mother and children frequented each other's stages, harmonizing their voices, impressing the audience with their intricate musicality. Whether solo or in ensemble, Parra showmanship commanded attention. Their costumed *cuecas*–danced by men in spurred boots and women rustling skirts, enlivened by *piropos* shouted by the musicians to praise the dancers and egg them on to greater flamboyance, the one-two-pause rhythm clapped by everyone in the room–was a spectacle worthy of fiestas in the Chilean *campo*.

Violeta's tiny room again attracted Chileans journeying through Europe–Nicanor Parra, Pablo de Rohka, Fernando Alegría, Nemesio Antúnez, as well as younger artists who relished her storytelling. Violeta was happiest when surrounded by friends.

Alone, she grew maudlin. Being in Paris again, missing a daughter, oddly paralleled the past. Depression overtook her. Even descending the staircase to go to work or run errands required conscious effort. She wrote blank verse, in which she relived the unforgiven tragedy.

She who always saw her hands as salvation puzzled over how they rebelled. Useful hands, working hands, suddenly divorced themselves from her will, as if the fragile bones and blood plotted war against their host. She grew fidgety.

> *Squeezing out of my ten little paths is a vitality*
> *that hides and then reappears like clouds in the wind.*

Sleep failed to refresh. In a morbid dream Violeta envisioned attending a wake, its smoky candles burning her eyes as she sang the elegies. Outside a little bird chirped.

Was she, who had been so distant from her infant's agony, the little bird?

She wished for tenderness. She wrote to Gilbert.

It took Violeta three months to scrape together enough money to send for Carmen Luisa, a remarkable accomplishment given how little she earned singing in the *bistros*. Even the young girl's trip to Paris was not without anxiety. Fog forced the plane to land at a different airport than scheduled. Nervously, Carmen waited for her mother, who arrived hysterical.

"Carmen, *mi hijita!*" Violeta hugged her daughter tightly, reassuring her, sobbing, stroking her black hair, asking a thousand questions. She serenaded her with an original song about a birdcage filled with twittering birds, out of which she could still pick "her very own little sparrow."

> *I gaze at the heavens . . .*
> *with a single desire in my thoughts*
> *that no one would prey on my little dove . . .*
>
> *Absent dove*
> *white dove;*
> *budding rose.*

Violeta had to work that night, so she brought Carmen Luisa to *L'Escale*, where the bewildered girl found herself amidst strangers who doted on her in a language she didn't understand. From the tone of the endearments, she sensed how much this evening meant to her mother, whose identity was suddenly transformed from that of a solitary middle-aged woman to mother of a teenage daughter. Violeta sang until nearly four in the morning, then took her sleepy daughter to visit yet another club in the Latin Quarter before going home.

Soon, Violeta's depression lifted, though she still craved intimacy. The girl settled into a routine at the *lycée*, where she tackled a demanding curriculum in a foreign language. Carmen Luisa's adolescence triggered all the moodiness and obstinacy of that stage of life. Arguments became slap-fests, with Violeta callous to the girl's feelings and blind to her own anguish.

Despite her late evening hours, Violeta awoke each morning by eight. She spent most of the day sitting on the bed sewing her pictorial tapestries, which she was beginning to believe she could sell.

In her heart, Violeta knew herself best as a peasant whose guitar allowed her "to let loose the song I know." She had only a vague idea what she was doing there in Paris or for how long she would stay. She missed Chile and happenings back home. She knew only that her music and art could be appreciated here, if only she could fathom how to generate the interest.

When the weather grew milder, she wandered the streets for hours and came home refreshed. Once, she took Carmen Luisa to the *Gare du Nord*, an enormous French railroad hub much larger than Santiago's *Estación Central*. Turning to her daughter she said, "Do you realize what it means to be here, the two of us alone, walking through the station?"

Carmen Luisa understood Violeta was seeing herself in her daughter, remembering her experience as a young girl arriving in Santiago.

Gilbert

Gilbert remained in Buenos Aires, "that immense city," without enough money to return home. Someone offered him work in a theatre in the Jewish quarter; but Gilbert soon found himself expected to stand guard duty after hours to protect the theatre's safety, because the entire district was under seige by perpetrators of anti-Semitic firebombings.

He quit and found work instead as a carpenter at a hotel, repairing furniture in exchange for room and board. Still he lacked money to pay his way back to Europe. He bought some art supplies and tried to earn money as a painter of modern art, but that merited little attention.

A fellow traveler he met had recently come from Bolivia and suggested Gilbert learn to play *quena*, the Andean bamboo flute. He figured, "surely it couldn't be all that different from playing clarinet" so he bought one, taught himself to play, and with two other men, formed a street-corner trio. Their busking, totally devoid of the indigenous syncopation that makes Andean music evocative, flopped.

Next, Gilbert looked for work on the docks. He landed a job on a Panamanian vessel whose cargo turned out to be arms and drugs. When he tried to get an exit work visa, the Argentines fined him because he had entered the country as a tourist. In a last ditch attempt, Gilbert stowed aboard an Italian cruise-liner, but was arrested by port authorities who released him three hours later. While studying at the Conservatory of Music in Geneva, Gilbert had worked as a stage hand for the *Theatre de la Comédie*. Now, desperate for a break that would get him home, Gilbert called the theatre to propose that they contract him as a member of the stage crew. The unusual tactic worked! He was hired and wired sufficient salary advance for boat fare.

Gilbert sailed to Genoa, then took a train to Paris, where he found Violeta at her hotel. The couple made their peace.

The miserable conditions in which Violeta and Carmen Luisa lived filled Gilbert with pity. "Their room was like none I had ever seen," he recalled, shaking his head as though even its memory was painful. "It was airless–lacking even a single window–and so tiny the bed monopolized the entire dark space."

After a brief stay, Gilbert departed for Geneva to repay his debt to the theatre company by building stage sets.

One day in late Spring 1962, Violeta called him frantic with worry: Little Cristina had tuberculosis. Commandeering his brother's car, Gilbert drove straight to Paris and brought Violeta, Carmen Luisa, Isabel, and Cristina back to Geneva. Once there, Violeta too required hospitalization, in her case for recurrent liver pains. When Violeta was released from the hospital, Gilbert invited her to live with him.

Ayúdame Valentina

An enormous willow dominated Voltaire alley where Gilbert lived. Set back from the street off a patio he shared with a goldsmith and a smithy, his dilapidated cottage consisted of two rooms and an attic, but in his words, "we lived a lot of life there." Partying and making music, art, and love, Gilbert and Violeta lived together from late Spring to early Winter.

To Violeta, the landscape of Switzerland resembled Chile because she could always see the mountains. Her body understood the air.

She taught Gilbert to play *quena*. She was an exacting teacher, requiring exact adherence to rhythm and tempo. He secured her recitals in Geneva and Lausanne and she became well-known regionally. Gilbert handled lighting and miking, and made sure she was properly paid for her appearances on Swiss radio. She recorded Chilean songs for the archives of the Museum of Ethnography in Geneva and negotiated a record contract. She felt cared for and her sense of well-being found expression in visual media and music.

Gilbert's attic became Violeta's studio, where she sculpted papier-maché masks and bas reliefs, some of which she painted, others not. She loved the immediacy of the material and its plasticity soothed her. According to Gilbert, "the reliefs were downright homely as they took form," but she never judged her output until the final appearance was evident. A prodigious number of works accumulated – enough for a gallery show. A dealer agreed to exhibit them in mid-January.

Until she could sell some of her art, Violeta had no means to support herself. Geneva sported no Latin Quarter bistros where she could perform. And, she was overstaying her welcome.

Gilbert came home late one day to find his cottage filled with an ashy cloud of smoke. "Violeta," he yelled, "What the hell are you doing?"

"I was cold. I made a fire." The room had a fireplace, but she had set a piece of scrap metal on the wooden floor right next to the fireplace and lit a fire upon it. It was not logical in any way. Squatting by the flame to warm herself, she ignored the smoke, which was not being drawn up the chimney.

"Put the damned thing out before you burn the house down!" She did as she was told.

Violeta returned alone to Paris for the winter. There amid the bistros of Rue Monsieur le Prince, she fell into the old routine of a solitary existence, oblivious to jazz and men's leers. She worked during Christmas. On New Year's Eve, she missed Gilbert's telephone call by a heartbeat, then wrote him a terrible letter alluding to her association of loneliness and death.

> *Darling:*
> *A second after you called [on New Year's Eve], I walked into la Candelaria, . . . your letter in my hand. . . . At 6 a.m. I went to bed exhausted and utterly sad. A new year without you. What bad luck. I have a phantom man. When will I have a*

*compañero at my side? I have to devour my sadness as if it were
a beast of the jungle. . . . All my life I have been very much
alone. . . . Who are you? Why do I call you so? And why don't
you hear when I scream? . . . I tell you, I'm dying. I need a
coffin and a ridiculous speech. . . . I hurt.*

*Threads weave themselves quickly. . . . Music pours out in
torrents, but my darling cannot hear my voice, doesn't understand
how cold I am. That's how Death is, ice cold inside and
out. . . . Winter has settled in the depths of my soul and I doubt
the coming of Spring . . . I am 46 years old, with the
disposition of a gale wind. . . .*

*What do you call yourself, darling? Gilbert Stone? Then I
am Mrs. Stone. Because one October fourth, you married yourself
to me. . . .*

*This cemetery that is Life keeps revealing to me its niches and
crosses. I'm scared. I want you to take my hand and lead me over
this dangerous bridge. A glass of water. A note of music. A piece
of bread. All I ask is that they come from your hand. Think hard
about it, darling.*

*Where is my darling? Who is my darling? I want to see him.
I want to hit him. I want to put my fingers right there, behind the
teeth. There, where it is so hot. Darling! I am yours*

Violeta Parra

Two weeks later, a feature article appeared in a Swiss
paper: "Geneva discovers Violeta Parra." Two photographs
accompanied the text, one showing Violeta with her family
ensemble, the other, her handcrafted masks.

A gallery poster announcing an "Exhibit of Masks
from Chile" caught a woman's attention as she walked down
the *Boulevard des Philosophes*. It beckoned her into a room usually reserved for modern painting. Instead, she saw masks
made of mirror, straw, *papier maché*, and hair, depicting
dreams or visions of sin. A small woman with big eyes,

pockmarked face and smooth black hair, the flush of youthful beauty "faded, but still full of life" sat in a corner gluing an aluminum-foil nose onto a long wooden face painted orange and coifed with raven feathers.

The visitor stood transfixed, and murmured, "Your masks hypnotize me."

"Would you like to visit my studio? I could teach you how to make them yourself."

So Raymonde Gampert found the address in the Saint-Jean quarter, and with some effort, climbed a steep stairway to a balcony in poor repair.

"Watch your step," a voice called, "or you'll break your neck!" The balcony was slick with pigeon droppings. Breathless, she followed the bamboo railing around to the attic studio, whose tapestry-covered walls led her into a room littered with newspaper, tangled skeins of wool atop a suitcase and crates of all sizes that served as furniture.

Strumming a guitar, Violeta Parra suddenly leaped forth with a dramatic twirling dance, followed by "a great devil of a man" playing flute. After three pirouettes, Violeta stopped. "This is how I greet my friends. Now, you and I will make masks together."

She set up their workspace on a crate, fetched a bucket of water, and added paste. She picked up some newspaper from the floor, added it to the mixture, then put it on a board and began to model it, all the while telling Raymonde what she was doing.

For her part, Raymonde was the mayor's wife of a nearby village. The women developed an immediate rapport and affection for each other. Raymonde did not finish her apple green mask with walnut-shell teeth and a broom-straw crown that day, nor the next. Others followed; sometimes she virtually hid out with Violeta making papier-maché masks.

When Violeta realized that Raymonde had theatre contacts, she pressed for a recital, which was held in March 1963 in the Theatre de la Cour St. Pierre of the old city. A reviewer characterized Violeta's delivery as "a superb stripping away of irrelevance," by which she evoked the true Chilean soul. An additional show was hastily scheduled for the next weekend, and thanks to the favorable publicity, Violeta sold many tapestries and masks, which she had hung in the lobby.

Other performances for political causes caused trouble at home. Gilbert returned one night to find Violeta busy making *empanadas* to sell for a Communist Party benefit being held that weekend at the University of Geneva. Though not a card-carrying member, Violeta felt a strong and long-standing duty to the Party.

"Why do you let them push you around? They don't even pay you for your work." Gilbert considered himself progressive, but he resented Violeta's being taken advantage of. Violeta ignored him, and spent the entire weekend working the poorly attended benefit. Afterward, Gilbert made no secret of his disgust.

"Who are the Communists of Germany, the East or West?" Violeta spit out the words as though they were a pebble in lentil soup. "You don't know the answer, do you? Yet you call yourself a European! *Ignorante!*"

And with that, she picked up a rock and whacked him on the back!

Gilbert groaned in pained shock, then found he couldn't move. "*Oh, pobrecito!*" Violeta squealed. "Get into bed, and I'll take care of you."

Violeta nursed him for three days, but her violence jeopardized their relationship.

She left Geneva and returned to Paris, where vacationing friends let her sublet their seventh-floor garret overlooking the fragrant Place de la Madeleine, locale of a flower market that convened every morning. Writing home after a month, Violeta confided her remorse, regretted her own destructive behavior. She was "suffering like a fool over Gilbert." At 46, she wandered the Left Bank daily. A butcher sold her a spoiled chicken disguised with vegetable oil, which made her so ill it cut "like a razor blade" in her gut. Weak, unable to sleep, she visualized her own funeral wake in a letter dated June 23, 1963.

> *The purchase of a coffin,*
> *and the receiving of friends,*
> *and the inevitable gloriado,*
> *and the family without a leader,*
> *and the work left undone,*
> *... and so many things yet to do.*

She'd put off writing to Nicanor, but finally poured out her misery.

> *Dearest Nica:*
> *By the time I left the eggshell and departed,*
> *my eyes were brimming over with my sorrows. ...*
> *Paris offers me not a single kiss, not the most superficial smile;*
> *its imposing structure crushes me ...*
> *I am growing extremely weary, I tell you in confidence,*
> *but do not repeat a word of it, not even under your breath.*
> *Keep it well hidden in the depths of your iron cookpot*
> *where the fire of your soul boils numerous verses.*

Nicanor wrote suggesting that she write a book of Chilean folklore for the French audience—advice she took seriously—and hinted he might visit that August. She wrote him back quickly, acknowledging his advice. She reminisced about eighty-year-old milkmaid Rosita, and wondered if doña Rosa Lorca in Barrancas was taking care of her heart, and how were faring La Lastenia, who had "spelled out thirty *cuecas* for me without stopping" and how the hands of doña Merche roamed over her harp.

A French Jew surfaced briefly as a love interest, but Violeta withdrew her affection when he meddled in her business affairs.

Isabel and Ángel came to Paris and performed with their mother at a gala workers' festival. After the concert, Violeta wrote a carefully worded letter to Gilbert, telling him about the frenzy of the event attended by 600,000 people and for which she was paid 1500 francs. She asked his advice on buying a tape recorder. The letter was newsy and conciliatory.

> *I'd love to see you and to sleep with you after having a good party. . . . Yesterday, I spoke to the Editor who's going to publish my book, so that it has two parts, Folklore and Revolutionary Songs, illustrated with my tapestries. . . .*
>
> *Please don't write me harsh letters. It's like cooking bad soup. Remember that you are writing to a woman who loves you … and needs the passion that a letter brings. Every character, every syllable, every word, should be a spark from the blood and heart of he who writes to his mistress.*
>
> *I am yours.*
>
> *VP*

By August, Isabel and Ángel had gone on vacation, Nicanor's European trip had failed to materialize, and seven years had passed since the infant Rosita Clara had died. For literally the entire month, Violeta imprisoned herself in grief. She became disoriented, and would awake frightened by a recurrent nightmare of suffocation.

> *Purple and black are the colors that haunt me.*
> *Purple flowers, black buds.*
> *black lines, purple dots.* . . .
> *Every afternoon the sky glows purple until*
> *the black of night dissolves it in its wake.*
> *. . . I have forgotten how to laugh;*
> *. . . words escape me in a tiny voice*
> *while the shouts of the orange vendor startle me.*
> *. . . I retreated into painting*
> *two wakes and an unsuccessful party*
> *so as not to feel the tightening in my throat.*
> *. . . I totter like a kite cut loose in dense space.*

Violeta, signed the diary entry *12 de agosto*, August twelfth, *día de la mamita*, the anniversary of the day she received the tragic news of Rosita Clara's death.

Gilbert visited. Afterwards, she wrote him, "Already you can see how everything changes. It could be that not even Death is eternal. I have no confidence in love."

Yet by the time she had to vacate 19 Place de la Madeleine, she had reanimated herself and was recording a new album whose songs attested to Violeta's mid-career virtuosity and political fervor.

In her song, *Ayúdame Valentina*, Violeta addressed Soviet cosmonaut, Valentina Tereshkova, the first woman in space, asking for all to see that Communists, Christians, and Capitalists alike gazed at the same wondrous heavens.

> *But of course, they adore the image of our lady Mary,*
> *without adoring any other woman or girl,* . . .

but to enter the kingdom of glory, one needs money,
my little mama.

Help me, Valentina, since already you have flown so far,
tell us once and for all that way up high
there are no Pearly Gates,
that tomorrow, man will be founded upon his reason,
my little mama.

At Gilbert's invitation, Violeta traveled to Geneva for a brief visit. With her earnings, she bought apparel, a tape recorder, a typewriter − lovely new things most of which she gave to her children. After returning to Paris, she wrote,

Gilbertito,

I arrived in Paris where Ángel was waiting for me. . . . Everything disappeared from my hands, but it isn't important. . . . It's a joy for me to be able to share my things with the people I love, and with those I don't love also. Ángel has promised to give me ten francs a day for food, so I can keep my little salary to spend it in time and to go on sharing things with those close to me. . . .

Tell me everything, Gilbert. After being together three years I want to know you better . . . in all tranquility. My children ask a thousand questions. They defend you and love you. . . .

When we said good-bye at the station, . . . I saw your little face behind the bars, you looked very pale. Suddenly, you raised your hand. . . . That was the last I saw of you. How was the cottage on your return? . . . Did you read the letter that I left you? . . .

Take up your clarinet again. . . . The sound you get from it comes right from your soul. Don't believe for a minute that you are not a musician. True, you have trouble with the Andean rhythm, but it is a completely curable problem. . . . The day you

can handle three or four pieces on quena we'll be set. Don't think
I'm angry at you darling, because I harp on you so much. It's for
your own good.

That evening, Violeta attended an elegant art opening
—an unusual occasion for her; she didn't circulate much at
openings. A Spaniard's flirtations made her realize how jealous she'd have felt if Gilbert were tempted by other women,
which prompted her to write him,

> *Absence doesn't cause forgetfulness*
> *When two people love one another*
> *Love increases even more*
> *When they cannot see each other.*

> *That's a stanza of a beautiful song from Chillán and I*
> *repeat it painfully, for I know nothing of what goes on beyond*
> *your closed door.*
> *600 km. to 16 rue Voltaire in Geneva. Visits from*
> *people . . . who play in the sacred bed. Harmful women who tell*
> *stories of love, who travel from bed to bed, obsessed with sex. . . .*
> *Look at the fire they spark. . . . the kisses they offer you. The*
> *saliva of our kiss is still not dry. . . .*
> *May you be deaf to the moaning that slips out. . . . Take*
> *care when mascara'd eyes gaze at you. Hundreds of years ago*
> *they belly-danced with any man. That is my mantra; I repeat it*
> *day and night to defend myself from shit on the path. . . . It is*
> *my blanket, my revolver, my power to scare away the enemy, and*
> *make my drawings strong when I stretch my tapestries.*

Gilbert replied, urging her not to be jealous. Amazingly, she
disavowed his charge!

Not jealousy! It is ridiculous to call me jealous, I who can fly away for months to other mountains. . . . Other eyes see you, others hear your laugh, receive your greetings. They see how you incline your head to Life. . . . How you flavor your soup with watermelon. I haven't even the strands of hair that you leave in your comb. . . . Don't call the absent flighty bird jealous. . . . The truth is that I am downcast.

Suddenly catching herself being self-indulgent, Violeta ended sweetly.

Keep my letters, darling. They will be of use later, when Titina wants to know her grandmother's secrets. Because in this world, not even deaths are tranquil. . . . You paid for my passage; thank you for that too. . . . I embrace you and kiss your testicles.
        Violeta

The Louvre

She sang in French–fluent by now–longing for home, but also inspired to create new visual art. Walking the streets of the student quarter surrounding the *Ecole des Beaux Artes*, Violeta scavenged for discarded clay, canvas, brushes, paint. Her treasure hunts yielded wool from knitting shops and fabric from dressmakers. She watched the artists capture impressions of the city on paper or canvas and render masterworks in chalk on the sidewalks of the Louvre bridge. She rummaged at stalls along the Seine, leafing through the etchings and lithographs for ideas.

The Paris art world in the early 1960s was in transition. New imagery suggestive of sex or psyche spilled into advertising. Though surrealism was deemed *démodé* and cubism too belonged to an earlier decade, galleries still banked on the works of established masters.

Critics applauded a retrospective of Henri Rousseau in 1961, but panned a show of Picassos painted in 1962 and 1963 because the aging Spaniard was said to be repeating himself. Violeta adored the work of Pablo Picasso (even tried to meet him once, without success). When Georges Braque died, his bier was laid out in the freshly scrubbed courtyard of the Louvre where a silent crowd of thousands paid him homage in the rain. The *Musée des Arts Decoratifs* honored

Mark Tobey as the first American artist to exhibit in their halls.

Concurrently, Algeria was wrenching loose France's colonial grip on Saharan oil. As France retreated from Africa, sub-Saharan "primitive" art became the newest find for collectors, who saw in its carved icons glimmers of Genesis, a purity of vision, *sauvage*, unsullied, elemental.

Steeped in this artistic bouillabaisse, Violeta embroidered, painted, made masks, and sculpted clay and wire. She recycled objects whose shape, texture, and color inhabited her emotional space. She stitched a length of wool into a bottle and gave it a brash face. Trees became doves. Flowers sprouted in a profusion of magical nuance. Her style was direct. Nostalgia evoked depictions of family and friends in masks, paintings, and *arpilleras*. Folklore animated vignettes of stories or events that haunted or delighted her –the circus, animals, the legend of the last Inca king, the Tree of Life, Don Quixote, warfare and heroism, an infant wake. Stitches and brushstrokes swept arcs suggestive of ocean waves or volcanic eruptions. Texture intensified. Violeta gave birth to the art of one peasant's reality that extolled the ordinary and fanciful.

Having accumulated a mountain of artwork she went looking for a place to exhibit. The oft-repeated story had Violeta meeting a man who send her to an address. When she arrived there, she found herself in front of the Louvre!

This magical anecdote is appealing, but evidence of letters from the files of the *Musée des Arts Decoratifs* library indicate that Violeta pursued her goal more pragmatically. She met the Chilean ambassador to France, Carlos Morla Lynch, from whom she secured a gracious letter of introduction to Jean Cassou, director of the *Musée National d'Art Moderne* in Paris:

Monsieur Director,

Permit myself to present to you by means of this note, Madame Violeta Parra, a Chilean artist who resides in Paris. Mme. Violeta Parra is a folklorist whose research and creations in the genre of Chilean peasant music have attracted tremendous interest not only in Chile but abroad, due to their authentic and original artistry. Mme. Violeta Parra's activities are valued in Latin America, and she is becoming known in Europe, where she has given several recitals. Her songs have also been recorded on disk.

In addition, Mme. Violeta Parra is a creator of tapestries, paintings, and ceramics of peasant inspiration. Besides her numerous exhibitions in Chile, she has participated ... in an exhibit of pictorial Chilean art shown at the Museum of Modern Art in Rio de Janeiro, where her works were received warmly by critics. She has had one-person shows in Geneva and Berlin, where the reviews of her creations were unanimously favorable.

I would be extremely grateful, M. Director, if you would accord a visit to Mme. Violeta Parra, for her to explain to you in person her desires, in the measure possible, for the development and diffusion of her artistic activities in France. I take this occasion to ask you, M. Director, to look favorably upon the assurances of my own most distinguished consideration. Thank you for welcoming my compatriot.

Carlos Morla Lynch
Ambassador of Chile

At the *Musée National d'Art Moderne*, a curator named Bernard Dorival received her. He examined the tapestries Violeta unfurled–her depiction of two couples, one in harmony the other in conflict; her *Negro Christ of Quinchamalí*. She sang him the song that inspired her canvas, *Parabienes a los Novios*.

Long live God, long live the virgin,
stars, heavens, elements,
long live those who receive
the seventh sacrament.

Although he did not deem her work avant-garde, M. Dorival found Violeta's embroideries indeed "worthy of interest, for she renews in them the tradition of Indian folklore from her country." By letter, he introduced her to Michel Faré, head curator at the *Musée des Arts Décoratifs* of the Louvre.

Violeta could not have hoped for a more receptive judge of her talent than Monsieur Faré, whose Gallic charm set her at ease. "Madame, these are very special. . . . Your use of color is like a jewel. Very lovely, madame." He won her trust. By the time she had left samples of her handicrafts in his office, she was certain she would have a show.

But when she returned days later, she received disappointing news. "I am so sorry," M. Faré began, "but the curatorial committee is unwilling to display the works of an unknown. They have rejected your petition for a show. I regret their decision."

Crushed, Violeta burst into tears, unashamed of her pain. "We are five people in my family living so meagerly, you wouldn't believe it. For the past three months I've done nothing but work day and night. Determination is like death itself for me. I stayed in Paris only for this chance. I rejected an invitation to East Berlin and gallery offers."

Nothing M. Faré said comforted her. Sentimentality was disparaged in sophisticated artistic circles, but Violeta's receipt of bad news so utterly departed from the norm, he was visibly moved.

"Madame, please understand that I admire your works and I regret that this has caused you to suffer so. I didn't want that." He added, "Listen, surely it was not a definitive rejection. In the long term, I am certain you will have your show."

Violeta gazed at him with childlike innocence. He touched her hand tenderly, stroked her hair, and then spoke with such resolve, she knew he was speaking from the heart. "Have faith in me and please be calm, madame. I think your works are amazing and deserve to be exhibited here." He resolved to bring the matter up again at another meeting of the curatorial committee. "Bring me all your works, quickly, immediately. I don't have much time, but I'll see what I can do for you. Bring me everything by four and with your works in hand I will defend your name and your show."

Clinging to this last hope, Violeta returned to the museum with Ángel and all her *arpilleras*, a wire sculpture of Christ, embroidered masks, and paintings. When she showed M. Faré *The Meeting of the Twelve Apostles,* he snatched it up with his hands, taken by its power. "Trust me, and you mustn't cry, " he said. He had another meeting with the commission the following Monday.

Violeta spent the intervening days crawling about like "a bloodless insect, without a backbone, without a brain, without anything," terrified of being rejected. Not even Titina or Carmen Luisa's company could distract her. She paced and fretted. Locked in a trance of self-doubt, lacking the conviction to sew or paint, she sang, oblivious to the complaints of neighbors, from early morning when she tuned her guitar to evening, when she left to sing in *La Candelaria.*

Monday when Ángel called, she appealed to him: would he go find out for her what had transpired at the museum? He agreed.

Violeta reckoned exactly how long Ángel would take to get to the museum, how much time he would spend there, and how long he would take to return. Then she distinguished his footsteps coming up the stairs. The verdict of her museum show loomed. She opened the door and saw Ángel climb to the landing, his face radiant. She cried.

No one was more astonished by her success than Violeta herself. "How could it be," she asked everyone she knew, "That I, who am the ugliest woman on Earth, from the furthest reaches of the world, I am going to exhibit at the Louvre?"

The show was scheduled for April, which gave Violeta two months to prepare. She persuaded Gilbert to come to Paris to frame her art. Carmen Luisa, who by now was fourteen, recalled that the one-room apartment became a claustrophobic madhouse, with Violeta "finishing off details, stitching here and there, and the *gringo* hammering and framing everything."

Before long, the three had no place to sleep. Gilbert made friends with the museum's carpenters and got permission to use their basement workshop. The arrangement was a godsend. While Gilbert built stretcher frames and stretched the tapestries, Violeta handed him tools, trimmed stray threads, and continued to stitch an ambitious depiction of the Naval War of Iquique that she did not complete in time for the show. At midday, Carmen Luisa arrived with bread and a pot of beans or soup that Violeta had prepared in the morning; everyone at hand convened for a hearty meal.

As opening day neared, Gilbert, Violeta, and the museum staff hung the gallery walls with a rainbow display of tapestry and acrylic color, jewel-like in its intensity. Spectral hues of green, blue, cobalt, yellow and chartreuse, pink, red. Shapes varied in scale from the intimate paintings no more than ten by fourteen inches and masks only slightly larger than the human head to expansive *arpilleras*, six-by-ten-foot swaths of jute stitched in colored wool whose figures were nearly lifesize. Perched on pedestals throughout the space stood a menagerie of three-dimensional creatures–llama, fish, flying dog, singing tree.

Violeta had externalized the world of her imagination and memory for all to see by tapping her beloved Chilean folkloric tradition. She treated every visualization as a direct outpouring of narrative and sentiment, in concert with nature. Children's stories, episodes from the Bible, historical events, figures from Violeta's personal life–all danced in place. In all, sixty-one pieces–tapestries, paintings, clay and wire sculpture, and *papier-maché* masks–exhibited for a month, from April 8 to May 11, 1964, at the *Musée des Arts Decoratifs*.

The opening reception of this, the Louvre's first exhibition to showcase a Latin American artist, was a gala affair indeed. Recorded music from Violeta's albums echoed the visual splendor–as one critic noted, "each song, a picture ready to be painted"–for surely it was impossible to separate her poetry from her pictures.

Violeta herself resembled any peasant woman of Chile, wearing a simple black dress, her hair loose, her unadorned face glowing. She chatted with the elegant men and women to whom she was introduced, glitterati who looked more natural in those surroundings than did she–collectors, critics, museum staff, other artists, diplomats–viewing Violeta's vivid imagery and discussing the unusual array of pictorial art while sipping wine and sampling the buffet. Isabel, Cristina, Ángel, Marta, Carmen Luisa all attended; Gilbert filmed the entire event with a 16mm camera.

In those exalted surroundings, Violeta's body of work stood on its own merits, an undeniable achievement. A contingent of high-bred Chileans attended who believed that Art occupied an elite strata in which the rustic Violeta Parra did notfigure. They were astonished that she had so captivated the esteem of a city renowned for its aesthetic as to warrant an exhibit at the Louvre.

Violeta beamed with satisfaction (she described it later as one of her greatest pleasures) when she spotted the director of the Santiago outdoor art fair. The same *cuecas* over which he had chastised her for making too much noise at the outdoor show now accosted him in this auspicious space. He looked like he wanted to hide.

Violeta walked right up to him and gestured expansively. "Some of these are the same little *arpilleras* I displayed at the *Parque Forestal*, remember?" The man flushed with embarrassment. He had "understood" that her work had hardly been of sufficient merit to be exhibited along the banks of Santiago's Mapocho River. Carmen Luisa watched the exchange and giggled at seeing her mother's delight at the man's comeuppance.

To the French, Violeta Parra's creativity made perfect sense. The museum's press release celebrated her as an original artist whose spark derived from the uniqueness of her personal experience.

Violeta is hardly unknown in France. Fans of folk music know her recordings of Chilean songs, collected during her travels of villages and countryside, the mountains and shores of her country. They know too that she enriched contemporary folklore, creating songs and poems in her own voice authentically Chilean yet profoundly personal.

For the first time in Paris, she presents another aspect of her talent, with a very original group of arpilleras, paintings, and sculpture.

Music and color are related for Violeta, who passes naturally from one to another, and who sees in each song a scene ready to be painted. On arpilleras or rough canvases, she embroiders lively images in wool with big stitches that illustrate a Chilean story or legend or . . . perhaps show a moving episode in her own life.

She uses a poetic and symbolic language, endowing significance to each theme, each color, without ignoring the plasticity, the aesthetic side of her work. Each one of her arpilleras is a story, a remembrance, or a visual protest.

Her small drawings are more intimate. They are intense and serious poems about her difficult and courageous life. With her wire sculptures, her dream occupies a universe of plasticity, woven of birds and doves, of bulls and llamas, of trees that sing and of legendary personages, such as Don Quixote.

Instinctive and willful, Violeta Parra appropriates the world and makes it her work. She animates all that she touches from a perspective that is precise, original in her words and sounds, form and colors. She is a total artist, musician, painter, sculptor, ceramist, a poet like her brother, Nicanor Parra, and her friend, Pablo Neruda.

P.-M. Grand, the art critic of *Le Monde* reviewed Violeta Parra in an article about three artists whose works were based on peasant themes.

"A lamb disguised as a wolf" according to her brother, poet Nicanor Parra, Violeta Parra stands alone as a solo ensemble of peasant art. This show displays a representative sampling of her works. Violeta is present . . . to play guitar, sing sad and expressive music, embroider inventively, and comment without guile. Petite, brunette, at once simple and complex like a figure

*from Lorca, or like her own sculptures, complicated twisted metal
wires made into golden flowers that bloom on a black tree.*

*Her embroideries plant astonishing scenes of misery and
poetry: . . . Cruxified Christ in a beautiful flowering tree.
Weapons disarm . . . with incorruptible liberty, in birds or
musical instruments.*

*Her masks evoke her children and familiar demons, as do her
violent little paintings. . . . Violeta, a wolf disguised as a lamb,
too.*

Critics from *Le Figaro* and *La Tribune* hailed Violeta as
the "embodiment of a distant yet universal experience." She
beamed when she told reporters, "Among us, everything is a
song. If a peasant sings to express his joy for having grown a
melon larger than the others, someone else will say, 'it's
nothing'; he's seen one the size of a house. Then like a
mountain, then like the world, then like the universe!"

Like all artists who come to Paris, Violeta was
broadened by the residency. Long before her European success, she esteemed contemporary Chilean artists Nemesio
Antúnez and Pablo de Rokha, and the Mexican painter,
Rufino Tamayo, all of whose works conveyed the peasant
not for the pleasure of the rich but for the piquancy of its
personality. Now, she came to know Roberto Matta, whose
two-dimensional spatial webs were as European as he was
Chilean. And she discovered Marc Chagall, for whom she
felt real affinity: Both grew up poor, both one of nine children, and both depicted the nostalgia of childhood.

Although she conceived art in terms of anecdote, she
conveyed ideas with a painterly eye. Her picture plane revealed spatial ordering. She chose deliberately the scale of
figure against ground. In *The Self-Absorbed Widower*, she
dwarfed the individual in a picture plane of light and dark
geometry suggestive of solitude. The color violet predomin-

ated. In *The Bald Singer*, executed as both painting and *arpillera* based on Ionesco's *Bald Soprano*, Violeta centered herself amidst a party of cubistically rendered revelry.

Alongside the intimate hung a depiction of war and peace, symbolized by rifle and dove in a tapestry that celebrated the brotherhood she experienced performing at international festivals. She told one reporter, "In my country there are many political disturbances. . . . At this time I cannot protest, but with my pictures I can do so."

Religious themes suggested a personal covenant with her savior that enmeshed nature and spirit, apart from the Church. In her *Christ of Quinchamalí*, the black figure symbolizes the color of the clay dug from the village riverbank, though it resulted from happenstance.

As her friend, Adela Gallo, told it, "One day I got to Violeta's and I had with me some black wool, because I was knitting a cap, which is the only thing I know how to do with my hands. Violeta spotted it and asked, 'What's this? What are you carrying in there? Ah, how nice that you bring me black wool! Let me see, give it to me!' And she took it from me, just like that, and from that she colored Christ black."

Her vivid characterizations in color, size, gesture, stitch or brush stroke grabbed viewers' attention. She painted as turbulently as Van Gogh and sewed quickly with long stitches, to cover large areas with color. She didn't like to sew as much as to paint, because it took so long and she wanted to tell as much as possible. And when she decided that her work was finished, often as not it was because she could not afford to buy more wool. Her ingenuity fascinated visitors, but her lack of formal training exasperated some.

> *Interviewer: But you knew how to embroider, didn't you?*
> *Violeta: Nothing could be simpler. But I don't know how to draw.*

Interviewer: Then you have invented it all anew?
Violeta: Yes, but everyone can invent; it isn't a specialty of mine alone.

Her technique was uniquely her own as well.

Interviewer: What is the theme of the tapestry that you are making now?
Violeta: It's an episode in the history of Chile.
Interviewer: Aren't you looking at the work as a whole.
Violeta: No, it will come out.
Interviewer: But I never see you stretch out the arpillera to look at it.
Violeta: That's because I have the theme in my head.

A radio interviewer once asked her whether she preferred to sing, make tapestries, or paint. She answered, "That depends on the day. Some days I want nothing to do with the guitar, nothing to do with making *arpilleras*."

Her voice became acerbic. "I don't want to see any of it. I move my bed to block the doorway and stew, because I can't bring life into my work: Life is harder, more intense than a mere picture."

The success of her exhibition at the Louvre had enormous impact on Violeta, but as her son Ángel noted, it didn't change her character. Violeta never pretended to be anything other than who she was. "She never hid her class, because deep down, she felt proud of her humble origins."

No work shamed her. Ángel recalled his mother setting up a paraffin stove in the doorway of their house and fried *sopaipillas* to sell. "For her, work represented the highest value of being human."

By now, Violeta's fighting spirit resembled like no one else. It fueled her will. "She never doubted that what she was doing was inspired, important, or unique." The Violeta who washed her clothes in a tin bucket full of drawn water outdoors on a winter morning was the same person who exhibited her tapestries in the *Musée des Arts Decoratifs.*

Violeta Parra was the first Latin American artist to be accorded a solo show at the Louvre in Paris.

Violeta Parra, Christ of Quinchamalí,
embroidered on green jute, 45" x 36". 1959.

To Gather a Bouquet

Through the entire month of the exhibition, Violeta maintained a very lively, savory atmosphere, spiked with Chilean music and *yerba maté* and cinnamon tea. Her presence was integral to the art. Seated on a straw chair, guitar in hand, surrounded by her ghosts, her peasants, her children, her demons, she embodied Creation indivisible from Imagination. Rarely leaving her pieces alone in the room, she presided and demonstrated her stitchery techniques to visitors.

Into Violeta's life streamed artists, collectors, gallery dealers, and representatives of museums, who lauded her work and tantalized her with proposals of new exhibits and prospective sales. The Chilean painter, Roberto Matta, who visited the show repeatedly, urged her to work in larger scale. The Czech ambassador wanted to exhibit her in Prague. Museum directors from Italy, Holland, and Belgium spoke of giving her shows. An Italian jeweler told her he could see her work hanging in a *palazzo* in Florence. An architect who worked with Le Corbusier fawned over her, enchanted by her exhibit.

She responded to all prospects with both delight and fear–thrilled by the acclaim and afraid of being deluded by false promises. She confided to Gilbert, "Now, we'll have to see what actually happens. If only I could believe a tenth of all this bouquet of flowers."

In fact, successful reviews for her Louvre show launched Violeta as an artist worthy of investment. Her lush paintings and "pictorial tapestries with ancient roots in southern Chile" became prized for their decorative, painterly qualities. Her art earned considerable income, a windfall to which she didn't feel especially attached. She remained wary of the wealthy buyers and their attention, always wondering when it would cease.

Gilbert returned to Geneva after the opening.

One day, Carmen Luisa answered a knock on the door and opened it to an elegantly dressed woman asking to see Violeta. Ushering her in, the girl watched bemused as the woman surveyed with dismay the tiny, windowless room occupied by the girl, her mother, musical instruments, and artwork.

The Baroness de Rothschild was in her mid-forties, about the same age as Violeta, and although her upper-class station was apparent in her tailoring and coiffure, her demeanor was unpretentious, good-natured.

It was mid-morning. Violeta was still lying in bed, wide awake; the radio, playing. She'd performed the night before and was in no hurry to get up. According to Carmen Luisa, "It was irrelevant that her guest was aristocratic and had come to buy. Violeta would've stayed in bed, baroness or not."

When Violeta asked her what she wanted, the patron explained she had seen her work at the Louvre, and so admired her craftsmanship and unique images that she wanted to purchase several tapestries.

Although they sold well, Violeta never made tapestries solely to sell. She had grown rather attached to the ones

Mme. de Rothschild desired, and since she was not eager to part with them, she quoted the woman inflated prices, hesitantly. Rothschild accepted the figure without argument.

This stopped Violeta cold. "You really do appreciate my work, don't you?"

"*Mais oui*," the woman agreed, and the warmth of her sincerity prompted Violeta to lower her price.

En route home from the Soviet Union, where his *anti-poemas* were being published in Russian, Nicanor showed up in Paris to revel in his sister's accomplishment. After he left, Violeta wrote Gilbert a newsy letter in French.

> *My Darling,*
>
> *I work night and day. . . . Nicanor left last Sunday. Mme. Rothschild is truly a great woman. She came last Wednesday and paid me 7000 new francs. Arturo Prat, my aristocratic Chilean friend, bought the yellow arpillera from me, the guitarist, you remember. But he'll pay Nicanor in Chile $500 dollars. Also, he took a mask.*
>
> *I'll make new ones of the two guitarists, black and yellow, the clown, the little bird, besides another that I started before the exhibition. . . .*
>
> *The Czech ambassador came to see me and spoke once again about the trip to Prague. I await his letter detailing his terms. I received your two letters.*

The letter marked an unusual juncture for the couple; this time it was Gilbert, missing her, who asked that she come to be with him.

> *I cannot go to Switzerland, my darling. I want very much to be with you. I am yours, but you well know very at this time I must remain here.*

After receiving no immediate reply, Violeta wrote again to Gilbert. By now she dreaded May eleventh, the day the show was due to close.

> *Darling,*
>
> *Did you receive my letter? Many days have passed since I mailed it to you. Here everything is going sweetly. We are in the last eleven days of my exhibition. The time is drawing near and I fear the eleventh will be a terrible day. I don't like to think about it. …*
>
> *I am kind of sad, but not too much. I seem to be preoccupied about not knowing exactly what might be my destiny after the museum.*
>
> Violeta
>
> Paris, May 1, 1964

Despite their recent harmony, Gilbert's silence troubled Violeta. She distrusted the episodic nature of their intimacy and wondered if he had another lover.

She resisted his advice that she move to a better room, at least one with a window. Though she had the means to do so, she decided instead to put her children's needs before her own and fund their return to Chile.

Likely the twenty-one-year-old Ángel and his young wife, Marta, had never intended to stay so long in Europe; they were anxious to get on with their lives. And it was only a matter of time before Isabel, age 25, would follow, taking with her the beloved nine-year-old granddaughter, Cristina, and teenaged Carmen Luisa, who wanted to go home to her friends. The prospect of being alone again in Paris weighed heavily in Violeta's mind.

As her Louvre exhibit ended, a new project beckoned. Earlier, Violeta had performed at a Latin American poetry reading. A reviewer singled her out as "the evening's revelation, that small woman who inclined her body humbly and when she stood up brought the entire universe with her." She sang the poems of Pablo Neruda, which she set to music, as well folkloric and original songs.

This led to her performance in a narrative celebration of Life called *Vivre*, featuring African poems, blues sung in French, puppetry, and Violeta's songs of Chile. Violeta's tapestries of Life hung in the entrance hall.

> *In the center of my heart*
> *is the rose,*
> *a tree of great mystery*
> *and fruit of passion.*

Violeta sang as though offering flowers to harmonize all humanity. She transported her audience. Yet their praise failed to anchor her.

Returning home from China in late May, Pablo de Rokha, a longtime friend, paid Violeta a visit. Ten years since they'd spent time together in Paris. His brashness had blackened with the shock of his son's suicide two years earlier. Violeta's lighthearted welcome cheered him. In an homage entitled "*Violeta y su guitarra,*" written in Paris on June 1, 1964 after seeing her perform, de Rokha praised her extravagantly.

> *Her art has that virtue of health from the robust,*
> *pharmacoepia of herbs scent Chilean mountains and hillsides and*
> *releases their scent of sweat from the world of the future, or the*
> *remote past, and are like whips of dialectical honey.*
> *   In the human common denominator, her folklore is roguishly*
> *Spanish, derived from the bowels of the people, a Catholicism*
> *more pagan than Christian. She cries, laughs, bellows from the*
> *subsoil of that happy wit; when sapped of courage she*

dramatizes her guitar. One so innocent becomes macabre, like a
gargoyle in a Gothic cathedral.

Once de Rokha left and her daughters prepared to depart for home, Violeta began to panic; she would be alone again in Paris. She wrote Gilbert a letter of bravura and longing.

> *Strength grows in me and Life seems more beautiful. I was*
> *invited to exhibit at an important gallery in Lausanne, on the*
> *30th of October. I accept, enchanted. It means I have to go to*
> *Lausanne. Near Geneva, the land of the gringo.*
> *The Parra family is going to Chile soon. . . .*
> *It seems to me that you were making a documentary (a short*
> *film I think) about a woman who exhibited at the Louvre.*
> *Someone seems to have come with a camera., one morning,*
> *awakening me with a. kiss. ... Oh, one more detail! He washed*
> *his feet every night. And he liked salami with bread and wine.*
> *How are you doing, Gilbert? Do you remember a folklorist*
> *in Chile whom you knew one night?*
> *Nobody here plays clarinet, yet here it sleeps peacefully in its*
> *case. . . . If you happen to see that fellow who washes his feet*
> *every night, tell him about the salami, the wine, the guitar and the*
> *clarinet. And how good it was then. . . .*
> *The Parra family is going to Chile very soon.*
> *Perhaps it played on its own. . . . Its wood is smooth, like*
> *the skin of someone who slept at my side and washed his feet. Is*
> *it possible that he was transformed into a clarinet?*

The day before they left, Violeta steeled herself against the inevitable pangs of her girls' departure. She took them shopping, cooked dinner while Carmen Luisa packed. They shared a final meal. Violeta gave Isabel money and instructions for repairs her brothers were to make to the house in La Reina. Isabel sang a new song to her mother. On a whim, noticing that Isabel's boots were worn, Violeta gave her the pair Gilbert had just bought her in Geneva.

As the three were gathering up their belongings (to leave from Isabel's in the morning), Violeta embraced Isabel with a fearsome squeeze and whispered, "*Bella mia*, take good care of my little brandies, will you please?" She sent Carmen Luisa and Titina off with big hugs and told them to be good. They left teary-eyed Violeta alone.

The next morning, Violeta awoke with an urge to paint. She arranged her palette and canvas, but was too distracted. She went walking by the Seine to look for driftwood, but in an instant she was standing at the door of Isabel and Titina's abandoned flat. "Tiny as an ant," she climbed the stairs to an unlocked door, entered, and lingered in the rooms empty but for bags and boxes of discards. Outgrown clothing. Crayon pictures. Isabel's brown boots. One by one, Violeta handled the items.

Suddenly, Violeta realized she had left herself without even enough money to pay the rent! Despite her earnings from art sales, she was broke. That very day she landed another Paris show to open almost immediately. Again she wrote to Gilbert asking for help, to which a small parcel soon arrived containing a Swiss billfold and a check. Violeta wrote back with heartfelt gratitude.

Weeks passed before she received any correspondence from home. When finally Isabel's letter arrived accompanied by a copy of Ángel's first solo record album, Violeta realized how desperately homesick she was. The letter hinted at goings' on that Violeta didn't quite approve of.

As a mother she worried that only she could straighten things out at home. She resolved to return to Chile after her Paris gallery show closed and before her October show in

Lausanne. She'd even be in Chile for the presidential elections.

Happily, her gallery show sold well.

For someone as impulsive as Violeta, lacking a car was a bother. So when she sold a large tapestry she spent the proceeds on a green Volkswagen camper van. Soon her high-spirited friend Adela was headed for Paris to chauffeur them around Europe.

The women's eccentricities were well matched and their adventures in Paris surreal. Both were generous to a fault, loved the company of people, thought nothing of cooking up meals for a crowd on a whim.

Adela almost killed off an entire supper party once with indigestion. While Violeta was out, Adela rummaged through her pantry (practically bare) looking for anything she could cook into a soup. She spotted what she thought was a bag of flour. It was gesso! The next day, she confessed that while it was cooking, the stew looked so pale, she had added a squeeze of some watercolor paint "to give it a little color."

Violeta's next letter to Gilbert apologized for her extravagance and again asked for help. She put great stock in promoting herself during her Chilean trip. She had appearances lined up, for which she had to look good.

> *I haven't even shoes. The little boots you bought me in Geneva I gave to Isabel. Could you ask for credit for me in a clothing store? I have no overcoat. Nothing. I need a coat (size 44), a pair of large black boots (size 35 or 36, although I prefer 35), two winter outfits, a little hat, a slip, and a suitcase.*
>
> *If you can get me this credit, don't send me money and you pay the credit little by little. Answer me right away, so I'll know*

where I stand. I don't want to go to Chile looking like one of the unfortunates.

Had he finished the film montage of her Louvre exhibition, so she could show it at the *Salon de Honor*, along with slides and photos? She acknowledged the estrangement was taking its toll.

> *Your letter is very scattered. I would say you don't love me anymore. You can't hide the truth from me. You're in Geneva, I'm in Paris. I've got a head of iron; your head's plenty hard. Maybe you're hurting, could be I'm hurting too. It could be that love has gone; maybe not. Cat and mouse – that's how Violeta and Gilbert play. That's the truth, no?*

Then she gave him a glimpse of her automotive progress.

> *So far, I've taken eight driving lessons. I'm already driving the car through the streets, though with the teacher at my side. I want to understand the very depths of the motor … an entirely new language.*
>
> *I would like to open up a man like a car. But the two things are impossible. If I were to open up a man he would scream; if I open the car's engine it would be so angry it wouldn't run.*

Despite her narcolepsy, Adela got a French driver's license. She'd fall asleep unpredictably and not even Violeta's most raucous singing could keep her awake. Adela ignored all gears but first, in whose "security" she preferred to remain.

They drove to Geneva (much to Gilbert's astonishment) and stayed for hardly a day. Violeta discovered no infidelity. Gilbert was a Saint, and Geneva, Paradise! The couple made music and love, and struck a deal: She'd have new clothes for Chile, he'd take the car when she left. The women drove back to Paris and the next day Violeta wrote,

> *Little saint:*
> *I traveled 1,200 kilometers in one day to surprise you. That's how I am. Now I'm going to Chile for just a few days. That's how I am. Actions speak louder than words.*
>
> *I think a lot about my little dress. I wear a size 42, not 44. I never know exactly if I am young or old. Sometimes I feel like a fifteen-year-old girl and other times I seem as ancient as the Earth.*
>
> *I don't like people who rob me of time. I passed by your side like a ray. I carried you a bit of joy and a bit of bother, but I did not rob you of your time. I traveled sixteen hours to see you for only one hour.*
>
> *I'm looking after my gallery, and since it's quiet I'm writing to you. . . .*
>
> *In September when I return from Chile, let's try a duo. Quena and tambor. Guitar and tambor. Cuatro and guitar. . . . Review the rhythms well.*
>
> *Don't complain about being alone. Remember, when you were very involved with other people you lost time.*
>
> *You'll need an immigration visa. Take care of the paperwork beforehand. You can take everything that way. I await your visit on the 12th, with my pretty little clothing.*
>
> *Love,   Santa Violeta*

The day her show closed, Gilbert arrived with Violeta's clothes. She loaded her art supplies and unsold works into the van and signed over its ownership to Gilbert. They departed–he for Switzerland, she for Chile.

Santiago Interlude

At a reception held in July 1964 at the elegant Hotel Crillon in downtown Santiago, Violeta reported her European accomplishments to the press. She showed photographs and news clippings of her exhibits at the Louvre and at Paris and Geneva galleries, of her concerts at UNESCO, the Sorbonne, in bistros and theatres. She displayed her albums and the book of folklore she had compiled of her Chilean research. She wanted every Chilean to know that in Europe she had brought honor to their culture.

Indeed, after the Louvre, Violeta Parra became a household name in Chile, legendary in her own time, like Gabriela Mistral, the rustic schoolteacher whose poetry won her the Nobel Prize in Literature in 1945. And like Mistral, foreigners valued her work more than her own countrymen, a fact that exasperated her.

To set disappointment aside, Violeta threw herself into politics, by volunteering to work for Salvador Allende, a physician who was running for President on a coalition ticket of the Communist and Socialist parties against Christian Democrat, Eduardo Frei. This was Allende's second run for the presidency.

Eduardo Frei's war-chest was bankrolled lavishly by the United States government and corporations, West Germany and the Catholic Church, all of them determined to prevent Marxism from spreading from Cuba throughout Latin America. At stake was Chile's very profitable high-grade copper ore, mined by two US multinational corporations, Kennecott and Anaconda. The *yanquis* had long-since recouped their investment and were robbing Chile blind, argued Allende as he campaigned to nationalize the copper mines. Frei advocated "Chileanizing the mines" by buying controlling interests and increasing production, which, he told the middle class, would improve people's standard of living. To the poor, he promised land.

Slick, anonymous campaign posters plastered throughout Santiago warned that if Allende won, Chilean youth would be indoctrinated to Marxism. Every half hour, melodramatic radio spots aired on all major stations:

> *Opening sounds of machine-gun fire.*
> *Speaker one: "The communists have killed my son!"*
> *Speaker two: "Stop this from happening in Chile!*
> *Let's elect Eduardo Frei for President!"*
> *Closing sounds of dramatic music.*

Allende campaigned tirelessly among the grassroots, calling for a more egalitarian society. His advertising was handwritten and posted by individual initiative, graffiti on public walls, or murals depicting a brighter future for children.

Prominent among Allende's campaign workers were many rising stars of the emerging *Nueva Canción Chilena*. The Parras joined with other young performers whose lyrics wed social criticism to traditional rhythms. By departing from traditional folkloric instrumentation and chord progressions, they achieved new harmonies and created a musical sound that was gaining popularity, especially among the youth.

Since Violeta Parra's trip home coincided with the culmination of the 1964 elections, she threw herself into the compaign fray and performed for Allende in union halls, schools, and plazas. How impressed she was to see all of San Miguel neighborhood waving little Chilean flags–factory workers from nearby warehouses and fabrication shops, housewives, young people, the elderly–and hear the port workers in Valparaíso cheer for their candidate, as the late-winter winds of September blew through the streets.

Against percussive clapping and shouted slogans, Violeta's voice galvanized audiences with new, outspoken songs, like *La Carta* (The Letter).

> *I just received a letter*
> *by early morning mail . . .*
> *that my brother's been arrested;*
> *they dragged him*
> *through the city in shackles.*
> *Yes!*
>
> *The crime Roberto committed*
> *was to support a workers' strike*
> *that had already been resolved.*
> *If that's a crime, sergeant,*
> *I too should be arrested!*
> *Yes!*
>
> *There's no justice in my homeland.*
> *Hungry people ask for bread*
> *and get policemen's bullets.*
> *Yes!*

Luckily, I have my guitar
and also my voice
and nine brothers and sisters
besides the one in chains.
All are revolutionaries.
May God make them strong!
Yes!

Violeta toured central Chile to cheering crowds during her month-long stay. But soon, the grinding pace of public life exhausted her. She rested amidst the comforts of her family. In a letter written to Gilbert over several days, she anticipated and then reacted to the outcome of the election.

Santiago, 2 September 1964

Beloved Gilbert:
    I have only enough strength and energy to write to you. Sick as a dog. My mother has come to take care of me. We have spoken much of you. She loves you. Isabel has worked in the presidential campaign and in recitals. Now she's taping records. I too intend to do that as soon as I get better. It's very cold, but there is a little sun. The house is lovely. Your dog is perfectly marvelous. Yellow and obedient, but very lazy. A cat is more lively than he is.
    At this moment the sun is setting and the teapot is boiling enthusiastically.
    Nicanor has asked me for drawings to illustrate the new edition of his Cueca Larga. I will get to work.
    Yesterday, the fourth, we were all greatly shocked. We lost the elections. Frei was elected. The Christian Democrats swept over the Allende movement. It's a very hard blow. We'll see what happens now. . . .

The only good thing is that we still have the yellow dog, so pretty and affectionate. A white cat keeps him company. The patio is completely covered with hair. The house is pretty as always.

I am better now. Tonight I'm singing on the radio. The kids too. A month-long contract. I believe darling, that I will be arriving there the first days of October. We'll make beautiful parties for two, if it's not too cold.

. . . I love you very much.

Violeta Parra

Though brief, Violeta Parra's trip home calmed her. She saw for herself that her children were thriving. She returned to Europe, content for the time being to live in France and Switzerland where her art was taken more seriously. Besides, she loved Gilbert and wanted to be with him.

Soul Food

Violeta arrived in Geneva in October 1964, for what was to be her final residence in Europe, a stay of less than a year.

She reclaimed the Volkswagen van from Gilbert, "My splendid little truck, my studio on wheels," she referred to it as affectionately as a pet. On a whim, she'd throw her belongings (clothes, guitar, flutes, and drum, her tapestries and wool, paintings still tacky to the touch, half-closed tubes of oil color) pell-mell into its curtained passenger area, and set off to park in Paris or Lausanne.

Yet Violeta could barely drive. Occasionally, Gilbert gave her vague driving lessons, though without much hope that she would master the rules of the road. She drove just as she embroidered–impetuously. Easily distracted, she was a public menace behind the wheel. The van became an object of contention in their already conflictive relationship.

"It's my car," she argued.

"Yes, but you don't have a driver's license so you will not drive it."

"We'll see about that." She'd grab the keys and leave.

To placate her, Gilbert drove her on the trafficked routes connecting Paris and Geneva, Geneva and Lausanne. Yet they'd travel scared, because they drove without a license, without insurance, often while drinking. Violeta had a permit and didn't know how to drive; Gilbert had no license and drove "like a veteran." When he tried to renew his driving privileges, he was reminded of a slew of unpaid tickets carrying a hefty fine.

Their chance pay up came soon, when Violeta's Lausanne show opened in February 1965. She mounted an ambitious display, filling the gallery's rear salon with brightly colored panels of cloth and canvas. In the main gallery were watercolors by another artist. Once Violeta installed her work, she parked herself conspicuously to meet prospective buyers and demonstrate her techniques, as was her practice.

Her vivid work caught the eye of a fashionably dressed browser. Unimpressed by the watercolors, she was about to leave when she spotted the petite woman in the hue-filled room stitching a tapestry. Violeta must have made a poignant site, her tresses of ebony hair falling on the rabbit-fur collar of her black coat, a valise and a guitar case parked beside her chair.

"Are you Violeta Parra?" she asked.

At having her concentration interrupted, the artist froze, startled. "Yes."

"Your work is beautiful." She was there to review the gallery offerings, but in that instant her response was simply visceral.

Violeta stopped sewing, stared at the woman, and asked in a hoarse voice, "Really? You really like it?"

"Yes, I do."

Violeta studied her for a long moment. "I believe you mean what you say. So listen to me." She gestured grandly with a sweep of an arm. "I will tell you about my work, here on these walls, by singing about it to you."

She took her guitar from its case, and led her guest to the first tapestry on the wall, which depicted a figure whose arms ended in flowers and from atop whose head grew a feathery tree. There she sang *La Jardinera*.

> *For my sorrow a blue violet,*
> *a red carnation for my passion*
> *and to know if you return my love*
> *I pluck the petals of a white daisy.*
> *Whether you love me wholeheartedly,*
> *a tiny bit, or not at all,*
> *my heart remains at peace.*

Violeta's voice transported them on an visionary tour of South America. The art critic wept, overcome by talents so generously exhibited. Of each work in turn, Violeta's guitar seconded her voice. Once she'd described it all, a church bell chimed noon. Nearly two hours had passed.

"Won't you join me for lunch," the woman invited. And she inquired politely where Violeta would sleep that night.

"Eat?" Violeta said to her, "I'm not hungry." Then looking into the woman's eyes with sudden malice, she added, "Besides, I've just swallowed your soul."

Marie-Magdeleine Brumagne had to admit, that was true. She invited Violeta to her home, where she rested for several days. That Friday's Arts and Letters section of the Lausanne Tribune carried the following review.

> *Some encounters with a being, a book, a picture, a song*
> *make an indescribable impression. This is why I am unable*
> *to speak of Violeta Parra objectively, because the tapestries*
> *she exhibits at the Galerie de Nouveaux Grands Magasins are*
> *more than aesthetically beautiful − they are magical. They*

escape the norms of meaning whose reasoned approach can be explained. Why do these personages of wool, animals, flowers, embroidery, tender and violent novelties move our sensibility? Doubtless because they are not decorative elements, but portraits of people beloved or not, memories of Chile that glorify and exorcise them. One witnesses the birth of deaf violence and fertile tenderness. Innocent works, primitive, but charged with experience, rich in technique and transcendence.

In her memoirs, Marie-Magdeleine referred to their friendship as having been born from the stroke of a reciprocal thunderbolt. Statuesque, olive-skinned, of North African ancestry that included a beatified missionary nun, Marie-Magdeleine viewed Life as a sequence of epiphanies. Violeta's vision of Destiny as trails and trials intrigued her. Everything Violeta created held emotion. Her characters came alive as she embroidered them.

When the captain of a ship emerged out of colored wool on the coarse weave of a burlap sack, Violeta spoke as though bringing him to life.

"He will be handsome and proud. We have to tell him nice things. I always talk to my figures. For me they are alive."

She stitched without a frame, holding the cloth tight against her knees, making no effort to match yarns from her basket of salvaged wool, but allowing nuances to organize themselves. When she finished, the two women spread out the cloth and discovered a coherent composition of unforeseen shapes and turbulent textures amidst balanced masses.

Violeta was a magician!

Being well connected in Swiss media circles, Marie-Magdeleine produced a television documentary about Violeta for Suisse Television Romande.

In it, a percussive *one-two-three* and *one-two-three* pulses as the camera pans a room of paintings, pausing at guitar, *charango* and flutes that hang decoratively on the walls.

A close-up on Violeta Parra then recedes to reveal her cloaked in woolen poncho, head tilted, eyes closed as she sings a lament about the pain of uncertain love, accompanying herself on *cuatro*.

> *What have I done with the moon, ay, ay, ay'y*
> *that we gazed at together? ay, ay, ay'y . . .*

> *What have I done with the iris*
> *that we planted in the patio? . . .*

> *Here is the very same moon*
> *and in the patio the same white iris*
> *. . . but you, ungrateful dove*
> *no longer coo in my nest.*

> *Everything changes in this world.*

A voice-over reports that after the Louvre exhibit, Violeta moved to Geneva, where she continued to create her prodigious art.

A wide-angle shot now contrasts the narrator, a neutral figure in a grey knit sheath and the artist, arrayed in a colorful broadcloth patchwork.

> *"What a wonderful dress you are wearing," says Marie-Magdeleine.*
> *"My mother sewed it of swatches like those I stitched as a girl. Then she edged it in lace, and gave it an apron to complete its peasant look."*

Violeta confides without guile that her mother, who bore ten children and taught them all to sing, taught her to sew.

> *"I am part-Indian," Violeta explains, "And I strive to be as much as possible like those indigenous people who can see the world's magic through the imagination spun right at home."*

Marie-Magdeleine asks about the figures in a nearly life-sized tapestry entitled, *"Against the War."*

> *"I've pictured people who love their country."*
> *"Why is the first figure - you, Violeta - mauve?"*
> *"Because it is my name, Violeta."* . . .
> *"The flowers growing from people's heads are their souls."*

She depicted them, she says, to vanquish war with love. They discuss a tapestry showing a man of heroic proportion, raising a hatchet overhead. His pants are tatters, he is shirtless, his skin is dark.

> *"He is a peasant rising up against the landowner. Sometimes, my grandfather told me, the peasants had nothing to lose."*

Strains from *La Jardinera* signals a change of subject, as Violeta pulls strands of wool swiftly through coarse fabric.

> *"What are you sewing?"*
> *"A scene from Chilean history . . . I have in my head."*

The right hand pulls thread through cloth as the left hand guides the needle down a chain stitch for a line in a picture that has yet to unfold. Violeta looks up wide-eyed at Marie-Magdeleine, who probes further.

"You're a musician, a painter, a tapestry artist, a poet. You have a constant need to create. What is that about?"
"I feel an urgency, like an illness. Tapestry shows life's beauty. Painting can show life quickly."

Violeta's eyes twinkle lightheartedly.
In another scene, the camera pans a wall of unfinished canvases, to which Violeta applies a single color to several in succession.

"All the pictures show the same figures, but tell different stories. I don't know beforehand which tales will emerge."

In the closing scene, Violeta dances a *cueca*, rustling her petticoats and dangling a handkerchief over her shoulder like a *campesina*, stepping deftly in white stockings and buckled shoes, pointing her toes, tapping her heels, deftly inscribing a figure eight on the plank floor.
She is ageless.

At the time the documentary was made, Violeta had two years to live. Already her voice revealed how vulnerable she felt in making manifest her art. She was already visualizing her own demise. She laughed mirthlessly, cried more often than ever. With tears came songs. Her moods shifted unpredictably. She was growing explosive, more abrupt.

How insecure she felt over the nineteen-year difference in age between herself and Gilbert. His apartment in Geneva had the air of a steamy love nest. He loved her (who didn't in those days?) with a silent, sullen, moody intensity. She matched his passion with a lust so hot it threatened to singe anyone who approached.

When they cohabited, music was a constant. Classical music, particularly that of Vivaldi and Bach, provided a backdrop to the day's activities. They didn't talk about the music, just listened, allowed it to be. And the couple made their own music constantly.

She played new songs for him right after she wrote them. Her songs varied tremendously. Some were topical, others purely folkloric, but as a whole they came across as her second voice, articulating a depth of sentiment that words alone missed.

For his own pleasure Gilbert played clarinet; but when he accompanied her he favored the *quena*, an Andean flute. They improvised music in the style of the Andean highlands.

Violeta loved the musical sound of words. She didn't speak Quechua, but she captured the inflection convincingly in nonsense syllables resembling the pattern of Quechua speech. *Saba tian' tibucana juana de inju!*

Besides guitar, she played the ten-stringed *charango*, an instrument the Incas fashioned from the shell of an armadillo, and a four-stringed *cuatro*. Always, against a percussive beat. Gilbert mastered the intricate syncopated variations, such as the one-two-*three-and*-four beat of the *taquirari*, which contrasted the constant pulse of a *bombo*. The couple developed a largely instrumental style that they recorded on a single record later that year; *El Tocador Afuerino* showcased Gilbert, The Foreign Musician.

Yet Gilbert's efforts on *quena* never quite met Violeta's hypercritical standards. She lambasted him, then regretted her own harshness. She found absurd his devotion to a style so foreign from his own roots. "Can you imagine," she'd say, "A *gringo* who wants to play like an Indian?" Nevertheless, Gilbert played admirably, very much like an Indian.

Sometimes Violeta reacted to her circumstances as though trapped. Marie-Magdeleine once visited to find her shivering in a frigid room, seated on bench, wearing a drab hat with earflaps.

"Oh, Magdalena, Gilbert will be angry. I'm afraid. He will be coming home soon."

"What are you afraid of?"

"I was so cold and it's bad for my throat, so I knitted this hat in the Indian style."

Then she burst out, "Oh Magdalena! I stole his last pair of socks to make it. When the poor guy comes in, he'll have to go barefooted in his shoes!" She cackled.

In fact, the hat still resembled the threadbare grey socks it once had been. Gilbert saw the humor in that incident, but not always.

About nine one morning, a friend of Gilbert's came to the house to borrow his guitar. The couple were still in bed, but the fellow knocked and knocked at the door. His insistence so angered Violeta, she picked up the guitar and answered the door by bashing the guy over the head with it —and it wasn't even her guitar, it was Gilbert's!

The episode sent Gilbert fleeing in the van, disgusted by her explosive temper. The couple lapsed into a period of mutual avoidance. Violeta wrote to Marie-Magdeleine:

> *I can't come to visit you on Wednesday. Everything is going badly here. I am very sorry. I am completely alone. The world is too big for me. I don't understand men. I must find a way to get out of this, it doesn't allow me to breathe. I want to see you.*

During their estrangement, Violeta prepared for her final return to Chile. Realizing it meant distancing herself from the lucrative European audience, Violeta set about selling as much of her work as possible before she left. Marie-Magdeleine introduced her to an art dealer in Geneva who sold four tapestries, including one exhibited at the Louvre called *The Peanut Seller* for 2000 francs, and offered to take others and market them for her once she left.

Mme. Raymonde Gampert, whom Violeta had met two years before and taught mask-making, sponsored two recitals at her estate, earning the artist 1,600 francs, which she sent home in a bank draft for the continuing repair of her house.

> *I sold the fish, the chicken, the little Christ, three masks, and three tapestries. Almost a quarter sold. They gave me an advance of 1000, but I haven't managed to find out which tapestry they want—one for 1000 or one for 4000. Can you imagine? That too is an element of hope. The woman liked two. A big one (2.5 meters) that you don't know, Naval War of Iquique, and the Christ with the black background; do you remember it?*

Knowing the fascination of the rich for primitive art, Marie-Magdeleine introduced Violeta to a Swiss celebrity couple, Charles-Henri and Marguerite Favrod, who quickly set into gear an exclusive party in their castle at Saint-Prex, where Violeta would display her talents before one hundred prospective buyers.

She put tremendous stock in what she dreamed of as a gala, profitable evening, though her vision differed from what was being planned. To Marie-Magdeleine she wrote, "It's a shame not to be able to print up invitations and programs. This way it will hardly be a recital, merely a gathering."

She sewed and rehearsed in the solitude of Gilbert's apartment, not eating much, going to bed very late. Gilbert was rarely home. She was having trouble motivating herself to work; then it occurred to her that if only the Favrods would put her up until the party, she might be spurred into full artistic production. She appealed to Marie-Magdeleine for help.

> *If the gathering goes well, I'll be happy; if it doesn't, I'll still be happy. I'd like to go to Marguerite Favrod as soon as possible. . . . There I can work like a queen.*
>
> *As to the price of the tapestries: for my friends, there's one price; for my enemies, another. The biggest will cost them 5000 francs, the smallest 2000. The same pieces to my friends, 3500 and 1500. If I sell a tapestry in Paris for 7000 francs, the price here cannot be less expensive. . . . Thank you for your letter to Gilbert.*

Marie-Magdeleine did write to Gilbert—she was fond of him—to ask that he give Violeta another chance, knowing full well that their temperaments would always clash.

As Violeta had hoped, the Favrods allowed her to take up temporary residence. But instead of feeling more entitled, Violeta felt burdened to toil like a fairy-tale princess set at an impossible task. The first night she slept well; but after three days of unaccustomed luxury, nightmares awakened her in fits of tears that soaked the sheets of her feather bed.

Ultimately, the fête proved an even greater disappointment to Violeta. To that magnificent setting decorated with sprays of tulips and lily of the valley in porcelain vases, apricot pink lighting, antiques, brocades, and Persian rugs came aristocrats who found each other and never stopped talking, even to accept canapés and champagne offered from silver trays by liveried servants. Coiffed and perfumed statuesque women in bare-shouldered gowns that accentuated their necklaces and earrings were squired by men of impeccable tailoring.

The Beautiful People took only passing notice of Violeta Parra's art and hardly fathomed how much the songstress bared her soul with each of her songs.

"I don't mean to be malicious," she confided later to Marie-Magdeleine, "but I thought I, Violeta Parra, should have been toasted as a celebrity."

All the accommodations so graciously extended led her to believe the party was for her, though of course it wasn't—she was the entertainment.

Whether Violeta sold any art at that party went unreported. She left behind several cumbersome tapestries and paintings and returned to what Marie-Magdeleine called "the simple straw pallet of her love nest in the ghetto" where Gilbert awaited her. The couple reconciled.

Soon thereafter, Gilbert helped Violeta transport some tapestries to Geneva. It was midnight and though no longer winter, patches of snow still spotted the mountainous terrain. She wrote her family,

Yesterday we went to retrieve the other tapestries at the Brumagne house in Lausanne. We were returning, driving at 100 kilometers an hour, when the bundle flew off the roof of the little truck. I screamed in terror. Gilbert hit the brakes.

Chilled by the Devil, we climbed down without any hope because at that speed the logical thing was for the tapestries to have landed in an abyss far below. Gilbert ran and I followed behind, crying hysterically of course. You can imagine—they were big tapestries. Since I never leave the house, I couldn't run. My commander let out with a tremendous whistle in the darkness, a whistle that I know very well, but that in that instant I didn't get its meaning.

> *"Here I come!" I screamed, overcome by emotion, struggling to slap my way through the snow and gulping hard in the cold.*
> *"Here darling, here they are all together, don't cry, they aren't ruined."*
> *We carried the tapestries to the car, where Gilbert delivered ferocious kicks to the wooden stretchers and loaded everything inside the van. With all that emotion, I didn't realize how cold I was, until we were seated again in my noble little car. Presently we got to the house, made a little fire, drank tea with aguardiente. We kissed and went to bed.*

Despite their strained relationship, Gilbert made plans to travel to Chile also. He had decided to film several events: the annual Andean festival of *La Tirana* in a tiny village in northern Chile, rustic Independence Day festivities, and possibly Santiago's Spring art fair.

Violeta wanted to bring home belongings far in excess of what an airline would permit her to carry without penalty, so she talked Gilbert into traveling by sea to transport her belongings as well as his own film gear. Her accumulated treasures included *bombo*, flutes, canvasses, and a steamer trunk. He drove her to Paris, where she stayed for a final stint to earn more money by singing in the Latin Quarter bistros.

A document dated May 12, 1965 and stamped with a seal from the *Canton de Genève* verified that Violeta transferred use of her Volkswagen microbus with French plates to Gilbert Favre. He then sold the van in Geneva and booked passage on a ship bound for Valparaiso, Chile. Though they planned to arrive at about the same time, Gilbert arrived at least a month before Violeta.

Once in Paris, Violeta had trouble actually leaving. She missed one flight, which was met in Santiago by a disappointed press contingent. When finally she arrived, she was carrying only her guitar and her battered suitcases, hungry now for the soul of her native land.

Violeta Parra, Against the War, embroidered on jute, 57" x 77", 1963.

La Peña de los Parra

Violeta Parra arrived home for the last time in Winter 1965, to a climate of great economic and social upheaval. Copper, revolution and counterinsurgency, land seizures, strikes, violence formed a backdrop for change in the fabric of daily life. With shifting economic dynamics came pressure for universities to educate more urban youth, a theme that inspired Violeta.

> *Long live students,*
> *garden of joys!*
> *They are birds unafraid*
> *of beast or police;*
> *neither bullets*
> *nor the growls of the dogs scare them.*
> *Hurray!*
> *Long live astronomy!*
> . . .
> *Long live students*
> *for they are the yeast of bread*
> *that will emerge from the oven*

ever so tasty
in the mouths of the poor,
who eat with such bitterness.
Hurray!
Long live literature!

Meanwhile, the costumed performance style called *neofolklore* persisted in the media as glamorized folk music. The fad featured sentimental songs sung by Anglo-looking performers, mostly men, costumed in tooled leather and silver spurs no peasant ever wore. The image ignored social realities; though ironically, the music primed the public for greater realism.

Out of its shadows emerged the more outspoken *Nueva Canción Chilena*, whose troubadours denounced misery and sang out against injustice and exploitation–even to exhort the peasants to seize idle land. The right-wing controlled media labeled the musicians *politicos* and refused to air them; nevertheless, their songs enlivened public debate and sold well. Like the protest songs of the Vietnam anti-war movement, *La Nueva Canción Chilena* turned news into art that called for radical change.

Ángel and Isabel returned to Chile in 1964, at least a year before their mother. They joined other singers campaigning for Allende and aimed for stardom in their own right. Their music grew wildly popular among Chilean youth, who were attracted to its vitality. Soon, young people everywhere were playing guitar and creating their own *Nueva Canción*.

After Allende lost his 1964 presidential bid, Ángel and Isabel sought commercial gigs. In Europe, they supported themselves as folksingers, but at home their style was too authentic for radio, restaurants, or night clubs. Twenty-two-year-old Ángel had to buy a dress suit and 26-year-old Isabel, an evening gown, to get hired by a show whose sponsor made liver salts. Oddly, their repertoire required no change, only their appearance, but even that accommodation to conformity was galling.

European experiences had broadened Ángel. He'd frequented literary bistros in Paris and the Spanish taverns called *peñas*, where the bullfighters gather to drink their wine and discuss the bulls. Back in Chile, he envisioned a *peña* centered around singers that could foster the same stimulating atmosphere. "Look, if they have *peñas de toreros*, why couldn't we have *peñas de cantores?*"

Ángel, Isabel, and two friends, Rolando Alarcón and Patricio Manns, rented a dilapidated house on Carmen Street, near downtown and two universities, that lacked amenities but was spacious enough for acoustic music. They set about inventing the *peña*—repairing the building, decorating it with posters, fishing nets, and handicrafts consigned by local artists, and creating an informal, noncommercial, uncensored environment whose character reflected what was happening in the streets and what was being sung in *La Nueva Canción*.

La Peña de los Parra opened in June 1965 with invitations to the press and other musicians; the first show was broadcast live over the university radio station. Overnight, the cabaret became a sensation. Crowds of intellectuals, artists, and youth queued up literally around the block to hear the shows. Tourists came. Within weeks, what began with audiences of fifty grew to one hundred; to accommodate them all, the artists gave as many as four shows a night.

Thursday, Friday, and Saturday nights, the patrons mingled in the congenial smoky atmosphere of the club, set up as a warren of rooms furnished with plank benches and tables. A dim corridor led to a straw-strewn patio, where members of the collective served savory *empanadas* and red wine, overseen by Ángel's wife Marta, who directed volunteers servers, who heated up and served the food and poured wine into rows of glasses.

As showtime approached and the performers tuned up, the candlelit interior grew intimate. Performers seated themselves on a central wooden platform under a single spotlight. They sang for hours, first in one room and then another, carrying their guitars and other instruments through the tightly packed evening's crowd.

A virtuoso of guitar and *guitarrón*, Ángel cradled his arms around his instrument and from his slight frame, produced explosive lyrics about Valparaíso and the streets of Santiago, the cities he knew well. Patricio Manns, a poet from southern Chile, sang of the sea, torrential rains, and the forested mountains of his childhood. Rolando Alarcón, singer, storyteller and teacher, set history to song.

Isabel Parra came into her own at *La Peña*, for while singing love songs, she learned to dominate the audience as a soloist. She and Ángel sang exquisite harmonies, introducing Santiago audiences to contemporary music of Venezuela, Uruguay, and Argentina, as well as to unfamiliar musical instruments—*cuatro* from Venezuela, *tiple* from Colombia, *quena*, *charango*, *zampoña*, and *bombo* from the Andean *altiplano*.

In no time, *La Peña de los Parra* became Santiago's premier music venue. As Manns described it, "I started with six songs about Chile; in three weeks I had thirty. It was crazy at the beginning—for me and everyone else. We wrote songs every morning to perform that evening, by the dozen. People were amazed that instead of plagiarizing from each other, we each developed our own style, while performing together every night."

Several months after the *peña* opened, Ángel introduced his friend, Victor Jara, to the audience and handed him a guitar. Victor was studying theatre, but also teaching students the fIeld work of recording peasant culture, much like Violeta Parra. His original compositions were strongly folkloric, but his voice was dramatic–particularly when he sang his satiric songs of social commentary. The audience applauded thunderously, earning Victor membership in the *peña* collective.

Of all his songs, *Plegaria a un Laborador*, A Worker's Prayer, with its radical union of prayer and petition, epitomized Victor Jara's unique gift.

Arise and look up at the mountain,
origins of the wind, the sun, the water,
you who direct the course of the rivers,
you who planted the flight of your soul.

Arise and look at your hands.
To grow, extend them to your brother;
together we are united in blood.
Today is the instance that becomes tomorrow.

Victor's genius made him difficult to approach, though much admired by other artists. Through music and agit-prop theatre, Victor Jara brought the politics of the poor into sharper focus, and it was that outspokenness that led to his murder by the military less than ten years later.

Music aside, *La Peña de los Parra*, its walls graffiti'ed with slogans and symbols, grew into an important forum for the airing of ideas. It gained a reputation as a hotbed of revolutionary fervor, frequented by Marxists, left-wing Christians, young men sporting beards as gestures of solidarity with the Cuban revolution, exiles from Brazil, Uruguay, and Argentina, and intelligence agents. Once, it hosted a peace delegation of Vietnamese women. The public thronged to its unique blend of musical vocabulary and political idealism, and some radio stations even found it profitable to broadcast the shows.

By now, *neofolklore* was losing popularity; its performers switched to an international style to survive commercially, while *Nueva Canción* was thriving. Other *peñas* opened, especially at universities.

As the grassroots movement gained momentum, it generated its own economic vitality, independent of the foreign model that already dominated the Latin American entertainment industry: *Nueva Canción* records began to sell as hits in Chile! Remarkably, these recordings often displaced international stars like Elvis Presley or the up-and-coming Beatles for top weekly listings on national hit parade charts.

Gilbert Favre arrived in Chile nearly two months before Violeta Parra. Ángel met his ship in Valparaíso, and together they hauled Violeta's belongings to Santiago and discussed their respective plans. With his camera gear and a portfolio of footage of Violeta's Louvre show, Gilbert intended to find work in television or documentary film. Though he spoke of abandoning music entirely, a newspaper clipping dated June 10, 1965 reported on his performance at *La Peña de los Parra* and recordings of *quena* solos.

At 29, Gilbert was closer in age to Ángel and Isabel than to his 47-year-old *compañera*; he sympathized with their need to separate from her and establish musical identities for themselves.

Violeta had strong feelings about her clan. Heated family arguments had erupted in Europe over her attempts to dominate and her inability to tolerate the independence that marked her children's maturation. Ángel and Isabel left

France as much to escape her overbearingness as to return home. Gilbert saw both sides of the conflict but was powerless to influence either.

The day before Violeta's arrival, Ángel announced at a meeting, "Violeta is coming home from Europe tomorrow, so let's make a special *peña* tomorrow night, and invite friends and the press."

This was to be Patricio Manns's first encounter with the formidable Violeta. He recalled that she sat up front, close to the stage with Gilbert. Ángel introduced Patricio to the audience, explaining largely for Violeta's benefit who he was. As Patricio adjusted the tuning of his guitar, he dedicated his first song to her. It was a song he had only just written, based on his experience as a coal miner in Lota, a city Violeta knew well.

He had not sung more than a verse when Violeta stood up and blurted out, "What a fine singer of *boleros* you are!" An unwarranted insult. She glanced around at the stunned silence of the audience and then took her seat. A dumbfounded Patricio continued singing.

Later, Violeta apologized. She was mistaken, she told him; she hadn't listened attentively. But the song reminded her of the countless Mexican *boleros* she had sung when she was younger. It made her indignant, because, she argued, 'that kind of music just wasn't folkloric.' Soon it became apparent that Violeta expected *La Peña* to be somewhere musicians performed *cuecas* and *tonadas*. Instead, it had the feel of a Latin Quarter bistro, with its own ambience and original music–avant garde, not at all traditional.

Reportedly Violeta enjoyed herself thoroughly that first evening and many that followed, yet weeks went by before she assimilated the entire picture. That crowds of people waited for hours in the rain to attend its shows, that all the artists jammed together in an improvised grand finale sometimes lasting long after the audience went home, that she herself had catalyzed these musical developments–all this impressed her tremendously. Though she had much to be proud of, Violeta found it difficult to accept the new musical climate.

Once she joined in, she contributed to the growth and rise in importance of *La Nueva Canción*, by bringing to it her own unflinching view of reality in simple language and with poetic dignity. Bread she called bread, wine wine. She baked *empanadas*, served up platters of *anticuchos*, prepared plates of *pebre* and pitchers of *mate con malicia*. Her *arpilleras* soon decorated the walls alongside posters of Cuban song festivals. In this milieu, Violeta's unsentimental depiction of rustic life among the poor now echoed in the restless music of a younger generation. She was being heard more profoundly than she realized.

A reporter for *El Siglo*, the daily Santiago newspaper of the Communist Party, described her set one Saturday night:

> *Suddenly everyone is silent. Through two French doors, creaking, heavy and old, pass a small woman of fine build, with loose, windswept hair. Her eyes fix on the public in whose midst she enters. Everyone seems accustomed to the semi-darkness. She looks from one end of the room to the other and smiles, satisfied, then climbs onto the improvised stage and seats herself. Voices whisper, "Violeta Parra, it's Violeta." She tunes her guitar, acknowledges greetings, and begins to perform.*
>
> *The music coming from her instrument and mouth merge, its grace and spontaneity filling the atmosphere with unexpected reminiscences–country scents, the penetrating aroma of green basil, sweet water, fragile, embraced with wet grasses.*
>
> *From far the soul senses*
> *the fragrance of fresh chicha*

Remembering back, it thinks
What a fabulous party.

She moves us with her limitless capacity to love, sadly, fatalistically.

Where did you go last night? …
I died when you didn't return.

People in the audience lose themselves in the infinite, oblivious
to the insistent flicker of the candles or the fisherman's net that
hangs precariously from the ceiling like an enormous cobweb.
Their eyes have turned inward. They commune with a distant
past, visualize Violeta's sisterhood with a poor peasant villager,
acknowledge blood ties to the Spanish and indigenous that is
Chilean.

The mood Violeta evoked was momentary. As she left the stage, the applause changed in tone, for next up was the one young people had come to hear–Ángel Parra. "Like his mother, Ángel is diminutive, with a serious, almost dour expression that barely acknowledged the enthusiasm of his fans." His personification of the anonymous worker made him one of the *Nueva Canción*'s most admired voices–masculine, forceful. "One cannot listen to Ángel Parra without stirring in revolutionary protest."

Ángel's songs impassioned the youth, and Violeta did not fail to notice. The popularity of her son and the other young musicians meant that she was becoming marginal. Never had the lyrics of a *tonada* she learned from her mother held more meaning than now:

When the priest recites your nuptial blessing
they'll bury my remains in the grave.

Violeta had done a superb job of imbuing her children with their rustic heritage—so much so that by now, her living legacy influenced an entire generation of young musicians. What she found hard to accept was that they were using what she taught in their own way. She felt displaced.

Gilbert tried to reconcile her to circumstance; they talked about it constantly. "Look, as adults, they have to make their own way," he'd say.

She'd argue that he was just taking their side and therefore didn't love her. She loved her children unreservedly, but her behavior toward them grew indefensible.

La Peña was not hers to run, but inevitably, she sought to preside over its entire fantastic assembly of song, night after night, and this posed problems. It irked her that *La Nueva Canción* derived from multiple influences besides folkloric Chile. Ángel and Isabel, for example, used *altiplano* musical instruments from Peru and Bolivia in their arrangements, which fascinated Violeta; but she argued against it on the grounds that truly authentic Chilean instruments were southern in origin, not Andean.

Musicians at *La Peña* were subject to Violeta's mentoring, whether or not they wanted her guidance. She disregarded, even disparaged experimental music. Each musician dealt with her in his or her own way. Patricio Manns recalled, "She guided many of our compositions of that era, with a character that synthesized the most tender feminine depths and an earthquake of will, aggression, dominance. When Violeta was right, it was best to be silent. And sometimes too, when she saw another side. Or when she didn't."

That year, both Ángel and Patricio composed thematic albums. Ángel's *Oratorio por el Pueblo* was a political response to the many *misas Criollas* (folkloric masses) then being released commercially. The Church and establishment media panned it to obscurity. Patricio composed his *El Sueño Americano* to denounce the plunder of Latin America by successive conquerors. Every commercial label rejected the album for being too controversial. When Violeta learned that Patricio was trying to tone it down, she was furious. "Don't you dare! Better it remains unpublished. Remember, all of you have become a mirror into which many Chilean youth are gazing." Eventually, Patricio managed a poor-quality recording, but the album never got air time.

On the heels of a bloody strike in *El Salvador* copper mine, Rolando Alarcón wrote and recorded a scathing indictment against police brutality that aired only once. President Frei himself phoned the radio station to warn that he would not tolerate the airing or distribution of the record. Some months later, Violeta chronicled the massacre more obliquely, in *Mazurquica Modérnica*, which she composed while conversing with reporters. In Spanish, the lyrics have an untranslatable soundplay of repeated syllables that emphasize both meter and disgust.

> *Various people have asked me*
> *if protest songs*
> *subvert the masses.*
> *What a foolish question!*
> *. . . when the belly craves food,*
> *the pious grow irate and warlike*
> *over onions and beans.*
> *No regiment can hold back*
> *the starving masses.*
> *. . .*
> *Stiff starched horsemen*
> *. . . comfortable in their armchairs,*

tell tales of massacres
as though farces or comedies.

History records many massacres.
You don't need revolutionary
songs to stage them.
Unfulfilled promises
cause discontent.
Neither workers nor police
are to blame,
Mister Bureaucrat.

As *la Nueva Canción Chilena* grew more outspoken, the communications media consolidated its blacklist. What few songs were aired were introduced with slanderous editorializing intended to impugn the musicians' credibility. Musicians had to find alternative means to reach their audiences. Grassroots promotion grew into commercial ventures, such as *Chile Ríe y Canta*, once a radio program, then a booking agency for concerts in the farthest reaches of the country.

By now, Violeta's songs were as idealistic as anyone else's in *Nueva Canción*. She denounced the Church, the inequity of poverty and authoritarianism. She enflamed live audiences by singing out the name of a landowner who sicked thugs on unarmed peasants. The album she recorded during this era contained these and quieter sentiments too.

Although she embraced the ideals of the young, Violeta could not abide her subordinate role. Blinded by her own celebrity, she set out hell-bent to launch a new cultural center for authentically rustic folklore. It was a project that would ultimately destroy her.

The Tent of La Reina

The summer of 1965, Violeta Parra performed at a new *Peña Universitaria*, in Valparaíso. It was her first visit to the port city in fifteen years. When word reached nearby Viña del Mar, booking agents at the posh *Casino* invited her to perform there too, but she refused; its audience was not her kind.

The day of the first show, fans from miles around thronged the *peña*, catching it unprepared. Guards had to be posted at the door to keep the place from being mobbed. All the world wanted to experience Violeta, a star not set apart from the world to glow but who reflected what could be plainly seen. She was beloved for that quality of communion with her audience.

That afternoon, she strolled through a plaza where children were playing ball. A photographer with an old box camera on a tripod stood poised to take pictures of vacationers. Violeta spotted him and was seized by a desire to own the camera.

"Won't you sell it to me?" she teased. The children's ball hurled toward her. She caught it, pretended to throw it right and left, then tossed it to a youngster on the sidelines. If only Violeta could manage other frustrations as easily!

Back in Santiago, a new venture beckoned with a phone call from Sergio Larraín, with whom she had worked years earlier. Sergio's publicity business had just landed a lucrative project. A landowner asked him to mount a concession on a parcel of land adjacent to the National Society of Agriculture fair, just two weeks away.

Sergio and his partner, Gretel, examined the site, the size of a basketball court, and saw it as suitable for a small cabaret—someplace gay and inexpensive. Gretel pictured it tented, to enclose a lively atmosphere of music and light refreshments, and at once Sergio thought of Violeta.

When they presented her with their idea, Violeta was delighted. "*Macanudo!*" And to Gretel, she said, "Your idea of a tent is brilliant!"

Sergio was skeptical.

Gretel pursued a canvas-factory owner until he agreed to make them an enormous yellow tent on credit, payable from their anticipated revenues.

Meanwhile Violeta organized the interior layout and venue: chairs, tables, *empanadas*, wine and soda. For entertainment, she enlisted all the Parras—her brothers, singer Roberto and Lalo, who performed as a clown; Hilda, who played accordion and sang. Isabel, Ángel, and all the other musicians of *La Peña* pitched in.

For the first three days of the fair, Violeta greeted the public, selling tickets. At day's end she lugged the proceeds into the office and set it before Gretel, who emptied it, counted it, and credited receipts against payables. The entire effort had generated many debts to repay.

On the fourth day, Violeta put the sack of money on the table and asked Gretel for money to cover her own expenses.

"Why no," Gretel answered. "The bills aren't paid off yet."

Violeta insisted. "I've collected plenty of money from the gate. Now will you please give me some money for my expenses?"

"Definitely not. You cannot have any money until the bills are paid in full." Violeta snatched the sack off the table. At this, Gretel stormed out of the office and quit, leaving Sergio to deal with Violeta and make good the letters of credit. Violeta conducted herself oblivious to the ill will she had generated. The rift widened between Violeta and a shrinking circle of friends and colleagues, grown contemptuous of her undisciplined behavior.

As the fair wound down, Violeta became secretive. She disappeared for periods of time without explanation; then on the last day, surprised everyone (even Gilbert) with an announcement: The mayor of La Reina had ceded her a parcel of land in *Parque La Quintrala*. She was going to move the tent there and use it to house a cultural center, *La Carpa de la Reina*, dedicated to the advancement of Chilean popular culture.

"Why should folklore be buried away in an archive as if it were dead, just to preserve it?" She wanted to revive what still flourished in the *campo*–stagings of the improvised verse contests sung by peasant poets, storytelling, rituals, such as the infant wakes. Customs could be studied and even reincorporated into urban life.

Violeta's vision was as vast as the tent was spacious. In a press conference at Carmen 340, she told reporters, "I believe that every artist should aspire to a goal of joining her work in direct contact with the public"–something she was very committed to do.

Although some were supportive of her effort, most people who knew Violeta thought she was making a colossal mistake.

She approached her old friend, José María Palacios, who was now working as station manager of *Radio Corporación*, and offered him a partnership in the project, but he refused. It wasn't feasible, he argued. How could she hope to lure audiences from Santiago to a distant neighborhood without public transportation? The tent was huge (over one hundred feet in diameter); why, just to keep it standing would require constant maintenance.

Members of *La Peña* collective argued too that the task was unrealistic, but Violeta refused to listen. *La Peña* and *La Carpa* were complementary venues whose joint presence would stimulate interest in folklore. Though she appreciated what the young people were doing, she wanted to preserve the stylistic purity of music native to southern Chile.

"With *La Carpa* I hope to accomplish much the same thing as *La Peña* in my own way. I'll show my paintings, tapestries, ceramics, sing my songs. Newcomers just starting out will have a stage. In this sense, *La Peña* is insufficient; that's why I am raising my tent."

Gilbert hated the entire idea. He was embarrassed by how poorly Violeta had handled her business dealings with Sergio and Gretel, and he doubted the new venture's viability.

"I tried to talk her out of it, arguing that it was impossible to attract customers there. This question became a perpetual bone of contention between us."

La Carpa jeopardized Gilbert's own career plans. He was beginning to get television work, for which he had to be available at a telephone call's notice. Her project threatened to monopolize his time. They argued, "but after an exchange of harsh words, she ended up convincing me to work with her."

Once Gilbert relented, he and the Parra men erected the tent in the parkland field—a Herculean task in service to Violeta's dream. Gilbert also built a one-room adobe hut of mud and straw, gessoed white, that was drafty and dark.

A patio out back served as an outdoor kitchen, with a path of stepping-stones leading to an outhouse. Beyond lay a meadow where Violeta kept animals—chickens, a dog, even a little *llama* Gilbert bought from a man in Santiago. "It was a mistake," he recalled. "*Llamas* ought to live in community. The animal should have had a mate; it suffered alone."

Early 1966, Violeta pushed herself to exhaustion, but work progressed very slowly. Seeing how hard she was working, Hilda tried to get her to scale back, but Violeta refused. "Look around you. Doesn't this look like the *campo*? I can re-create it all."

"But my God, Violeta, things could go badly for you. You'd be here all alone."

Hilda suggested a smaller, mobile tent that traveled from neighborhood to neighborhood, 'like the circuses we knew as children,' but Violeta was adamant. "*Ave Maria*, we'd find her out there in the heat all flushed. Anyone who came by, she put to work."

La Carpa had disturbing undertones for Ángel; Violeta had once told him she wanted to die in the circus. This resembled that vision.

Nearly every day, Violeta visited her children. Marta, Ángel's wife, was now pregnant. At Isabel's house, Violeta played with Tita, listened to Beatles music (which fascinated her), and tried to talk Isabel into moving onto the land with her. "Luxury is foolishness," she'd say; "people are consumed by problems of their own making." Whether with lightness or violence, she reproached them for living bourgeois lives. As always, arguments.

As the project took shape, Violeta gave interviews and tours, showing off the handicrafts that decorated the tent in cloth, *papier maché*, leather, basketry, ceramics, tooled copper. Next to the tallest, central tent-pole stood the stage, with a table for Violeta's guitar, *guitarrón*, harp, and *bombo* and a stove for heat. Tables and chairs were arranged as in a supper club, and behind them, cushionless risers for additional seating.

When questioned, Violeta denied that the name represented her own grandiosity. *"La Carpa de la Reina* does not mean that I'm Queen, but that it's located in the neighborhood of La Reina."

Inevitably, reporters compared *La Carpa* unfavorably to *La Peña*. Its physical dimensions lacked *La Peña*'s intimacy. It was difficult to reach by public transportation. Its weekend operations were a major undertaking that might have succeeded with more people and money–but while five young musicians ran *La Peña*, *La Carpa* was the burden of Violeta alone.

Artistic differences sharpened as well. Whereas Violeta had performed at the Carmen street *peña*, the younger musicians did not reciprocate. Musical contact between them decreased.

Word spread that the tent was cold. Very soon after its inaugural evening, *La Carpa* wanted for patrons. Gilbert attempted to insulate the tent by wood-paneling the canvas walls. Violeta bought individual braziers to radiate heat and on which to serve hot food. Slowly, a curious public ventured back for a visit.

All the while, Violeta worked at folklore. She recorded an album of her memoir, *Décimas Autobiograficos*, which was published posthumously as a book.

Then Violeta took ill. She developed shingles, a painful, persistent burning outbreak whose prescribed medication had an alcoholic base that Violeta ill-tolerated. Sleepless, she scratched until her skin bled and became infected. She consulted a specialist, who told her she was too high strung and prescribed medicine that let her sleep restfully for the first time in weeks. Soon, Violeta was overmedicating herself.

Violeta's druggy state alarmed her fifteen-year-old daughter, Carmen Luisa, but Violeta paid her no mind. Finally in disgust, Carmen Luisa grabbed the pills away from her just in time "to keep her from doing herself harm," and threw them down the privy.

Violeta cried and asked for forgiveness. The encounter troubled Carmen Luisa. "Why couldn't she understand that people worried about her?"

Every day, Carmen Luisa helped Violeta cook over a wood fire for the evening's show, never knowing how many people to expect. They filled *empanadas* with meat, raisins, olive, and egg, and baked them in a wood-fired oven; they skewered *anticuchos*, which took "not only meat but also kneaded bread, heart, kidneys, sausage, and fried rinds—fifteen little pieces on every *anticucho* in a good variety, making them ready to grill."

For dessert, Violeta made *sopaipillas* from winter squash, fried in hot oil and sweetened with syrup, topped with lemon peel or cinnamon. To drink, they prepared *mate*, mulled wine, and a *mistela* brewed of cinnamon, sugar, and *aguardiente*. They fueled the stove and braziers, and set the teapots to boil atop beds of coal. All this was a lot of work.

One Saturday night when quite a few people were seated and yet no one was eating, a friend of Violeta's set out a brazier topped with the succulent *anticuchos*. She started nibbling, savoring the food before the audience. In two minutes everyone was asking for *anticuchos*.

According to Nani Venegas, who attended *La Carpa* as a teenager, "Violeta greeted whoever showed up, then called Carmen to seat them, take their order, set out a brazier and serve them tea. Carmen was an acrobat carrying multiple braziers of hot coal, but it was Violeta who liked to present the food itself. Nothing was fancy; the cups and plates were serviceable, the food honest, delicious."

Like her food, Violeta's appearance in that tent space resembled the stark spirit of a survivor. Nani recalled, "She wore no jewelry; her hair was pulled back, unadorned. A black dress, dark stockings, sensible shoes. Violeta always performed in black. Perhaps the dress sported a ruffle around the three-quarter sleeve, but even that much ornamentation was unusual for her."

Once Violeta had seen to her guests, she mounted the stage under one spotlight, seated herself in a wooden chair, took up her guitar or *guitarrón*, and played for long sets. She was untiring, capable of singing all night long.

Typically, she began with a *canto a lo divino* learned from the peasant elders. Then something upbeat, perhaps a *parabienes*, a good-humored toast to fiances celebrating their marriage, rife with innuendo. Sweet songs followed, a *tonada*, a ballad. She serenaded her audience with an *esquinazo* or shifted to dance songs, climaxing with *cuecas*, as everyone kept time by clapping the *one-two-pause* rhythm. She urged people to get up and dance the *cueca* and teased them to flirt.

Often other family members performed too. Even Nicanor, by profession a math teacher and poet, recited poetry and told stories. Hilda performed, but not as often, because Violeta insisted that her accordion repertoire was too commercial. Frequently, Roberto joined in to sing *cuecas* and tell stories.

Audiences delighted in outrageous finales such as *El Sacristán*, a folkloric polka that poked fun at religious prudery.

> *. . . A pious woman who has not loved*
> *the sacristan*
> *cannot know cinnamon,*
> *anise, chocolate, flan.*
> *. . .*
> *How my heart throbs when the sacristan*
> *rings the church bell*
> *tilín tin tin*
> *tilín tin tan. . . .*

By now, Gilbert had a stage name, *El Tocador Afuerino*, the Musician from Afar. Young women Nani's age were fascinated by his aloofness.

"He looked at nobody, but exuded an aura of mystery. We stared at him, watched the introverted artist brood. Whether or not he would play on any given night was always an iffy proposition. When he performed, he threw back his head, shut his eyes, and breathed into the *quena* as a shepherd to the wind. And his steady *taka taka boom, taka taka boom* – he was very very good at the *bombo*, particularly for a non-Chilean – anchored Violeta's songs. Their rapport was tangible as a subterranean river."

In private, Gilbert and Violeta waged war. She screamed at him if she saw him so much as glance at another woman. In fact, he performed with his eyes closed so as not to antagonize her.

Gilbert grew resentful, felt taken for granted. "I had to give up my film work to devote myself to that sacred tent. As I'd predicted, it was a total fiasco."

Finally, Gilbert had had enough.

One hot summer Friday morning, Violeta was waiting to be photographed for a magazine interview she had given two days earlier. She paced impatiently. Gilbert was painting a door, blue. She wanted it painted red. He continued painting. She grew angrier, more agitated. He left the house to buy red paint. While he was gone, Violeta swallowed pills.

By the time the two reporters arrived, Violeta was struggling to stay awake. She had taken too much medicine, she said, and felt sick. They seated her and got her a glass of milk, which she refused. Moments later, she grew faint. Alarmed, the men rushed her to a nearby hospital. Violeta was treated promptly, but she remained unconscious for three days.

Every newspaper and radio news broadcast reported that Violeta Parra had tried to kill herself with barbituites. Gilbert denied rumors he was seeing another woman. "It was a stupid matter of paint," he said.

According to the family, Violeta's nervousness led her to take too many pills, but she never intended to overdose. A vigil gathered at the hospital.

Lautaro Parra told reporters that just the day before, he had been rehearsing a new song with her. They had talked about producing a new show. "She was nervous, especially about the tent." But he did not think she wanted to end her life.

Throughout her coma, Gilbert stayed at her hospital bedside. But when she awoke and saw him, she directed her first utterances at him. "If you don't do what I tell you, I'm really going to kill myself."

Gilbert was appalled. "That was it! I left the hospital, sold my clarinet in downtown Santiago, boarded a train, and left her."

When friends and family visited Violeta, they found her sedated, discouraged, wired with tubes for intravenous feeding and medication. Carmen Luisa saw her mother in bed, with her swollen mouth and sallow complexion, and she cursed "the damned barbituites."

Héctor Pavez reprimanded Violeta sternly. "What kind of ridiculous shit is this, *vieja?*"

"Don't talk to me like that *Negro*, I'm burned out."

"Okay then, . . . what about your work? And the tent?"

"What tent? Oh, it's nothing." Her voice faded, and then abuptly, "*Negro*. . . . would you work with me in the tent?"

"With you, Violeta, I'd work on anything. I'm here to help you."

"Really? You'd work with me?" Hope brought color to her face, as though blood had decided to circulate again through her sluggish body. She raised herself up and said, "Seriously, can we erect a *ramada* in the tent?"

"We'll put up a *ramada*," he reassured her, "and make a memorable fiesta. But first you must get well, because here you can't do anything."

> *Here madame,*
> *have a handkerchief,*
> *dry your flood of tears.*
> *Nothing. . . .*
> *can bring you consolation.*
> *Give up that downcast look*
> *and look me in the face.*
> *. . . Egotistical oblivion*
> *is driving you to the abyss.*

A week later, Violeta was active as ever, running around the tent organizing the next show. News of the suicide attempt actually increased attendance. Many younger musicians pitched in to help out. Among themselves, they arranged to watch her by taking turns sleeping there.

Héctor Pavez visited the tent every evening, and often stayed overnight. Usually she was cooking when he arrived; but one moonless night, he came to find the entire encampment dark. He groped his way around the structures, following the sound of her singing to the semi-darkness of her bedroom. He called, "Violeta."

"*Negro*, come in." Only then did she light a candle.

"Get up, Violeta. You have to make the *empanadas*."

"Okay," she said. "Right away. Pass me my shoes." She moved about dazed. Soon she was kneading dough for the *empanadas*. Héctor lit a *lantern* and busied himself preparing the *anticuchos*. While he fried them, Violeta made the *mistela*.

When he finished, she said, "Okay, *Negro*, now get out there and sing for the people who come!" He washed and dried his hands and grabbed her guitar, to play as people began to arrive.

At first no one acknowledged him; but then from the rear of the tent came, "Bravo! Bravo!" Violeta applauding wildly to provoke audience response. "Bravo *Negro*, encore!" She had him sing for an hour.

Violeta was prone to comedic flights of fancy with Héctor. "Today, I'm going to be an old paralyzed woman." As she danced, she moved her hands and feet spasmodically to the rhythm. She challenged his seriousness by acting ridiculously. They pantomimed. He had studied ballet, which she mimicked by making farce of his leaps, jumping onto a table, then tumbling off as if she were a rag-doll fallen out of a little girl's arms.

Many who saw her animated believed her happy. But the interview published in *Aquí Está* on January 20, 1966 painted a darker portrait.

Q. What satisfactions have marked your artistic career?

A. Absolutely none. Everything you see here is the product of my own sacrifice. In Chile, people just don't understand.

Q. Do you agree with the new style of Chilean music? If so, who do you believe best reflect its evolutionary quality?

A. No. I don't agree. I do not judge anybody. Who am I to do that? But one thing I'd like to see is for writers and singers to let down their masks for once. . . . Are the new folk musicians toying with our music or wanting to make money? That they are doing effectively.

Q. How would you define folklore?

A. I am no more than a humble singer who can scarcely speak. The public . . . must answer this question. I sing to keep from crying . . . There's great truth to the saying, "song is the lament of the people."

Q. How do you account for the fact that your entire family is dedicated to some form of national culture? Heredity? Living together?

A. All Chileans are artists and we are of the people. . . .

Q. Of your travels abroad, what impressed you most?

A. Being far from Chile and my Chillán.

Q. Do you think some folkloric songs have a notorious affect on the attitudes of the people?

A. What can water do to a fish, when she's grown up in it?

Q. Ángel and Isabel have become prominent in the current folkloric wave? How would you rate them? To what would you attribute their success?

A. As Ángel and Isabel's mother, I cannot define them artistically. It would be a little unseemly for me to promote my family. In every case, as my children they have given me nothing but satisfaction.

Q. Then how would you rate your own triumph?

A. I haven't triumphed at all. If you call triumph to have won a few prizes and recorded several records, this for me is nothing more than washing dishes.

Q. Who would you define yourself as woman, wife, mother, and artist?

A. As woman and wife, my gringo has the last word. As a mother, I ought to be a seven-headed demon, and as an artist I am a tiny ant who looks from beneath the earth where you can shelter your heart.

Run-Run se Fue

Gilbert headed North by train to Bolivia. At the southern edge of the Atacama Desert, flash flooding had washed out the railroad bridge over a ravine, forcing everyone on board to disembark, cross the chasm on foot with their belongings, then board another train to continue their journey. It was a dramatic, unexpected event. Gilbert wrote Violeta of the mishap.

Clutching to this iota of connection with Gilbert, Violeta set the story to music, weaving into it a lament about their love's demise. She called him Run-Run, a name said like Gilbert with a pulsing cadence.

Crossing Purgatory, Run-Run bore his cross. He withheld himself from her (she told herself) to consider their fate. What he wrote dispassionately, she read as tragedy. He had separated; she had not let go.

Run-Run went North,
I remain in the South:
Between us lies an abyss
without music or light
ay ay, woe is me. Time crawls
by the wheels of the train,
over the sharp edge of track.

The more turns in the iron,
the more clouds in the month,
the longer are the tracks,
the more sour is the aftermath.

After seven days' travel, Gilbert reached La Paz. Exhausted and penniless, he put up in a fleabag hotel and the next day went looking for camera work. The government film studio verged on bankruptcy and the only other wasn't hiring.

"Hungry, I remembered I could play *quena*," said Gilbert sheepishly. "It was an absurd thing to do in the Land of the *Quena*, but I had no recourse." He performed in a plaza, where he met two other musicians, one of whom played *charango* and suggested they audition for a radio program.

By nine o'clock that night they were on the air. The three called themselves *Los Jairas*, which in Aymará means "the lazy ones." It was a joke, for all of them were "appreciated laziness, but had no time to practice." Soon, *Los Jairas* became famous for their renditions of Andean music.

Gilbert's long association with the Parras had atuned him to the antagonism between folkloric and commercial music. One heard accordion, not *quena*, on the streets of La Paz; and as in Santiago, folklore was absent over the airwaves. Everyone told him, "Festivals are the only times you hear folk music." This bothered him, for he esteemed Bolivian music as emblematic of Latin America.

Admiration drove him to an ambitious undertaking. Since folkloric *peñas* were so popular in Chile, why wouldn't they catch on here? Gilbert pawned his camera and went looking for a suitable site. He found it in *Galería Naira*, an art gallery whose Aymará name means "eye," centrally located in the old part of town next to a colonial church.

The gallery dealer was intrigued by the idea and helped Gilbert get started. They built a low platform for a stage, assembled chairs, wooden benches and tables to accommodate an audience. *Los Jairas* became the resident musical group, though soon many street musicians were congregating and jamming there.

Reports hailed *La Peña Folklórica de Galería Naira*'s opening night (March 4, 1966) as a tremendous success. A radio station aired the show out across the *Altiplano*, the high Bolivian plain, reaching a huge audience. Quickly, *Peña Naira* became a mecca of Bolivian music, a meeting place for composers, singers, and artists, frequented by tourists, diplomats, and intellectuals, a magnet for anyone interested in indigenous culture and the ideas that percolated in that secretive fertile ground.

Gilbert wrote Violeta, telling her about his new venture and inviting her to visit. She flew to La Paz immediately, the first of three trips she made to Bolivia. *Peña Naira* impressed her deeply. She listened, allowed herself to get caught up in the Bolivian rhythms, and took a turn on stage with her own music, for which she was warmly received. But the evening also saddened her terribly, for she felt alien in an ambience created by her estranged lover.

Later that night in Gilbert's tiny room behind the gallery, Violeta caressed Gilbert's hand and asked him sweetly to return to Santiago. Gilbert turned away. "I'm not interested. I'm pursuing my own destiny."

She pleaded with all the power of her heart, but her flood of tears failed to move Gilbert. The convulsive strain of her body and grimaced face touched him, but only to pity. "That was Hell for me. It wasn't any fun. I'm having fun now, all the time."

Violeta was crushed. It showed in her entire person. Gilbert comforted her; she washed her tear-streaked face.

The entire confrontation lasted no more than five or ten minutes. "Then we visited La Paz."

They attempted to spend a companionable week together. Violeta took every opportunity to evoke their past intimacy of working together. She'd brought only her guitar. He got her a stint on the radio, broadcasting from *Peña Naira*. She even put together in two days an art exhibit of oil-crayon paintings. Gilbert bought her a *charango*, a ten-stringed Andean instrument fashioned like a miniature guitar from an armadillo shell. Weeks later back in Santiago, Violeta composed her most famous song, *Gracias a la Vida*, on that instrument.

By the end of the week, Violeta had invited a group of *zampoña*-playing bootblacks who called themselves *Los Choclos* to perform at *La Carpa*. Gilbert had promised to help them raise money for the trip and accompany them.

One more fact marked her stay. Since Gilbert left *La Carpa*, Violeta felt unsafe. Local ruffians had taken to congregating near the tent at night, drinking. Their rowdiness frightened her; she feared one day they might put muscle behind their idle insults.

Would Gilbert help her buy a gun? Yes. They selected a revolver, a .38-caliber Brazilian-made *Tigre* and ammunition. Gilbert swore she bought it to protect herself. He never once thought she would use it as she did.

Violeta returned to Santiago alone, devastated by the finality of having lost "her husband." Their divorce was her most wretched shame. She clung to the hope of his promised visit, when perhaps he might relent and return her love as he had before.

Little Darling,

I received your letter that was so long in coming. How terrible that you are sick! Pride separates people. Everyone fights to be valued, but it alienates family, lovers, friends.

Do you love me, little darling? . . . I await anxiously until the end of April to receive you with your Choclos. . . . I feel your presence in the little charango. Always I have you in my bed by my side. I kiss you and I play you the sweetest music.

Saturday I had 150 people in the tent. We had plenty of food, drinks and music. If we could serve fondue it would sell. . . . I made a round oven, quite large, in the earth near the central pole. Ten little teapots and many grills filled with meat. What a marvel my tent is now!

Yet in her poetry, Violeta admitted defeat.

The man I most love
has ice running through his veins.
He leaves me stripped naked
knowing it's going to rain.
. . .
The river I most love
has no wish to be stopped.
The roar of its waters
drowns out my thirst.

Alone, Violeta ran *La Carpa de la Reina* as a truly rustic cultural center. No color photos in the Sunday magazine section of *El Mercurio* lauded its virtues; attracting an audience every weekend was a major chore.

Besides vying with *La Peña* for an audience, *La Carpa* competed with discotheques playing rock'n'roll. On a date night, if high school or university students had use of a car, they might come to *La Carpa*. But if they wanted to dress up and dance, they might go to *Las Brujas*, a dark nightclub just a little further uptown where you could dance suggestively close or stroll along a lakeside footpath.

To everyone who came, Violeta was welcoming, affectionate. She quipped without ridicule. Sarcasm no longer seeped into her performance space, for she had only gratitude now for people who made an effort to come. Gone were her demands that an audience give her undivided attention. At *La Carpa*, if talkative patrons caused others to turn and glare at them, Violeta would remark, "It's okay! Better that they be here and learn about Chilean folklore than be up the street with the rock'n'roll."

She sang of the man who still occupied her heart. She expressed herself poignantly, made people laugh. On icy nights in La Reina, heat from the braziers radiated to warm her guests. Between sets, she circulated, asking after their comfort. She was a gracious hostess and a consummate performer who generated good times.

> *Life pleases me, florid rosebush.*
> *Its handsome thorns need not prick me,*
> *and if one does, so be it.*

Violeta performed her *Décimas Autobiográficas*, which articulated in narrative poetry the themes she was grappling with in song: death, destiny, faith, time, the world as theatre, love as a redemptive force.

The turmoil of her personal life lay submerged.

Too many evenings *La Carpa* remained empty. Violeta and Carmen Luisa waited until midnight for patrons. If no one showed up, the girl retreated to her room, leaving Violeta to pace around the tent, worrying about money. Whatever she earned on the weekend supported them for the rest of the week. Every evening after the public left, Violeta collected the uneaten pieces of leftover *empanadas, anticuchos, sopaipillas,* to feed them in the coming days.

A priest came to visit her one rainy day and was struck by how tenuously they lived in a drafty adobe hut and unheated tent. "Her vision crashed against the hard rock of indifference. Few people lent a hand. . . . Violeta was alone, discouraged, with plenty of glory but sometimes without a cent."

She unburdened herself by playing guitar and singing, seated close to the stove.

> *Answer me heart:*
> *Why do you throb. . .*
> *like a bell that is rung? . . .*

> *Don't you see that I spend*
> *the night sleepless . . .*
> *in a violent sea . . . ?*

> *What is my crime*
> *that you so mistreat me, . . .*
> *You want to kill me!*

> *. . . you let my blood run . . .*
> *through your nets. . . .*
> *Why don't you let me go?*

She embroidered, worked in clay, and painted. She told anyone who asked that she was moved to create from a deep inner space, and to surrender her creations to the fire of their intended owner.

She told Patricio Manns that the worst sin of the creator was to be stingy with what you made ("to make and keep it in your balls," she said) while the patron's worst conceit was to make the artist beg to be seen.

She grew even harder to get along with. Violeta was frequently having to borrow money to live on, let alone pay her bills.

She still owed Sergio Larraín the cost of the tent. He went to see her to settle the matter. She had lent him a tapestry depicting a famous war hero, which he hoped to keep in exchange for forgiving the debt. But Violeta flew into a rage.

But how could this occur to him! The tapestry was hers and so was the tent! She ordered him to return the tapestry. After removing it from a stretcher frame, he rolled it up and brought it to her. The fact that he brought it back without the stretcher frame made her furious. Go to Hell, she told him. She never wanted to see him again.

As Larraín put it, "I loved Violeta but I never did see her again. Two hours, she looked me in the face, insulting me."

Gilbert visited Santiago in June 1966, bringing *Los Choclos* from Bolivia. The entire group's expenses were underwritten jointly by the Bolivian and Chilean Offices of Tourism. The eight young men of *Los Choclos*, speaking Quechua and Aymará among themselves, must have made an unusual sight, their slight physical size garbed in colorful woolen hats and ponchos. They performed first in Antofagasta and then Santiago, demonstrating their dances and songs on wind instruments exotic to most Chileans.

During his stay, Gilbert busied himself with the Bolivians and avoided spending much time alone with Violeta. Hoping to keep things lighthearted, he brought her a gift– a monkey, who did not thrive in the Santiago climate or with the *mistela* that Violeta gave it to drink. The press handled the couple's altered relationship decorously. When reporting on the group's show at *La Carpa de la Reina,* a journalist noted that Violeta's husband now had his own *peña* in La Paz. Nothing more was said.

Tempest

One night, shortly after Gilbert left, an enormous rain cloud settled low over all of Santiago, dumping drenching rains on the city, heaviest in the outlying mountain regions. Thunder resounded, the heavens lit with lightning, noisy with gale-force winds that battered trees and structures. Violeta awoke in terror. Her screams awakened Carmen Luisa and also Héctor Pavez, who was sleeping in the tent that night.

The massive tent was faltering in the storm. Never secured tightly enough, soaked guy ropes stretched and loosened their support of the immense center mast, which swayed treacherously. The roof sagged under the weight of accumulating water; in some places water ripped through the canvas, streaming off the weakening structure to dig holes in the mud and undermine the tent stakes.

As one, Violeta, Carmen Luisa, and Héctor gripped the center mast and stilled its motion. Then Héctor tied the guy ropes taut to stabilize the tent. They poked the roof with poles to drain it. A hysterical Violeta raced around baling water, writhing in fear, shrieking over impending disaster.

Once they had the tent secured, the three slogged around its perimeter in the slippery mud, drenched, shoring up one portion after another, as the tent weathered the storm. The downpour lasted until five in the morning, then subsided to a drizzle.

That weekend, Osvaldo, Violeta's gypsy friend from Valparaíso, showed up for a *peña* at *La Carpa* with a young Uruguayan named Alberto Zapicán. As was customary at the show's finale, the scant audience applauded enthusiastically. Alberto watched, but didn't clap.

"Who do you think you are not to applaud?" Violeta asked pointedly when Osvaldo introduced them. To her confrontational tone, Alberto remained silent, which piqued her curiosity.

Conversation switched to the subject of the tent. Alberto had grown up in the *campo* and he wanted to work for her. He knew how to make the kind of repairs the battered homestead needed. From the few words they exchanged, Alberto recalled, "Her tone changed when she realized I was as brutish or more so than she. You could see that this pleased her!"

She hired him to sew up the canvas and build a bathroom in exchange for lodging, and in the months that followed–the last months of her life–Alberto became the man who cared for her with devotion when she was depressed or drunk, when she couldn't or wouldn't wash herself or eat, when her bed was no more than a nest of tangled sheets.

Ever since he was a boy, Alberto loved to make noise. Whenever Violeta was out, he practiced playing his barrel-sized *bombo*. When she heard him she said, "From now on, you must leave the hammer behind, take up the drum, and play with me." Alberto was the only man to sing on any of her recordings, for his was an authentic peasant voice.

On stage, Alberto's drumming created a dramatic opening. The *bombo* would signal such reverent hush, even young children quieted. Violeta opened with a lament, followed by something raucous to intensify the show. She segued to *cueca*, and from there, set a lively and happy tone, until at the end, she closed with something serious or poignant.

> *The carefree butterflies, on seeing the pretty little angel,*
> *flutter very quietly for him around his cradle.*
> *When the flesh dies the spirit ascends directly*
> *to greet the moon and in passing, the morning star.*

With Alberto now handling the tent maintenance, Violeta once again dedicated herself to mentoring musicians who were just beginning to perform professionally.

One such group called themselves *Chagual*, for a plant that grows in the *cordillera* amid the rocks. They were ten primary-school teachers from southern Chile, who enjoyed singing and dancing the country dances, complete with native costuming and choreography. When they asked Violeta's permission to interpret some of her material, she worked with them until every word, every tone and gesture conveyed her intent.

Their relationship changed with time. She auditioned them, seated quietly for two and a half hours, as they sang songs from the North, peasant songs, *criollos*, and from Chiloé. "You'll perform the ones from the North and from Chiloé," she said in planning their show. She directed the effort, praising what the group did well and criticizing what didn't work for her. She herself danced a *sirilla* and a *cueca* to demonstrate how they were to be done.

Chagual took intense instruction from Violeta every Tuesday from 7:00 p.m. until midnight. "She had us repeat a stanza up to thirty times. Our fingers would get bloody, but we had to stay there until she said we could leave." Yet once she was satisfied with their delivery, her approach changed.

"You fly solo now," she told them. "Use the rhythms as they present themselves, try different instruments, destroy the meter, free yourselves. The song is a bird without a flight plan, that hates mathematics and loves the whirlwinds."

Violeta was willing take artistic risks based on authenticity, but had no patience for what she considered phony. Three Mapuche Indian men and a woman introduced themselves to her as *Huenchulyan*. They sang and played their indigenous instruments, the ancient *trutruka*, fashioned from a long hollowed bamboo and a bull's horn, and the ceremonial drum called *kultrún*.

The young woman in the group, however, left Violeta incredulous. To the men's music, she danced in the manner of classical ballet with great leaps and twirls.

"What kind of shit is this?" Violeta ordered the men, "Here, you play by yourselves and that *huevona* has got to go!"

The Mapuches fell silent; then played and sang as she insisted, with complete authenticity and without the woman. Unaccustomed ears may have found the Mapuche music monotonous, but the young people who frequented *La Carpa* knew it was important to Violeta. She was proud of her Mapuche blood.

Matinees catered to the children who came to *La Carpa*. Two puppeteers performed many afternoons. One day as they'd come to the end of a fairy tale with a happy ending, they were surprised to hear Violeta sobbing. "What's wrong?" they asked.

"The blind king made me cry," Violeta blurted out. She was growing very emotional, all the time. Something happy might animate her with manic glee; then in a flash, she'd burst into tears or fly into a rage, unpredictably.

Amidst her family, she basked in the pleasure of her first grandson, born to Marta and Ángel. She embroidered dreamy images into gigantic *arpilleras*. She was composing brilliant songs that had new textural complexity of lyric depth and musical intonation.

But Violeta's vision for *La Carpa*–to create a living museum of peasant culture in urban Chile–wasn't materializing. True, musicians respected her and *campesinos* revered her; but the *Universidad Católica* denied her a grant for folkloric research. She detested record companies, radio stations, and television studios for patronizing her, when what she wanted was for Chile, not for herself. She grew bitter.

Sometimes, Violeta provoked conflict seemingly for sport. One night after working at *Radio Chilena*, she invited Alberto to dine with her at one of downtown Santiago's posh restaurants. No sooner did they walk in when the maitre d' approached and explained that he could not seat them because of the restaurant's dress code.

"Why not?" Violeta demanded, and dumped her purse onto a nearby table. "See, I have money." Clearly, Violeta had entered the restaurant expecting to be thrown out.

On another evening, Violeta and Alberto were in the tent when a man entered. He was well dressed, clearly a gentleman. Violeta turned belligerent. "What do you think you're doing, coming in here without permission?"

"Violeta, I've come from Buenos Aires to see you." Without thinking, she threw something that hit him. He left.

Seconds later realizing who he was, she ran after him, brought him back, and introduced him as the Chilean ambassador to Argentina. They had met in Paris. But Violeta was no longer the artist he knew as an admiring collector. She'd changed.

Dead of night, gunfire rang out close to the tent. An unknown assailant, thought to be a malicious neighbor who resented his evening solitude disrupted by loud music, shot the llama.

The killing stunned Violeta. She accepted it passively, then redoubled her efforts to interest radio stations in scripts for new programs. A few projects got produced, but their proceeds were insufficient to sustain her financially.

Meanwhile, neighbors escalated their pressure. They petitioned the municipality to rescind Violeta's permit to reside in the tent in a public park. From all sides they made her life miserable, by launching complaints about the noise— her music as noise.

As Alberto put it, "The nearest houses were about 40 meters away, so the noise that carried wasn't that strong, except if I were beating the *bombo*—and then it would be a good noise, wouldn't it?

"So there we were, fighting with people who didn't even know how to dance the *cueca*." Except for a poor little grocer, all of them were well off economically. Maybe today some of them regret never having visited the cabaret, but none of them ever came.

What neighbors saw as a circus, a nuisance that disturbed their tranquility, nevertheless was frequented by educated people. This remote performance space had some prestige. At night it was like a gala party, but by day they saw an unkempt peasant woman in blue stockings and yellow shoes. How could peasants have installed themselves in this neighborhood?

Despite having permitted Violeta to pitch the tent, the municipality cut off her electricity. She chased down signatures to get it turned back on, while her friends tapped power from existing lines–likely from the very people who had pressured the government to cut it off. The police searched the premises repeatedly for illegal substances, without finding anything.

Violeta traveled to Bolivia again to see Gilbert. As soon as she had the chance, she thrust Alberto's photograph in his face. "See," she said, "I have a new lover. What do you think of that?"

If anything, Gilbert was relieved. *Peña Naira* was burgeoning, and with it, his own social and musical life. *Los Jairas*, the group he had organized with *altiplano* Indians when first he arrived in La Paz, was becoming so popular, they had just signed a record contract.

Tempted by Violeta's offer to get them television exposure, Gilbert brought *Los Jairas* to Santiago. The group was well received, but the couple argued constantly. She wept and raged. He distanced himself. No one dared interfere in their bruising tussle. Violeta was jealous of his happiness and terrified of losing his love, yet her behavior was pushing him away. Their relationship had grown too tense.

When Gilbert left, Violeta fell into a bitter silence. She depicted him in poetry as a trapped lion desperate to escape. She mocked his dependence on pleasure, accused him of selling out. "Your gaze seems like a joke, your laughter like a scream."

Even so, she held out for a promise of "new wine to sweeten the bitterness of bile."

Alberto observed with compassion Violeta's self-loathing, but was unable to comfort her. She lashed out with a fury that was like being kicked into barbed wire. "Or you have a lamb that is drinking water and you kick it without knowing why. Being what you are infuriates you."

As he saw her, Violeta was deteriorating in a spiritual loneliness of her own making. "By the time you reach age of fifty, like Violeta did, to reach that point in life and lose your companion" was a terrible humiliation.

At sixteen, Carmen Luisa had blossomed into a troubled adolescent. She was hyper-vigilent; her dark eyes saw everything, unlike girls her age whose lives were more sheltered. Her mother's desperation terrified her. Violeta always treated Carmen Luisa as if she were older. And she was rough with her, abusive.

For much of her childhood Carmen Luisa lived with her grandmother and her father, but after Gilbert left, she lived at *La Carpa*. Violeta needed her, but they fought constantly.

The girl took to running away to stay with her father, grandmother, or friends for two or three days at a time. She lied to Violeta about her whereabouts. Whenever Carmen Luisa disappeared, Violeta panicked, terrified that something untoward would happen.

Finally after an unexplained absence, Violeta overpowered her daughter, chained her wrists, tethered her to a tree, and cropped off her thick black hair with scissors, like a woman shamed. Violeta was determined to dominate Carmen Luisa, to deny her adolescent beauty so she would not leave home.

In Switzerland, Marie-Magdeleine Brumagne received a letter from Violeta, written in the third person as a cry for help.

Once upon a time there was a little animal who was black and dirty, and so wild, no other animal wanted to play with him. He cried, because he too wanted to be beautiful, at least one day in Winter.

What could he do? His mother knew nothing of her little monster. He never came home for meals like the other children. He was forever hunting wild flowers for a bouquet that he kept on the window in a jelly jar. The poor little creature wanted to sing and play guitar. His mother couldn't afford to buy him one: She barely managed to buy bread to feed all ten of her children!

One clear and starry night, Violeta (like her little black hero, dirty and sad) steals her godmother's guitar. She needs it to sing to a dead little angel, so the good woman lends her guitar and the girl disappears into the blackness of time.

When she sings, she becomes beautiful, with the eternal song of the slippery road of Life. But there was no place for Violeta's song, so she sings to the walls. Loudly, bitterly. I want to sing, Magdalena. Outside. For everybody, the song of the living angels.

The stones must be moved, but they are hard and cold.

Again, Violeta's verse foretold her intent.

The heavens I most love
Have begun to cloud up;
My eyes serve no purpose:
The darkness kills them.

Without shelter, without shadow,
without water, without light,
I lack only a knife
to deprive myself of well-being.

Violeta slit her wrists.

Alberto heard her moaning inside her locked room. He busted open the door, saw her bleeding, bandaged her up. News that Violeta Parra attempted to take her life a second time scarcely moved some. She was not dead. She obviously recovered. Someone brought her flowers. She told people she felt happy again.

Gracias a la Vida

I thank life, which has given me so much.
It gave me two eyes, which when I open them
see clearly the black and the white,
and in the heavens high above, the celestial depths,
and among the multitudes of humanity, the man I love.

Having lost Gilbert Favre, Violeta idealized him. She imagined returning to his patio, gazing into his eyes. In her perfect song, *Gracias a la Vida*, Thanksgiving to Life, she gave homage to the ordinary–"crickets and canaries, dogs barking, hammers," the compassion of "mother, friend, brother, and light shining over . . . the spirit that dearly loves me." She voiced pride in sentiment, intellect, and honest work, recalled her own travels through cities, mountains and prairies collecting folklore. Any fruit of human endeavor reminded her of the "good so distant from the bad." In every verse, love anchored her.

I thank life, which has given me so much
It has given me laughter and a flood of tears;
to distinguish between happiness and heartbreak,
the two elements that form my song

and your song, which are the very same song
and everybody's song, which is my own song.

Only in the final verse did she reveal her vulnerability —"happiness and heartbreak, the two elements that form my song" – then quickly she submerged it into a communion of universality. Strumming the guitar-like *charango* Gilbert had given her, she sang in a voice of rare, eloquent wisdom. The first time she performed *Gracias a la Vida* she confused the verses with those of another song. Laughing, she explained that it was "fresh from the oven and still very hot." She hadn't memorized it yet.

The few people who attended *La Carpa* that evening didn't realize they were hearing the folklorist's testament.

In mid-November 1966, springtime in Chile, Violeta performed in Arica with a group of musicians as part of a cultural tour. It was an odd trip for her, going north nearly to Bolivia without visiting Gilbert. As they boarded the DC-3 to fly home to Santiago, one of the other women remarked, "Well, if we go down today, that would be the end of *La Nueva Canción Chilena*." Enough of its proponents were present for the point to have resonance.

Departure from the hot, arid region was scheduled for 11 a.m. A non-stop flight would have reached Santiago in under three hours; but their puddle-jumper was scheduled for six stops en route before reaching Santiago in early evening.

Violeta seated herself on the aisle next to one of the members of *La Peña's* collective, Patricio Manns. She was manic. Once the plane was aloft, she walked up and down the aisle, made loud jokes, questioned, chatted, sang. She got off at every landing.

At about 8:00 p.m., the plane approached Santiago's airport for domestic flights. Passengers stowed their gear for the final landing. The repeated landings and takeoffs had made many queasy, irritable; everyone looked forward to landing for good. The aircraft descended, and then, just as everyone was expecting the little jolt of contact with the runway, the DC-3 gained altitude.

Out the window, dusk glinted red in the vapor that settled over the mountains. Half an hour later, the plane repeated the maneuver.

"How did that song go?" Violeta asked, completely out of context.

"What song?"

"The song about my little sculpture."

The night before, Patricio had sung a new song about a clay figurine of a peasant woman strumming her guitar that Ángel had found in a corner of *La Peña*. He decided to give it to Patricio as a gift.

But as he handed it over, the sculpture fell from his hands and broke. The left arm and the guitar disappeared, leaving the shard of the right arm curved around an invisible instrument, the figurine distorted by impact, head thrown back, mouth open as if screaming. Its new form, like its old, could have been Violeta herself.

"Don't change a single line. It's perfect. Sing it again."

Patricio sang slowly. Violeta hummed, keeping a *tonada* rhythm with her hands on the armrests of the seat.

Forty minutes later, the plane again descended, this time at a military airfield, then without touching down, ascended over the rooftops of nearby buildings as before.

Over the loudspeaker, the co-pilot asked everyone to remain calm and seated. "We are trying to solve a little problem."

Below them lay Santiago, all lit up at 10:00 p.m. Someone was sobbing. Every eye stared toward the closed door of the cockpit.

"People are taking stock," whispered Violeta as she eyed her traveling companions. "What they'll leave behind. I have neither house nor lover. My children are grown. The wind might carry my tent away at any time. Besides, I've only borrowed it."

As the plane descended for its fourth landing attempt, passengers could see silhouettes of ambulances and firetrucks lining the airstrip. As before, the plane was obliged to ascend. By now, some were crying inconsolably.

"Are you happy?" Violeta asked Patricio.

"I wouldn't say so."

"You know, people hear us or read us to experience our sufferings and to suffer a little bit themselves in some new way. No one suffers alike. People don't understand us, and often, we don't understand them. Yet they approach like children to fire knowing they'll burn their hands, yet reaching out to touch."

"Look out the window, Violeta." Patricio gestured to a great yellow moon that lit up the mountain peaks, creating a chiaroscuro panorama.

The pilot addressed everyone by loudspeaker. "You are not in mortal danger. The landing train is malfunctioning. If we cannot land next time, we'll drain off fuel in flight and land on the belly of the aircraft. Stay calm and follow the crew's instructions to the letter."

Violeta gazed in awe at the fantastic vision out the window, for with the plane's ascent, a moonlit landscape of midnight blue mountains became visible. She touched Patricio's arm and asked, "Why aren't you scared?"

"I am scared."

"Show it."

"I can't."

"Impossible," she said. "You know how to express yourself. How come you can't express fear?"

He stared at her. "And you, why aren't you afraid?"

She laughed weakly, then pulled her shawl around her shoulders and sat silently for a long time before she replied. "Death is not as important as Life. People are only afraid if they haven't sown anything."

The pilot landed the plane safely.

Back home, Violeta learned of Gilbert's own recent drama. In September 1966, *Los Jairas* competed in a music festival in Cochabamba and swept the awards: best song, best ensemble, and best presentation! They recorded their first LP album and their prize-winning song was soon heard all over Bolivian radio.

Another record producer offered them a lucrative deal if they would break their record contract and sign with him. The group refused.

A few nights later, Gilbert was awakened by one of the band members, who reported that the producer had released a pirate recording, which he had apparently taped during the competition. The sound quality was atrocious and the record was issued despite the group's express refusal.

Enraged, Gilbert stormed the producer's house and pistol-whipped him black and blue, an act that earned him the nickname, *El Gringo Bandolero*, the Foreign Gunslinger. Gilbert was arrested and charged with attempted murder.

News of Gilbert's arrest unleashed unprecedented protest. Every radio station and newspaper denounced the actions of the recording company. Lawyers offered to defend Gilbert free of charge. Residents of a slum neighborhood began a hunger strike to petition his release. Amazonian Indians began a 400-kilometer walk to La Paz to demand justice! Gilbert Favre became a *cause celebre.* By the third day, the vice-president of Bolivia, Dr. Siles Salinas, intervened on Gilbert's behalf. The police released him and dropped all charges.

Gilbert wrote Violeta what happened and invited her to Oruro to run a folkloric *peña* with him during Easter carnival week. He also planned to film *La Diablada,* the colorful pageant of Good and Evil whose staging culminated the festival of *Semana Santa.* Violeta accepted the invitation and said she'd visit in January to make further plans.

For Christmas 1966, Violeta arrived at Isabel's house laden with gifts. "I'm thinking of touring Magallanes province, although they wouldn't be paying me what I'm worth," she told them. Everyone encouraged her to make the concert tour, hoping that a trip might cheer her up.

The 150-mile drive between Puenta Arenas and Puerto Natales paralleled the Straits of Magellan along on a rocky road slick with mud and moss, then turned inland up a gravel road. The squawking of marine birds along the austral coast died away. Sun shown on a vast bristly grassland, framed in the distance by a jagged spine of rock chiseled by icy wind and relentless rain—the southernmost extremity of the Andes.

Though it was summer, temperatures the night before had plunged below freezing. In one tiny frozen lake, Violeta saw a flock of flamingos trapped in ice, their pink heads and black feet protruding sculpturally in the telling indifference of death.

The southern trip provided Violeta's first contact with the Patagonians. In a large theatre in Puerto Natales, she sang before an enthusiastic audience of coarse shepherds from the steppes, fishermen and peasants of the tiny rural hamlets nearby. Because she was so far from Santiago (1500 miles), she believed she would be foreign to them, so she undertook to explain herself excessively.

"I have never come here," she began, "but perhaps some of you know me."

A youth stood up and said, "Everyone here knows you. You sing on the radio and you're named Violeta."

Violeta blushed with embarrassed pleasure.

She repeated, "I want to tell you about myself. I live by touring Chile, although I've never ventured here. I collect songs of our country and perform them far from where they're found. So, the songs I collect in the south are those I want people to know in Chile's northern desert plains; and the songs of the desert plains should resound here. It's one way to unite this country from within—by the sound of its music."

Then she announced a song, a *cueca*. She strummed her guitar, interrupting herself several times with commentary in verse.

> *The priest doesn't know how to plow*
> *nor yoke an oxen*
> *But with his saintly law*
> *He harvests without sowing a seed.*
> *Yeah, I said, yeah!*

The auditorium exploded in laughter, astonished by her irreverence.

Over thirty years, Violeta had forged a musical style richly textured by regional sound. A virtuoso guitarist, she drew forth a stunning lyricism. Her last compositions were unlike any before: metaphysical, penetrating through time. On this, her last tour, Violeta Parra had reached a pinnacle of achievement in conveying her compassion for the human condition. Her emotional depth touched everyone for whom she sang.

Little or nothing remained of the raucous vocalizations of her youth; her stage presence was now peaceful, gracious, inviting a new intimacy. Her exhausted voice rendered her songs smoothly, sweetly, with perfect control. When she sang her face lit up, her eyelids lowered. She played long preludes to her songs and concluded in silence, listening to the ovations, and then, opening her eyes to receive her public's adulation.

En route to their final concert in the port of Punta Arenas, the tour bus had to stop to let pass a great flock of sheep. Violeta got out to meet the herdsmen.

A single shepherd on horseback and his trained dogs can herd 5000 head, they told her. They spoke haltingly about the winter solitude that transforms every man into a lost island in the sparse immensity of Patagonia, of the scarce women who lived with them (generally aged prostitutes), of friendships and the loyalty of the animals. She listened without comment, with her dark eyes veiled by the discovery and intense emotion. The panorama and its people made a profound impression on Violeta.

"I knew that you existed," she said to her audience that night, "but I didn't know how. This is Chilean land on which I've never walked. It's all new to me. I don't understand why, with this beautiful and terrible experience that is your lives, you have no songs of your own. Chile is a country of music in every region, yet Magallanes has no music."

Among all the songs she sang that gala night, at the end of 1966, no other provoked the wild acclaim of *Hace falta un guerrillero*:

I wish I had a son
Brilliant as a carnation
Fleet as the wind
To name Manuel,
with a surname Rodriguez,
The most precious laurel.

The very mention of Manuel Rodriguez brought the audience to their feet. The *guerrillero* commander had exchanged magistrate's robes for disguises and a sword, to fight for freedom during the wars of Chilean independence. Violeta's song sanctified that beloved young hero, revered even today, nearly two centuries after his death.

At the end of the recital, she received a tumultuous standing ovation. Then, a little girl climbed the steps to the stage, carrying a stool, finely crafted of wood and woven grass. Violeta walked over and bent down to greet her. The audience fell silent.

"Since you sing seated," said the child, "we want to give you this stool that my father made to your size." Violeta accepted the offering gratefully, but it took her several moments to regain her composure.

"You don't know how dear this gift is for me," she said to the audience. "I have always sung with my feet dangling in the air, because as you know, I am very short. Now, in this little chair made to my own size, I will be able to sing, finally, with my feet planted firmly on the ground."

The next day, Violeta gave her last performance to an audience of parents and children. When asked whether she was affected by the cold, she admitted, "a little."

The speaker said, "It appears," said the speaker, "that the *Centro de Madres* intuited your problem, because they've made you a shawl of thick wool." Overcome with emotion, she thanked them and received their heartfelt applause.

The Punta Arenas concert tour marked Violeta's final public appearances. She returned home from Magallanes unrecognizable, according to her brother, Lautaro, "without wrinkles, radiant, with really good energy."

One Sunday in Heaven

Violeta's cheerfulness was short-lived. During the trip south, she had had an affair with a young man to whom she declared her love on radio. But when he disappointed her, Violeta grew bitter.

> *To return to age seventeen*
> *after having lived for so long*
> *is like deciphering the signs*
> *without becoming the wiser.*

Alberto remained her loyal companion at *La Carpa*, though they were not in love. She clung to the notion of recovering Gilbert.

She had only to look at Carmen Luisa in the full flush of adolescent beauty to recognize herself as a woman growing older alone. "My footsteps have retreated while yours are advancing," she sang in her *sirilla*, *Volver a los 17*. In song she longed for innocence long-ago gone.

> *To again be suddenly*
> *as fragile as a second,*
> *to again feel as insubstantial*
> *as a child before the Lord,*

that is how I feel myself to be
in this fertile instant.

When her father had died, Violeta had characterized Death as a fearsome animal that "arrives like a whirlwind" and from whose desire there was no escape. Now love and death stirred passions from which Violeta could not disengage.

One becomes entangled, entangled;
Like the ivy growing in a wall,
ever blossoming, blossoming
Like the tiny moss upon a stone.

In mid-January 1967, Violeta released her last album, *Las Últimas Composiciones de Violeta Parra.* She sang of love's grip, the sorrow of an infant's death, the resilience of life.

Human beings are formed
of a spirit and a body,
of a heart that beats
to the tones of sentiments.

I cannot understand love
of the soul alone,
when the body is a river
of such lovely waves.

The record was a masterpiece. Violeta acknowledged her breakthrough when she gave a copy to a life-long friend and wrote on the jacket, "As a gardener offers his best flower, I surrender to you my best songs."

Soon another depression manifested itself. Carmen Luisa dreaded her mother's mood swings. "One day she'd wake up happy, and the next she was an ogre who saw everything in the worst possible light. She'd cry, and when I'd ask her what happened, she'd tell me to go to Hell. When she got depressed, she'd go to see my uncle Nicanor and complain that everyone abandoned her. She was hard to live with. You never knew what was going to happen. I can say this because I was the only one who was with her until the end."

Few people ventured to *La Carpa*. Without an audience, Violeta convinced herself that she was unworthy.

> *I curse the word Love*
> *with all its foolishness:*
> *How great is my pain!*

She closed her tent to the public and began composing what she envisioned as a great folkloric symphony. She spent hours alone writing, playing music, singing, particularly on the *charango*, *Volver a los 17* and *Gracias a la Vida*. She lost weight. She drank. She gloried in agitated moods.

Everyone close to her knew she had a gun. She showed it to her closest friends, to gain attention. The revolver was on the table one day when she turned insulting toward Alberto. He stood up to leave when she screamed, "If you walk across that doorway, I'll kill myself!"

He left, barely closing the door behind him. The moment passed.

Alarmed by her deterioration, Alberto and Nicanor looked into organizing another concert tour, this time to Buenos Aires. "Have her stir up some Chilean dust in Argentina."

Meanwhile, Violeta prepared to visit Gilbert to arrange for their Oruro *peña*. At a press conference held at her departure, she announced ambitious plans: an exhibit scheduled for April in Geneva, an Argentine trip, a recording of *cuecas*, and a tour with Nicanor to the United States of America. They would hold concerts and readings at universities, she would exhibit *arpilleras*. Together, they would present a multi-faceted vision of the Chilean people through poetry, song, and art.

In La Paz, Bolivia, a photograph of Violeta and Gilbert published on January 20, 1967 showed Gilbert embracing an adoring Violeta. The image was meant to quell gossip of their definitive separation. "Perhaps we will be together elsewhere," she was reported as saying. "It's always been this way. I leave or he leaves, but the other soon follows." The accompanying article lauded their joint venture for its folkloric importance.

Violeta performed at the *Peña Naira*. Gilbert admired her newest music, wondering how much of it was about him.

Gilbert's much celebrated arrest had catapulted *Peña Naira* to radical chic, now popular among intellectuals across the political spectrum, including sworn enemies.

Government, military, and embassy personnel, wealthy progressives such as Pierre Cardín said to be bankrolling leftist activities. Che Guevara met there with Regis Debray and rendezvoused with his lover, Tania. All were seen in the audience. With the cachet his cabaret had acquired, Gilbert grew cockier, basking in his separate destiny.

Back in Santiago, Violeta raged at Carmen Luisa for staying out late with her boyfriend, when Carmen stopped her cold. "You're boring me. All you want to do is kill me with your hysterics."

"Look, Carmen Luisa," she said. "When someone wants to kill herself, she does it silently. I'll never announce it to you."

Yet Violeta warned everyone of her intentions in her own way. To Héctor Pavez, she asked, "*Negro*, do you ever think about your own death?"

"Yes," he answered. "But I never believe it. . . ."

"When you die you are going to look like this," and she showed him a clay figurine she had just made of a corpse.

"Everyone dies," she said. "Some people decide to die, even order it! Not that *that* death comes to everyone."

Violeta's friends hid everything potentially lethal: knives, razors, even scissors. A married couple moved into the tent to keep watch that she not harm herself. They confiscated the gun and locked it away where they figured she wouldn't find it.

On Friday, February third, Violeta invited her sister, Hilda, to join her for a Turkish bath before Hilda left for a vacation at the seashore. By Hilda's recollection, Violeta seemed content. "I knew her nerves were shot, but she was as cheerful as I've ever seen her." The women talked animatedly for hours.

"This is the best song I've ever written in my life. Listen," she said to Hilda, as she plugged in the record player to play *Gracias a la Vida*. She told her that the trip to Punta Arenas had warmed her heart. She believed that she, a country girl who always said things simply as she felt them, had created her most flawless songs.

When the record ended, Hilda asked, "Why did you choose to name the album *Las Últimas Composiciones* (Final Compositions)?"

"Because they are the last."

Hilda laughed, not taking her seriously. "Will you give me your record as a gift?"

"You have to buy my records," Violeta teased. But she retrieved an album from a carton and autographed it, something she had never done. Later, Violeta sent Hilda home with a large tapestry and other belongings she'd bought in Europe. "Here, take this suitcase, take this tape recorder, this typewriter."

Hilda drew back. "How can I ever pay you all the money these cost? I don't even have steady work." Violeta argued she didn't need the money. Only in hindsight did her family recognize that Violeta was consciously giving away her possessions during those early days of February.

Despite his great affection for her, not even Nicanor realized Violeta's intentions. He had invited her to a luncheon gathering on Sunday. But Saturday noon, *el día de San Gilberto* according to the ecumenical calendar, Violeta dropped by with a friend; the three ate together. She was cheerful, but distant.

"Listen, Violeta," he began. "Chile has very few novelists. Why don't you write a novel, Violeta? You're the voice of our clan." It was an absurd idea, but Nicanor hoped to kindle a spark of enthusiasm, even for the ridiculous.

She laughed. "No *guachito*, you'd write a much better one. I'm tired."

"Okay," Nicanor said, "then go someplace to rest. Why don't you vacation at the seashore before going to Argentina?"

She remained pensive for a while. "All right," she said in a rare voice. "I'll rest." Then she grew animated. "I want to sing you a song called *Un Domingo en el Cielo* (One Sunday in Heaven).

"No. Sing me a different one, *una chilota*." She sang a song from Chiloé, but then insisted on singing *Un Domingo en el Cielo* too.

When she finished singing, she got to her feet. Nicanor protested, "Stay, Violeta, a while longer."

"No." She had to go to *La Peña*. And with that she left. It was the last time Nicanor heard her sing.

That night, Violeta and Alberto performed until late. Violeta grew more irritable as the evening droned on.

Sunday morning, she awakened Alberto at six, asking him to bring her tea. Annoyed, he brought her *yerba mate* and left her alone. She spent the morning writing, while listening repeatedly to a recording by her daughter Isabel of a Venezuelan song she liked very much.

> *Rio Manzanares, let me pass*
> *My ailing mother is calling me.*

That same morning, Sunday, February fifth, Nicanor realized that he didn't have any wine to serve his luncheon guests. He was about to go to ask Violeta, whose tent was nearby, but on a whim he stopped to see Clarisa, who now lived in Violeta's little wooden house. He drove there and honked the car horn, which brought Carmen Luisa outside into the garden.

"Does your grandmother have any wine?" he asked.

"No." He started the engine and said he'd ask at the tent. "No uncle, don't bother. My mother doesn't have any either." So Nicanor went to the store and didn't look in on Violeta.

Violeta stopped writing at about 2:00 p.m. to join Alberto, Carmen Luisa, and a woman who was living in the tent as a caretaker, for lunch. She ate in complete silence,

poured herself some tea, then retreated to her room and
shut herself in. According to Alberto, "She was giving free
rein to her writing. She wasn't playing guitar."

What happened later that afternoon remains unclear.
An argument started. Alberto and Carmen Luisa both left
the tent compound. At 4:00 pm, Violeta ordered the caretaker to go buy some corn, telling her she wanted to make a
pastel and *humitas*. That left Violeta alone at *La Carpa*, which
gave her the opportunity she was waiting for—a chance to
look for the gun.

When Carmen Luisa returned, she heard Violeta repeatedly strumming chords on the guitar. "I was putting
things in order in the tent–it would have been about 6:00
p.m. –when suddenly I heard a gunshot.

"I ran into the bedroom and found my mother
slumped on top of her guitar, with the revolver in her hand.
I approached and touched her. I talked to her, but she didn't
answer me. Then I realized that a thin stream of blood was
running out of her mouth. I was paralyzed. I don't know
why, but the most instinctive thing to do was to take the revolver from her.

"I went outside the tent and screamed to some people
who were walking by. Suddenly the tent was full of people.
Detectives arrived and then an ambulance came to take her
away."

In the room was found Violeta's letter of departure,
written the day before:

> *I bid you farewell ladies and gentlemen.*
> *The essence of Truth is what I come to say.*
> *Now I leave you, singing, with all the voice I can muster.*
> *Do not deny me the land on which to strew my torment*
> *nor the bird that bears my memories.*

It soars through the air and to all the elements
and keeps the stubborn heart pumping blood
and softens the language of every vulgar remark.
See you tomorrow compadre.
Everything has its time
so here ends the letter you are reading today.
Look at me in my serenity.
Care for me, angelic, through the night.
Close my unseeing eyes.
Today is Saturday and it is raining.
Tomorrow is another day; we'll see what happens.

The site of the tragedy resembled a peasant encampment in Violeta's girlhood Chillán. Behind the tent stood the spartan adobe living quarters with its kettles, canvases, sewing machine, straw chairs.

Family members gathered beneath the canopy of poplars and willow in *La Quintrala* park. Carmen Luisa sobbed hysterically. Isabel stood numb in shocked disbelief. Ángel, emaciated, wearing dark glasses, paced. Nicanor stood apart, mute, stooped, unconsolable. Marta, Violeta's half-sister, wept in her husband arms. Lautaro arrived shrieking, "Where is my little sister? Let me see her!" That night after learning the news, Roberto attempted suicide.

Homicide investigators interrogated witnesses, paying particular attention to the disturbance that afternoon between Violeta and Alberto.

Shortly after 1:00 p.m. Monday, Violeta's remains were returned to family at the tent, where they washed and dressed her for final repose. She was laid out with her guitar beside her in the coffin, positioned on stage.

Around her were placed the projection of peasant life that she held so close to her heart. Her drawings, poplar and willow boughs, a bench of cattails.

The Parra family kept vigil.

Once the scene of so much Chilean song, the tent now stood in deep mourning. Violeta Parra had strummed her terrible finale for which there was no encore.

Hundreds of wreaths and condolences arrived from across society—from President Eduardo Frei, from Senator Salvador Allende, from members of the folklorists' and circus workers' unions, from celebrities and ordinary people who knew her only through her music.

Thousands came to view Violeta Parra's open casket, to touch it, to gaze upon her now-tranquil face, to bid her good-bye and thank her for all she had given to the poor and to Chile. Her paintings and tapestries hung nearby drunk with color—portraits of simple men with guitars and birds captive in enormous woven skies. Her rope-soled shoes sat out on the patio waiting to be worn. The atmosphere hushed in terrible awe.

Saturday, Hilda had taken her children on vacation to the beach town of Cartagena. They were returning home by bus Tuesday morning, when inexplicably Hilda grew anxious.

As her daughter disembarked to help her mother off the bus, a neighbor's child saw them and called, "Carmencita. Carmencita, your Aunt Violeta is dead. They're going to bury her today!"

Hysterical, Hilda dropped everything in the street and took off running. She never knew how she reached the cemetery.

The sun broke through an overcast sky as the funeral cortege carrying Violeta's remains passed before the Orfeón

Theatre, which broadcast Chopin's funeral march into the street.

As the sad procession crossed the bridge over the Mapocho River, florists strewed rose petals before the path of the hearse and upon her coffin.

On the radio one could hear *Casamiento de Negros*, *Volver a los 17*, *La Jardinera*, *Gracias a la Vida*.

Crowds of people whose lives Violeta had touched gathered to see her pass and joined the procession through the gates of the *Cementerio General*–ordinary citizens of modest and high bearing, musicians, artisans, tradespeople, peasants who traveled from outlying villages.

At the gravesite, the clarion call of a trumpet silenced the wailing laments. Once Violeta Parra was buried, a human sea of grief spilled into the streets.

Don't cry once the sun has set;
your tears will blind you to the stars.

Violeta Parra

Book Notes

The Commandment (May 1960)
Much of the text derives from Patricio Manns' memoir, *Violeta Parra: Una Guitarra Indocíle.* Silvia Urbina verified the uncanny cable. The boat capsizing was reported by Fernando Alegría, brother of don Julio Alegría, who helped rescue those who couldn't swim.

Destiny's Child (1879-1929), The Circus Years (1929-32)
Violeta revealed her childhood stories in poetry. I cite *Aquí presento a mi abuelo, Mi abuelo por parte 'e maire, La cena ya se sirvió, Cayeron grandes y chicos, Por suerte, la inteligencia, El jardín de la Totito, Válgame Dios cómo están,* all from *Décimas:* an autobiography in verse. Nicanor Parra's poem, *Defensa de Violeta Parra,* depicts his sister as only a brother would see her.

In their scholarly studies (*Violeta Parra o La Expresion inefable* and *Violeta Parra: Santa de Pura Greda*), authors Marjorie Agosín and Inés Dölz-Blackburn analyze how Violeta's world-view, way of life, and poetic tradition (even her rhyme scheme) descend from Hispanic literature traceable to the Middle Ages.

In *Gracias a la Vida: Violeta Parra, Testimonio,* Bernardo Subercaseaux and Jaime Londoño published interviews with members of Violeta's extended family, including the Parra children's circus years.

Adolescence in Santiago, Ten Years of Hell, Less Protection than the Color of Milk (1932-53)
Violeta documented in *Décimas* her earliest experiences in Santiago, in *Llega el tren a la Alame'a, Mi vestido uniforme,* and *No lloro yo por llorar.* Nicanor Parra's accounts of events are told in interview material published in *Gracias a la Vida: Violeta Parra, Testimonio.* Accounts of Violeta's marriage to Luís Cereceda derive from Violeta's biographers, and from her own poetic account in *Décimas, Verso por matrimonio.*

Isabel Parra's biography of her mother, *El Libro Mayor de Violeta Parra*, provided remembrances of growing up as Violeta's daughter – how her mother raised her children, how she and Ángel performed with their mother from the time they were very young. Her traditional music derives from her *Poésie Populaire* and its subsequent Spanish edition, *Cántos Folklóricos Chilenos*.

Luís Cereceda and Violeta's sister Hilda detailed their recollections in *Gracias a la Vida*. Alfonso Alcalde's anthology, *Toda Violeta Parra*, published in Argentina during the 1980s, provided anecdotes of Violeta's development as a young musician. Throughout, Patricio Manns, in *Violeta Parra: La Guitarra Indócile*, provided the political and social landscape of the times.

In *Gracias a la Vida*, Violeta's sister, Hilda, her brother Lautaro, and folkloric musician, Héctor Pavez provided vivid descriptions of the sisters' dual career as entertainers in Santiago. Violeta's second husband, Luís Arce described their marriage and life together.

According to Carmen Oviedo, in *Mentira Todo lo Cierto: Tras la Huella de Violeta Parra*, Violeta was so steeped in traditional music that she had to prove to critics the originality of her own compositions. Similarities can be seen in many of her early songs, for example *La Jardinera* (the Gardener) Violeta's original composition, when compared to the folkloric *tonada*, *Un Hortelano de Amor*; both were published first in *Poésie Populaire*.

Song to a Little Ángel, The Songs of Elders, Canta Violeta Parra (1953-54)

Violeta's early folkloric efforts and her rise to national celebrity was recounted by family and professional associates, in depictions of her interviews with elders, as well as in a transcript published in *Gracias a la Vida*. Violeta documented folkloric songs, attitudes she encountered, and her earliest original songs in *Poésie Populaire des Andes* and *Cantos Folklóricos Chilenos*.

The practice of *velorio del angelito* was observed in the countryside well into modern times. A Chilean woman living in California recalled such a vigil in her home town of Chilcolco, in south central Chile in the 1960s. The deceased infant was dressed in white and held a bough of jasmine in his hands. Violeta later synthesized the pathos of the tragedy in one of her most perfect late songs, *Rin del Angelito*.

Violeta imbued folklore with more importance than domesticity. Everyone who knew her at this time told of her drive, and how those close to her enabled her to conduct her work. The way of life she documented would have remained obscure were it not for these accounts.

Radio professionals, Jose Maria Arguedas (in *La Mayor Libro de Violeta Parra*), Jose Maria Palacios (in an author interview, 1995), Ricardo Garcia (in correspondence shortly before his death), Sergio Larraín, Gaston Soublette, and Fernando Alegría (in author interviews) all corroborated stories of Violeta's radio days. Her ability to recreate a rustic event had the paradoxical brilliance of spontaneous performance art. Her award-worthy productions contributed to enriching her nation's understanding of its own folkloric heritage.

Rosita Clara and *Little Jasmine Flower (1954-56)*

Violeta herself recounted the circumstances surrounding the death of her infant daughter and her self-imposed exile in Europe. The narrative draws from *Décimas*, specifically *Salgo de Chile, En l'Argentina, En Río, Llego a París, Viví clandestinamente, Aquí tiene mi pañuelo, Rosita se fue a los cielos*, and *Cuando yo salí de aquí*. Violeta's own self-judgment was evident in interviews, such as one cited in *Mentira Todo lo Cierto: Tras la Huella de Violeta Parra*, conducted by the magazine *Eva*, 1955: *Vida y andanzas por el mundo de Violeta Parra*. Friends and family detail the events as they unfolded in *Gracias a la Vida: Violeta Parra, Testimonio* and *La Mayor Libro de Violeta Parra*.

Paths (1956)

Décimas poetry, specifically *Cuando regreso al país, Me fui por un senderito, A los dos años cumplidos* and *La muerte con anteojos*, provided insights to this year. *Gracias a la Vida: Violeta Parra, Testimonio* had accounts of Violeta's extensive fieldwork.

Concepción (1956-58)

In an unpublished author interview, Mireya Mora Muñoz, a student in Violeta's class, corroborated the story of Carmen-Luisa's role in the theatre workshop. She remembered Violeta's ability to intimidate those who challenged her and her sweetness when nurturing students who responded to a gentler approach. She also recalled hearing Violeta play instrumental compositions on guitar in a classical style in the privacy of her room.

Eventually, Violeta won over Panchita, who taught her a nineteenth-century courtship dance, *la cardita*. The account of *cueca* danced in the brothels derives from Pablo de Rokha (pseudonym of Carlos Díaz Loyola), *Genio del Pueblo*; Fernando Alegría corroborated the story. The museum languished for lack of funds; the collection was eventually stored in the *Museo Hualpén*. Violeta wrote of Concepción in *Décimas*, *Engaños en Concepción*, *Con mi litigio de amor*, and *Veintiuno son los dolores*.

By the Whim of the Wind (1958-60)

RCA Victor recorded Violeta's *Casamiento de Negros* as an instrumental tune, "The Crazy Melody," by the Les Baxter orchestra, which was known for bringing exotic music to 1950s U.S. audiences. Under the terms of the contract, Violeta was paid for the song's copyright and reliquished it.

Joan Jara's biography, *Victor Jara: An Unfinished Song*, explains that Victor convinced the members of his performing group, Cuncumén, to give up typical costuming of poncho and spurs in the style of the *patrón* and instead, dress as peasants, wearing the sandals he knew from childhood. This had enormous impact; in polite society, to make poverty visible was considered an affront. Violeta's unique training techniques were recalled in Osvaldo Rodriguez Musso's article, *"Violeta, influencia y fuerza moral,"* in *Araucaria de Chile*, no. 38, (a cultural journal published in Spain during the Pinochet years); her role writing music for documentaries, is discussed in *Araucaria* no.37.

The *milonga* is a traditional Argentine ballad rhythm. Atahualpa Hupanqui (pseudonym of Héctor Roberto Chavero) was an Argentine folkloric musician,who like Violeta herself, is much revered among Latin American musicians. *Quenas*, *sampoya*, *charango*, and other traditional instruments are integral to contemporary Latin American folkloric music, but it was Violeta Parra who first brought them out of obscurity.

Outbursts (1960)

Pablo Neruda, Nicanor Parra and Pablo de Rokha wrote elegaic introductions to *Décimas*. They may be found online at the *Fundación Violeta Parra*. Allen

Ginsberg described his meeting Violeta in an unpublished diary, found in Allen Ginsberg Papers, archived at Stanford University. The May 1960 earthquakes were reported widely by the press.

What Things Life Holds, Zambitay! (1960-61)

Carmen Oviedo cites the review published in *El Diario Ilustrado*, Santiago, 7 Dec.1960. How Gilbert Favre met Violeta Parra derives both from *El Libro Mayor de Violeta Parra* and author's extensive interviews with him in August 1994.

Zambitay combines the name of an Argentine dance rhythm (*zamba*) and a suffix common to Quechua and Aymara (*itay*), which connotes endearment.

Absent Dove (1961-62)

Carmen Luisa recalls her reluctant trip to Paris, in *Gracias a la Vida*; other family members and friends recalled time spent with Violeta in Europe. Patricio Manns anthologized Violeta's most emotive or outspoken songs (such as *Paloma Ausente* and *Miren cómo Sonríen los Presidentes*) in *Violeta Parra: la Guitarra Indócile*. A page from Violeta's journal, published in *El Libro Mayor de Violeta Parra*, shows a drawing of her own coffin, with flowers, votive candle, her dog sniffing.

Gilbert (1961-62)

Gilbert Favre recounted these events in interviews with the author.

Ayúdame Valentina (1962-63)

Violeta's letters to Gilbert, published in *El Libro Mayor de Violeta Parra*, paint a visceral portrait of her passion for him and the degree his love grounded her. Yet Gilbert recalled too Violeta's increased propensity for violence. These extremes increasingly characterized their relationship.

During her European stay Violeta Parra composed *Composiciones para Guitarra*, a classical composition for guitar in sixteen movements. The work, though recorded, has never been edited or released. Carmen Oviedo, in *Mentira Todo lo Cierto: Tras la Huella de Violeta Parra*, tells of Violeta's friendship with Raymonde Gampert, the first of several women who promoted her in Europe. In correspondence with José María Palacios dated June 4, 1963, Geneva, Violeta refers to *Trés Marías*, the three stars of Orion's belt, visible in the Chilean sky.

Violeta refers to *Poésie Populaire des Andes*, her only book published during her lifetime. *Ayúdame Valentina* was published in *Violeta Parra: la Guitarra Indócile.*

The Louvre (1964)
Much of the information in this chapter was furnished by personnel of the Louvre archives. They provided me with copies of letters, the exhibition catalog, and published reviews. Recollections of family members and friends were published in each Violeta Parra biography.
Inés Dölz-Blackburn and Marjorie Agosín's book, *Violeta Parra: La Expresion Inefable*, provided a wealth of information about Violeta's visual aesthetics.

To Gather a Bouquet (1964)
Enrique Bello recalled Violeta's presence at her show, and Carmen Luisa described Violeta's acquaintance with the Baroness de Rothschild, in *Gracias a la Vida*. Gilbert Favre concurred. Violeta's excerpted letters to Gilbert were published in *El Mayor Libro de Violeta Parra*. Excerpt from *En una barca de amores*, derived from *Violeta Parra: La Guitarra Indócile*. The excerpted *Violeta y su guitarra* derived from Pablo de Rokha's introduction to *Décimas*.
Recollections of Adela Gallo came from an article by Irene Dominguez and Cristian Vila Riquelme published in *Araucaria de Chile*, as well as from remarks by Gilbert Favre.

Santiago Interlude (September 1964)
Depiction of Violeta's brief stay in Santiago and her letters to Gilbert derive from *El Mayor Libro de Violeta Parra*, with factual background from Fernando Alegría's biography, *Allende: A Novel*, Thomas Skidmore and Peter Smith's *Modern Latin America*, and German Marín's, *Una Historia Fantastica y Calculada*. Lyrics of Violeta's *La Carta* were translated from *Violeta Parra: La Guitarra Indócile*.

Soul Food (1964)
Gilbert elaborated on their episodic relationship in interviews, and provided the videotape portrait of Violeta. Violeta's letters to Gilbert (which he meant to have published in this book) were abridged from *El Libro Mayor de Violeta Parra*. Lyrics of *La Jardinera*, were published in the book, *Volver a los 17*.

Details of Violeta's friendship with Marie-Magdeleine Brumagne is drawn from correspondence with her as well as from her memoir, *Qui se souvient de sa vie?*

La Peña de los Parra (1965-66)

The founding of *La Peña de los Parra* as a distinctly Chilean response to international pop music trends is told by anecdote in *El Libro Mayor de Violeta Parra*, *Gracias a la Vida*, *Violeta Parra: La Guitarra Indócile*, and *Victor Jara: An Unfinished Song*, as well as in numerous articles. Personal accounts of these formative years were related by Patricio Manns in author interview, 1980. His biography of Violeta Parra assembles the most politically focused anthology of her songs, including *Me gustan los estudiantes* and *Mazurquica Modérnica*. Information about Victor Jara derives from Joan Jara's biography, *Victor Jara: An Unfinished Song*, as well as numerous contemporary publications. Reportage of Violeta's set was translated from *El Siglo*, Sunday 14 November 1965.

The Tent of La Reina (1966)

How Violeta came to have the tent and how it affected her was told principally in *Mentira Todo lo Cierto: Tras la Huella de Violeta Parra, Gracias a la Vida*, and remarks by Gilbert Favre. Her vision was detailed in *El Mayor Libro de Violeta Parra* and in an interview with R. Largo Farias, 1966, published in *Gracias a la Vida*. Dianna Nani Venegas described the atmosphere in Violeta's tent in an author interview. Gilbert Favre described the end of his relationship with Violeta in author interviews. Violeta's song, *El Sacristán* appears in *Volver a los 17*.

Run-Run se Fue (1966)

Gilbert Favre recounted tales of his trip to Bolivia, establishment of *Peña Naira*, and Violeta's visit in author interviews. Violeta's letter to Gilbert excerpted from *El Mayor Libro de Violeta Parra*. Impressions by 6those close to Violeta after her return from Bolivia were published in *Gracias a la Vida*. *Violeta Parra: Santa de Pura Greda* explores the themes of *Décimas* concerning her worldview and ideas that synthesized in her last songs. Lyric excerpts are from Violeta's songs, *Run-Run se fue pa'l Norte*, *Lo Que Más Quiero*, *Qué tanto será*, and *Corazon maldito*.

Tempest (1966)

    Gracias a la Vida provided accounts by those who aided Violeta during the rain storm, her mentoring of Chagual and Huenchulyan, and her personal shame over Gilbert's abandonment. The letter Violeta wrote to Marie-Magdeleine Brumagne was published in Brumagne's memoir, *Qui se souvient de sa vie?* Lyric excerpts are from *Rin del Angelito, Cantores que reflexionan,* and *Lo Que Más Quiero.*

Gracias a la Vida (1966-67)

    Accounts of Violeta's northern Chile concert tour and Magallanes trip derives from Patricio Manns, *Violeta Parra: La Guitarra Indócile.* Violeta's brother Lautaro, interviewed in *Gracias a la Vida,* described Violeta's expressions of gratitude on her last trip. Marjorie Agosín, in *Violeta Parra: Santa de Pura Greda*, analyzes the relationship between her songs and their thematic meanings about rustic life, including her testament, *Gracias a la Vida.* Carmen Oviedo, in *Mentira Todo lo Cierto: Tras la Huella de Violeta Parra,* elaborated on Violeta's increasing fatalism and loneliness. Lyric excerpts are from *Gracias a la Vida* and *Hace falta un Guerrillero.*

One Sunday in Heaven (February, 1967)

    An account of Violeta's demise drew from *Toda Violeta Parra,* by Alfonso Alcalde, and and from testimony of Carmen Luisa, Alberto Zapicán, Héctor Pavez, and Violeta's siblings, Hilda, Nicanor, and Lautaro, published in *Gracias a la Vida.* News accounts included *El Siglo,* 7 February, 1967 and *La Nación,* 8 February, 1967. Lyric excerpts are from *Volver a los 17, De cuerpo entero,* and *Maldito del Alto Cielo.* Violeta's last letter was excerpted from *El Mayor Libro de Violeta Parra.*

Sources

Books

Marjorie Agosín, ed. *A Dream of Light and Shadow: Portraits of Latin American Women Writers* (Albuquerque, New Mexico: University of New Mexico Press, 1995).

Marjorie Agosín, ed. *These Are Not Sweet Girls: Poetry by Latin American Women* (Fredonia, New York: White Pine Press, 1994).

Marjorie Agosín and Ines Dölz Blackburn, *Violeta Parra: Santa de Pura Greda, un Estudio de su Obra Poetica*, (Santiago de Chile: Editorial Planeta, Biblioteca del Sur, 1988).

Alfonso Alcalde, *Toda Violeta Parra*, (Buenos Aires, Argentina: Ediciones de la Flor, 1985).

Fernando Alegría, *Allende: A Novel*; Frank Janney, transl. (Stanford, CA: Stanford University Press, 1993).

Fernando Alegría, "Violeta Parra," a chapter in *Retratos contemporáneos*. (New York: Harcourt Brace and Jovanovich, 1979).

Carol Andreas, *Nothing Is As It Should Be: A North American Woman in Chile*, (Cambridge, MA: Schenkman Publishing Co., Inc., 1976).

Anonymous, *Arpilleras*, (Santiago, Chile: likely, *El Comité Pro Paz*, 1982).

Fernando Barraza, *La Nueva Canción Chilena*, (Santiago, Chile: *Editora Nacional Quimantú Ltda.*, 1972).

Bernard Bessière, *La Nouvelle Chanson Chilienne en Exil*, (Toulouse, France: Editions d'Aujourd'hui, Thèses et Recherches, 1980) vol. 2, songs.

Ines Dolz Blackburn, *Antologia Crítica de la Poesia Tradicional Chilena*, (Ciudad de Guatemala, Guatemala: Instituto Panamericano de Geografia e historia, organismo especializado de la OEA, 1979).

Inés Dölz-Blackburn and Marjorie Agosín, *Violeta Parra: La Expression Inefable* (Santiago, Chile: Editorial Planeta Chilena S. A., 1992).

Marie-Magdeleine Brumagne, *Qui se souvient de sa vie?*, (Lausanne, Switzerland: Editions L'Age d'Homme, 1992).

Renato Cárdenas A., ed., *25 Años Andanzas ... Mariguanzas y Jodiendas*, (Castro, Chile: Centro Cultural y Artístico Conjunto Folklórico Magisterio de Castro, 1993).

John A. Crow, *The Epic of Latin America*, (Berkeley, CA: University of California Press, 1980).

Charles Darwin, *The Voyage of the Beagle*, (New York: PF Collier and son, 1909).

Howell Davies, ed. *The South American Handbook*, (Bath, England: Trade and Travel Publications Ltd., 1972).

Ariel Dorfman, *Widows*, (New York: Pantheon, 1983).

Agustín Edwards, *My Native Land: Panorama, Reminiscences, Writers and Folklore*, (London, England: Ernest Benn Ltd., 1928).

Pedro Bravo Elizondo, *Cultura y Teatro Obreros en Chile 1900-1930*, (Madrid, Spain: Ediciones Michay, S.A., 1986).

Manfred Engelbert, *Violeta Parra: Lieder aus Chile*, (Frankfurt, Germany: Verlag Klaus Dieter Vervuert, 1978).

Clarissa Pinkola Estés, *Women Who Run With the Wolves: Myths and Stories of the Wild Woman Archetype*, (New York: Ballantine Books, 1995).

John Felstiner, *Translating Neruda: The Way to Macchu Picchu*, (Stanford, CA: Stanford University Press, 1980).

Janet Flanner, *Paris Journal*, (New York: New Yorker Magazine, Inc., 1971).

Raymonde Gampert, *A la decouverte du theatre. Le petit creve-coeur.* (Geneva, Switzerland, 1979).

Marie-Lise Gazarian Gautier, *Gabriela Mistral: La Maestra de Elqui*, Alberto R. Cellario, transl., (Buenos Aires, Argentina: Editorial Crespillo, 1973).

Inéz Dölz Henry, *Los Romances Tradicionales Chilenos: Temática y técnica*, (Santiago, Chile: Editorial Nascimiento, 1976).

Luís Miguel Hernández Hernández, *El Vendedor de Cochayuyos* (Concepción, Chile: Universidad del Bío-Bío, 1990).

Joan Turner Jara, *Victor Jara: An Unfinished Song.* (NY: Ticknor and Fields, 1983).

Dale L. Johnson, *The Chilean Road to Socialism*, (Garden City, NY: Anchor Press/Doubleday, 1973).

Enrique Kirberg, *Los Nuevos Profesionales: Educación universitaria de trabajadores, Chile: UTE, 1968-1973*, (Guadalajara, Mexico: Universidad de Guadalajara, 1981).

Meri Franco-Lao, *Basta! Chants de Témoignage et de Révolte de L'Amérique Latine*, Gonzalo Estrada, transl., (Paris, France: François Maspero, 1967).

Suzanne Jill Levine, *The Subversive Scribe: Translating Latin American Fiction*, (Sain Paul, MN: Graywolf Press, 1991).

Brian Loveman, *Chile: The Legacy of Hispanic Capitalism*, (New York: Oxford University Press, 1979).

Patricio Manns, *Violeta Parra: La Guitarra Indócile*, (Barcelona, Spain: Ediciones Júcar, 1977). *Violeta Parra: la Guitare Indocile*, (Paris, France: Les Editions du Cerf, 1977).

German Marín, *Una Historia Fantastica y Calculada*, (Mexico, D.F.: Siglo XXI Editores, S.A., 1976).

Earl Chapin May, *2000 Miles through Chile*, (New York and London: The Century Co., 1924).

Gabriela Mistral, *Selected Poems of Gabriela Mistral*, Doris Dana, transl. and ed. (Baltimore, MD: The Johns Hopkins Press).

P. Ernesto Wilhelm de Moesbach, *Voz de Arauco: Explicacion de los Nombres Indígenas de Chile*, (Chile: Imprenta San Francisco, Padre Las Casas, 1976).

Humberto Baroni Muñoz, *Latigos de Luz: Poemas*, (San Carlos, Chile: Grupo Literario Toquihua, 1986).

Pablo Neruda, *Memoirs: Confieso Que He Vivido*, Hardie St. Martin, transl. (London and New York: Penguin Books, 1978).

Carmen Oviedo, *Mentira Todo lo Cierto: Tras la Huella de Violeta Parra*, (Santiago de Chile: Editorial Universitaria, 1990).

Luís Hernandez Parker, *Catástrofe en el Paraíso: Reportaje al Sur de Chile*, (Santiago, Chile: Editorial del Pacífico, S.A., 1960).

Isabel Parra, *El Libro Mayor de Violeta Parra*, (Madrid, Spain: Ediciones Michay, S.A., Libros del Meridion, 1985).

Nicanor Parra, *Antipoems: New and Selected*, David Unger, ed. (New York: New Directions, 1985).

Nicanor Parra, *Obra Gruesa: Texto Completo*, (Santiago, Chile: Editorial Andres Bello, 1983).

Violeta Parra, *Cantos Folklóricos Chilenos*. Musical transcriptions by Luís Gastón Soublette, photography by Sergio Larraín and Sergio Bravo, (Santiago de Chile: Editorial Nascimento, 1979).

Violeta Parra, *Décimas*, (Barcelona, Spain: Editorial Pomaire S.A., 1976). *Décimas: Autobiografía en verso* (Santiago de Chile: Editorial Sudamericana, 1988).

Violeta Parra, *Poésie Populaire des Andes*, Fanchita Gonzalez-Batlle, transl., (Paris, France: François Maspero, 1965).

Violeta Parra, *Violeta del Pueblo*, Javier Martínez Reverte, ed. (Madrid, Spain: Visor, 1976).

Violeta Parra, *Volver a los 17*, Juan Andres Piña, ed. (Santiago de Chile: Editorial Los Andes, 1995). Published earlier as *21 Son los Dolores: Antología Amorosa*. (Santiago, Chile: Ediciones Aconcagua, 1976 and 1977).

Violeta Parra. (Paris, France: N. F. C, 1980).

Violeta Parra: Composiciones para Guitarra; Rodolfo Norambuena, Rodrigo Torres, Mauricio Valdebenito, eds., (Santiago: Fundación Violeta Parra, 1993).

Mariano Picón-Salas, *A Cultural History of Spanish America: from Conquest to Independence*, Irving A. Leonard, transl., (Berkeley, CA: University of California Press, 1962).

Pablo de Rokha, *Pablo de Rokha: Nueva Antología*, Naín Nómez, ed. (Santiago, Chile: Editorial Sinfronteras, 1987).

Ernesto Saul, *Pintura Social en Chile*, (Santiago, Chile: Empresa Editora Nacional Quimantu Ltda, 1972).

Yolando Pino-Saavedra, *Folktales of Chile*, (London, England: Routledge and Kegan Paul, Ltd. and Chicago, IL: The University of Chicago Press, 1968).

Thomas Skidmore and Peter Smith, *Modern Latin America*, (New York: Oxford University Press, 1984).

Robinson Rojas Sandford, *The Murder of Allende and the End of the Chilean Way to Socialism*, Andrée Conrad, transl., (New York: Harper and Row, Publishers, 1976).

Bernardo Subercaseaux and Jaime Londoño, *Gracias a la Vida: Violeta Parra, Testimonio*, (Buenos Aires: Editorial Galerna, 1976).

Bernardo Subercaseaux, Patricia Stambuk, and Jaime Londoño, *Gracias a la Vida: Violeta Parra, Testimonio*, (Chile: Editorial Granizo-CENECA, 1982).

Alain Touraine, *Vida y Muerte del Chile Popular*, (Mexico, Spain, Argentina: Siglo Veintiuno Editores, 1974).

Turismo y Comunicaciones S.A., ed. *Chile Confin del Mundo Guia de Turismo*, (Santiago, Chile: Editorial Lord Cochrane S.A., 1992).

Foreign Area Studies, *Chile: A Country Study*, Andrea T. Merrill, ed. (Washington D.C.: The American University, 1982)

Samuel Claro Valdés, *Oyendo a Chile*, (Santiago, Chile: Editorial Andres Bello, 1979).

Periodicals and Papers

Marjorie Agosín, "*Violeta Parra: Cantos Folkloricios Chilenos*," review in *Literatura Chilena: creación y crítica*, Los Ángeles, CA: Ediciones de la Frontera, no. 15, 1981.

Marjorie Agosín, "Bibliography of Violeta Parra," in Inter-American Review of Bibliography, Washington, DC, vol. 33, 1982.

Isabel Allende, "*El compromiso del escritor latinoamericano*," in *Araucaria de Chile*, Madrid, Spain: Ediciones Michay, vol. 25, 1984.

Aquí Está, #149, January 20, 1966, pp.6-7.

Gustavo Becerra, "*Música chilena e identidad cultural*," in *Araucaria de Chile*, Madrid, Spain: Ediciones Michay, vol. 2, 1978.

Klaus Muller-Bergh, "*Fulgor y Muerte de Violeta Parra*," in Inter-American Review of Bibliography, Washington, DC, vol. 28, 1978.

Soledad Bianchi, "*La política cultural oficialista y el movimiento artístico*," in *Araucaria de Chile*, Madrid, Spain: Ediciones Michay, vol. 17, 1982.

Soledad Bianchi and Luís Bocaz, "*Discusión sobre la música chilena*," in *Araucaria de Chile*, Madrid, Spain: Ediciones Michay, vol. 2, 1978.

Inés Dölz-Blackburn, "*Introducción a la poesía amorosa de Violeta Parra: recolección, reelaboración, y creación*," in *Literatura Chilena: creación y crítica*, Los Ángeles, CA: Ediciones de la Frontera, no. 47/50, edición anual, 1989.

Inés Dölz-Blackburn, "Violeta Parra: Singer of Life," in *A Dream of Light and Shadow: Portraits of Latin American Women Writers*, Marjorie Agosín, ed. (Albuquerque, New Mexico: University of New Mexico Press, 1995).

Marie-Magdeleine Brumagne. Review published in the Arts and Letters section of the newspaper, Tribune, Lausanne, Switzerland. Feb. 5, 1965.

Yvonne Brunhammer, catalog of Violeta Parra exhibition. Musée des Arts Décoratifs, Palais du Louvre, Pavillon de Marsan, 8 avril – 11 mai 1964.

Centro de Indagación y Expresión Cultural y Artística (CENECA), "*La Canción Popular Chilena.*" Seminar proceedings, Santiago, Chile, October 1979.

Eduardo Contreras, *Violeta Parra, el Origen del Canto*. México City: *Cuadernos Casa de Chile*, 27:7, n.d.

Irene Dominguez and Cristian Vila Riquelme, "*Despedida a Adela Gallo*," in *Araucaria de Chile*, Madrid, Spain: Ediciones Michay, no. 26, 1984.

Jorge Edwards, "*Vida y andanzas por el mundo de Violeta Parra*," in Eva, Santiago, 1955.

Pedro Bravo Elizondo, "*El teatro obrero en Chile: Algunos antecedentes*," in *Araucaria de Chile*, Madrid, Spain: Ediciones Michay, no. 17, 1982.

Juan Armando Epple, "*Notas sobre la cueca larga de Violeta Parra*," in *Araucaria de Chile*, Madrid, Spain: Ediciones Michay, no. 5, 1979.

Juan Armando Epple, "*Cronología historica y literaria de Chile*," in *Araucaria de Chile*, Madrid, Spain: Ediciones Michay, no. 19, 1982.

Stefano Gavagnin, "*Sobre la 'orquesta' en la nueva cancion*," in *Literatura Chilena: creación y crítica*, Los Ángeles, CA: Ediciones de la Frontera, no. 35, 1986.

Allen Ginsberg, Allen Ginsberg Papers, Stanford University, box 10, page 171. March 6, 1960.

P.-M. Grand, *Le Monde*, 17 April 1964.

J. H., "*Violeta Parra, el arte contra el sistema*," in *Cine Cubano*, Havana, Cuba, 1972.

Inter-Church Committee on Human Rights in Latin America, "Mapuches: People of the Land," Report on a fact-finding mission to Chile, November 1979.

Joan Jara, "*Los manos de Victor Jara*," in *Araucaria de Chile*, Madrid, Spain: Ediciones Michay, vol. 2, 1978.

Victor Jara, in *El caiman barbudo*. La Habana, Cuba, no. 54, March 1972.

Victor Jara, *Victor Jara: su pensamiento, sus canciones*. La Habana, Cuba: *Musica de Casa de las Americas*, bulletin no. 40, n.d.

Victor Jara, in *Hemos dicho: Basta!* Barcelona, Spain: Hogar del Libro, S.A., 1977.

Naomi Lindstrom, "*Construccion folklorica y desconstruccion individiual en un texto de Violeta Parra,*" in *Literatura Chilena: creación y crítica,* Los Ángeles, CA: Ediciones de la Frontera, no. 33/34, 1985.

Patricio Manns, "*Los problemas del texto en la Nueva Canción,*" in Araucaria de Chile, Madrid, Spain: Ediciones Michay, vol. 30, 1985.

Régine Mellac, "Isabel et Ángel Parra: *Un répertoire, reflet de vies et d'histoire,*" in Paroles et Musique, no.2, 1981.

José Morales, "*El canto nuevo,*" in *Araucaria de Chile,* Madrid, Spain: *Ediciones Michay,* vol. 2, 1978.

Leonidas Morales, "*Figuras literarias, rupturas culturales: modernidad e identidades culturales tradicionales,*" Santiago, Chile: Pehuén Editores, 1993.

Albrecht Moreno, "*Violeta Parra and La Nueva Canción Chilena,*" in Studies in Latin American Popular Culture, New Mexico State University, Las Cruces, vol. 5, 1986.

Nancy Morris, "*Canto porque es necesario cantar:* New song in Chile 1973-83," University of New Mexico, 1984.

Jacqueline Mouesca, "*Variaciones sobre el cine,*" interview of "*Sergio Bravo: pionero del cine documental chileno,*" in *Araucaria de Chile,* Madrid, Spain no. 37, 1987.

Nain Nomez, "*Pablo de Rokha: El tigre que no era de papel,*" in *Literatura Chilena en el Exilio,* Los Ángeles, CA: Ediciones de la Frontera, no. 11, 1979.

Osvaldo Rodriguez Musso, "*Violeta, influencia y fuerza moral,*" in *Araucaria de Chile,* Madrid, Spain: Ediciones Michay, no. 38, 1987.

Ángel Parra, "*Preguntas por Violeta Parra,*" in *Mundo: Problemas y confrontaciones de política, cultura, filosofía, literatura,* Mexico City, vol. 1, no. 3, 1987.

Violeta Parra, unpublished letter to José María Palacios dated June 4, 1963, Geneva.

Anny Rivera et al., "*El publico del canto popular.*" Santiago, Chile: CENECA, 1980.

Rodrigo Torres, "*Perfil de la creación musical en la Nueva Canción Chilena desde sus orígenes hasta 1973,*" Santiago, Chile: CENECA, 1980.

Rodrigo Torres, "*La urbanizacion de la canción folklórica,*" in *Literatura Chilena: creación y crítica,* Los Ángeles, CA: Ediciones de la Frontera, no. 35, 1986.

Magdalena Vicuña, *Violeta Parra, hermana mayor de los cantores populares,* Revista Musical Chilena, año 12, no. 60, 1958.

Alberto Zapicán and others, *El Mercurio, Revista del Domingo,* no. 828, 31 Octubre 1982.

Selected Discography and Film

Violeta and Hilda Parra as "*Las Hermanas Parra,*" in single recordings by produced by RCA Victor, Santiago, 1949-52.

Violeta Parra, *Qué pena siente el alma* and *Casamiento de negros* (single). Santiago, Chile: Odeón, 1953.

Violeta Parra, *Cantos de Chile*. Paris, France: Le Chant du Monde, 1956.

Violeta and Isabel Parra, *Cuecas* (single). Santiago, Sello Demon, 1965.

Violeta Parra and Gilbert Favre, *El Tocador Afuerino*. Santiago, Chile: Odeón, 1965.

Violeta Parra acompañada de guitarra. Series "*El folklore de Chile*," vols. 1,2, Santiago, Chile: Odeón, 1956.

La cueca presentada por Violeta Parra. Series "*El folklore de Chile*," vol. 3, Santiago, Chile: Odeón, 1957.

La tonada presentada por Violeta Parra. Series "*El folklore de Chile*," vol. 4, Santiago, Chile: Odeón, 1957.

Toda Violeta Parra. Series "*El folklore de Chile*," vol. 5, Santiago, Chile: Odeón, 1957.

Violeta Parra, (long-play album produced, then suppressed and not distributed; contained the first recording of *Porque los pobres no tienen*), Buenos Aires, Chile: Odeón, 1961.

Violeta Parra and her family, *Los Parra de Chile*. Berlin, R.D.A.: *sello Amiga*, 1962.

Recordando a Chile: Canciones de Violeta Parra. Santiago, Chile: Odeón, 1965.

Violeta Parra: Bordadora Chilena, documentary film by Radio-Television Suisse Romande, 1965.

Violeta Parra and other artists, *La Carpa de La Reina*. Santiago, Chile: Odeón, 1966.

Violeta Parra accompanied by Ángel and Isabel Parra and Alberto Zapicán, *Las Últimas Composiciones de Violeta Parra*. Santiago, Chile: RCA Victor, 1966.

Posthumous Recordings

Canciones de Violeta Parra. Series "Music of this America," Havana, Cuba: Casa de las Américas, 1971.

Violeta Parra, *Canciones Reencontradas en Paris*. Santiago, Chile: Dicap, 1971 and Dortmund, Germany, 1975.

Un río de sangre, Le Chili de Violeta Parra. Paris, France: Arion, 1974.

Violeta Parra, *Presente / Ausente*. Paris, France: Le Chant du Monde, 1975.

Violeta Parra, *Décimas*. Santiago, Chile: *Alerce*, 1976

Violeta Parra, *Santiago, penando estás*. Dortmund: Plane, 198_.

Violeta Parra, *Cantos de Chile*. Mexico: Discos NCL, 198_.

Violeta Parra, *La Magia de Violeta Parra*. [s.l.]: EMI, 1991, 2003.

Violeta Parra, *Que Cante Violeta Parra*. Chile: EMI, 1992.

Violeta Parra, *El Hombre con su Razón*. Chile: Alerce, 1992

Violeta Parra, *Obras de Violeta Parra*. Chile: Columbia, 1993.

Violeta Parra, *Décimas y Centésimas*, Chile: *Alerce*, 1993, 2003.

Violeta Parra, *Las Últimas Composiciones*. (CD) ANS, 1993, 2003.

Violeta Parra, *El Folklore y la Pasión*. (CD) *Chile*: EMI Odeon Chilena, 1994, 2005.

Violeta Parra, *En Ginebra*, Chile: Warner Music Chile, 1999.

Violeta Parra, *Décimas y Centésimas*, Chile: *Alerce*, 1999.

Violeta Parra, *Composiciones para Guitarra*, Chile: Warner Music Chile, 1999, 2003.

Violeta Parra, *Serie de Oro: Grandes Exitos*, EMI Europe Generic, 2004.

Violeta Parra, *Haciendo Historia: La Jardinera y su Canto*. (CD) Chile: EMI Odeon Chilena, 2005.

Selected Covers by other Artists

Isabel Parra and Inti-Illimani, *Canto para una Semilla: Décimas Autobiográficas de Violeta Parra*. Music by Luís
  Advis. Santiago, Chile: Dicap, 1972 and Rome, Italy: Vedette, 1978.

Joan Baez, Here's to Life, A & M Records, Inc., 1974.

Mercedes Sosa, *Homenaje a Violeta Parra*. Polygram; Buenos Aires, Argentina, 1991.

Placido Domingo, *De Mi Alma Latina*, EMI, 1994.

Lichi Fuentes, *Quien Soy — Who I am*, Bisu Records, 2003.

Digital Availability

The website of the *Fundacion Violeta Parra*, <http://www.violetaparra.cl/>

Author's website, <http://karenkerschen.com> has links to many Violeta Parra resources.

Glossary

abuelita/abuelito — A term of endearment toward the elderly (little grand-mother/grandfather).

aguardiente — An alcoholic beverage distilled in Chile from wine.

Altiplano — The high Andean plateau, partly in Northern Chile.

arpillera — Pictorial tapestry created with wool thread on canvas or jute. Violeta's *arpilleras* were sewn flat, in the manner of Chiloé, rather than the style of Isla Negra, which features three-dimensional doll figures.

anticucho — Shish-kebab skewered with meat, sausage, rinds, bread, heart.

bandurria — A stringed instrument smaller than a guitar, pear-shaped, and strung with twelve strings.

Barrio Alto — The upscale neighborhoods of Santiago, at a higher eleva-tion than downtown and smog.

bolero — A Cuban dance popular throughout Latin America in the 1940s; typically its lyrics were exaggeratedly sentimental. Violeta used the term *bolero* to insult phony folkloric music

bombo — A large barrel-shaped drum capable of being heard for great distances.

caballero — Horseman in spurs and poncho, a sentimental figure of an idealized *campo*.

campo — The rural countryside. Peasants of the *campo* are *campesinos* and *campesinas*, typically living on the *hacienda* (landed estate) of the *patrón* (landlord).

canto a lo divino — Songs of God and Heaven. These are sung at *velorios del angelitos* (wakes held to mourn the death of an infant or young child) and other solemn gatherings. The night of a *velorio* is passed by singing the following sequence of themes: First, *por saludo*, to greet the parents and gathered friends. From midnight to 3:00 a.m., *por padecimiento*, to acknowledge the suffering of grief through songs of the sufferings of Christ. From 3:00 a.m. until dawn, *por sabiduría*, taking comfort from the wisdom of the Scriptures. Finally, before leaving for the cemetery, *por despedida*, songs symbolizing the departure and letting go of the deceased.

canto a lo humano — Songs of Humanity and Earth. These songs include improvisational ballads, serenades, songs of personal foible, fantasy, sacrilege, and humor.

canto a lo pueta — According to Violeta, poetic song is inspired by two basic themes — the divine and the human.

cazuela — Meat and corn stew.

charango — The *Altiplano* version is a small guitar-like instrument whose sound-box is traditionally made from the shell of an armadillo (or carved from wood into that form), strung with five pairs of metal strings. In southern Chile a primitive *charrango* (variant spelling) might consist of a flat board and two bottles (for resonance), over which wires are strung.

chicha — Corn liquor.

Chiloé — The largest island of Chile's southwest archipelago. Residents and objects of Chiloé are referred to as *chilote*.

copihue — *A* red bellflower that grows in the Chilean south; Chile's national flower.

cordillera — A mountain ridge of the Andes.

corrido —A Mexican ballad form.

cueca — The national dance of Chile, performed to a *one-two-pause one-two-pause* rhythm. Men and women dance apart facing each other, each waving a handkerchief, their steps strictly sequenced in a series of steps and turns. The overall impression is said to resemble a rooster and hen in courtship; he advancing, she, brushing him away until the end.

curandera — *A* healer, one who ministers to the sick with herbs; often the midwife.

décima — A poetic form with verses of ten eight-syllable lines.

empanada — A savory pasty of meat, onions, olive, raisin, and egg.

escudo — Unit of Chilean currency; the national seal.

esquinazo — A traditional serenade.

guagua — An infant or baby who is still breastfeeding.

guitarrón — A bass guitar with a large sound box strung with twenty five strings grouped in fives, plus four supplementary strings called *diablitos* (little devils).

gloriado (gloria'o) — Fruited wine served at a wake.

gringo — In Chile, a foreigner whose native language is not Spanish.

humitas — Fried cornbread.

kultrún — A consecrated drum of the indigenous Mapuche, shaped as bowl and stretched and lashed with leather or horse skin. Because it is believed to possess its own magic, the *kultrún*'s construction and use are prescribed by ceremony.

La Peña (de los Parra) — The cultural center of Ángel Parra, Isabel Parra, Victor Jara, Rolando Alarcón, and Patricio Manns, on Carmen street in downtown Santiago, which became the cradle of *La Nueva Canción Chilena*.

La Carpa (de La Reina) — Violeta Parra's encampment in La Reina, which she envisioned as a living museum of authentic folkloric culture.

Mapuche — "People of the Land," the indigenous people who live in southern Chile; also called Araucanian.

maté — Tea brewed from *yerba maté* leaves. *Mate con malicia* is *mate* spiked with *pisco* or *aguardiente*.

mistela — A sweet wine beverage made with *aguardiente*, water, sugar, and cinnamon.

mote con huesillos — A summer drink/dessert of sundried peach or nectarine and juice with limed corn or husked wheat.

muletillas — Vocal taunts, syllables, and exclamations shouted to animate a *cueca* or other rousing song.

neofolklore — A sentimentalized version of folkloric music and dance, typically idealizing the *campesino* and his *huasa* (country girl) sweetheart.

Nueva Canción Chilena — The "New Chilean Song" that emerged as a folk music of protest and change in the mid-1960s. Violeta Parra was a seminal figure in the development of this style.

parra — Grape vine.

pastel de choclo – A shepherd's pie made with ground corn and beef.

patria — Nationhood.

pebre (salsa) – A salad or condiment of onions, peppers, and tomato.

peña — A nightclub or cultural center; the term derives from *las peñas de toreros*, the bars where bullfighters congregate in Spain.

pituco — An educated snob.

popular — In Spanish, connotes the idea "of the people."

quena — A wooden flute, played vertically, typical of Andean music.

rabel — Pastoral instrument of Arabic origin, resembling a three-stringed violin and bowed vertically.

ramada — A temporary shelter built for *fiestas*, as at the end of a harvest. Typically decorated with boughs of greenery and strings of flags.

rancho, ranchito — The modest house of the *campesino*.

sirilla — A ballad form native to Chiloé. Violeta composed *Volver a los 17* in this style.

sopaipillas — A fried dough confection, served with sugar syrup.

tonada — A traditional ballad-style song about passion, sung by a woman in a minor key.

velorio del angelito — A funeral wake held for an infant or child younger than five years. In Violeta's time, the all-night gathering was marked by singing a sequence of songs, termed *cantos a lo divino*.

zampoña (sampoya) — A wind instrument of the *Altiplano* consisting of ten to twelve bamboo canes of graduated length, lashed to two supporting canes, and played vertically by blowing across and into the top of the hollow reeds.

Acknowledgments

This book calls forth ghosts– *¡El pueblo unido jamás sera vencido!* – workers, students, *campesinos* of whom Violeta Parra once sang, whose fates dangled by the whim of the wind. The people whose spirits manifest in the echo of automatic weapons fire. How many died in the Chilean *coup d'etat* of September 11, 1973 or suffered heartbreak in its aftermath? I testify to their sorrow.

I shuddered in the Santiago cinderblock basement of *Investigaciones* where, with my late ex-husband, John Clements, I heard the shrieks of someone being prodded with electricity. We were detained as suspected subversives, then forced to flee. A friend, Frank Teruggi, was not so lucky.

I honor the tireless work of Amnesty International, the Institute for Policy Studies, North American Congress on Latin America, the many regional grassroots organizations and labor unions that fought for a full accounting of the human rights violations and to reveal the fates of *los Desaparecidos* (the Disappeared). And the gutsy individuals who smuggled handicrafts such as *arpilleras* (pictorial tapestries depicting life under dictatorship) out of Chile by diplomatic pouch.

I remember the late Father Cuchulian Moriarty, priest of the Sacred Heart Church in San Jose, California, who transformed his parish into a reception center for Chilean refugees and gave them a decent start in a foreign land. I remember the women I came to know only shyly, who cooked the *empanadas* and with their men, played the music and danced the *cueca* at fiestas.

Paradoxically, as the *exiliados* swelled to nearly a tenth of Chile's population, their musicians spread *La Nueva Canción Chilena* as a genre of defiance worldwide. Isabel and Ángel Parra, Patricio Manns, Inti-Illimani, Quilapayún gained international fame and kept alive the music of martyred Victor Jara and of their godmother, Violeta Parra, in concerts such as those held in *La Peña* and Mission Cultural Center, in Berkeley and San Francisco, California.

Spurred by the music, I probed further. Violeta Parra's own *Décimas*, I discovered, chronicled rustic life in the early to mid-twentieth century, from strategies for survival to prayerful decisions that shaped her life. Her quest to revive age-old customs had me appreciate the intelligent roots of modernity, whether in Chile or in the American Southwest. And when I realized how under-appreciated she was as a visual artist, poet, and serious musician, I undertook to write her story.

Many people helped me. Linda Vaughn, a reference librarian at the Sunnyvale, California public library, retrieved obscure texts from university libraries nationwide. The research staff of the Louvre archives sent me material on file about Violeta's one-woman show at the *Musée des Arts Decoratifs*, in Paris.

I am grateful to Patricio Manns, Isabel Parra, Carmen Oveido, Raymonde Gampert and Marie Magdeleine Brumagne for sharing their biographical insights. I integrated the recollections compiled in Bernardo Subercaseaux's valuable *Gracias a la Vida* to characterize further this complex, brilliant woman.

I owe an enormous debt of gratitude to the late Gilbert Favre, who answered my author's query published in a Swiss magazine. Thanks to his American wife, Barbara Erskine, I had the privilege of interviewing him. He shared glimpses of life with his fabled companion, always with respect and admiration for her and her family.

I remember fondly the late Fernando Alegría, of Stanford University, who as a young poet was an ardent admirer of Violeta and who regaled me with recollections.

I thank Sergio Maraboli, who let me taste the tiny berry of a *calafate* shrub, which some say ensured my return to Chile. On that trip in 1995, I met many people who drew forth their memories to bring Violeta Parra to life. None were surprised by a foreigner asking about one of their own.

In Concepción, a university town like Berkeley, I met librarian Mireya Mora Muñoz, who had attended Violeta's *cueca* workshops. She recalled her spontaneity, her boundless energy for composing and collecting, her rapport with the timid as well as the poised, her warmth toward her children and Violeta's brutality toward the arrogant. I want to thank Jose Maria Palacios, for insights into Violeta's radio career and on how she drew on her own life for performance art. I applaud the San Carlos community of *Grupo Literario Toquihua*, for having erected their commemorative statue. Violeta would have found them to be "dear as cousins." I thank Dante Montiel Vera, folklorist of Chiloé, and the potters of Quinchamalí, a village where I found figurines of a *guitarrista* named Violeta. I recognize the anonymous artists whose copper pictures, handmade books, broadsheets of her songs demonstrate how she lives on into the present.

I want to thank the Parra family members who helped me, particularly Leonora Parra, daughter of Violeta's brother Roberto, who I was told greeted every day with happiness and accorded dignity to the simplest people; Nano Parra, son of Violeta's sister Hilda; and Eduardo Parra, Violeta's brother. I want to acknowledge the fine work of *La Peña de los Parra, la filharmonia de los pueblo*, the People's Philharmonic.

To bring the ideas to the printed page, I owe debts of gratitude to many more. I had two brilliant teachers, the late book designer George Salter and physicist Richard M. White, to whom I'm grateful. I wish to acknowledge psychotherapists Irene Lazarus, the late Marianne Pomeroy, and Devi Dyal Khalsa for helping me understand the emotional aspects of this project. I thank visionary Daniel del Solar, who touched me with the emotions captured in Violeta's poetry, particularly in *La Jardinera*.

Articulate prose demands strenuous rewriting. I appreciate deeply the time and effort expended by Meredith Angwin, Lisa Asato, Helen Park Bigelow, Kathy Clay, Annie Cooperman, Patrick Daly, Naomi LaBouff, Dickie Magidoff, Karen McChrystal, Jane Staw, Sarah Stromeyer, Nani Venegas, Roxanne Wales, Juanita Wolff, Margaret

Zuanich, and others in suffering through rough drafts, reading, reviewing and commenting on my efforts.

I was blessed with the mentoring of Marjorie Agosín, of Wellesley College, who encouraged me in my project, who saw the breadth of my work when I was still focusing on detail, and who published some of my translations. Thank you too, to Wayne Crawford, publisher of *Sin Fronteras: Writers without Borders.*

Thank you to Harlen Campbell for computer advice and to Amanda Marie Campbell for her collaboration and artistic wizardry in bringing my cover ideas to fruition.

This book culminated in publication thanks to the grace, patience and understanding of Judith Van Gieson, whose editorial acuity sharpened my prose and kept me out of trouble.

To my cousin, Phyllis Trager Hyman, I offer infinite thanks for her lifelong artistry, intellect, empathy and support.

I dedicate this book to Sandy d. Sommers, my tender soulmate, who helps me accept myself as I am, delights me with his imaginative wit, and sparkles my day with his smile. His many kindnesses enabled me to bring this project to fruition.

Gracias a la vida contigo, mi amor.

Karen Kerschen
Ojo Caliente, New Mexico
January, 2010

Index

CPSIA information can be obtained
at www.ICGtesting.com
Printed in the USA
FFOW02n1249060417
34310FF

9 780984 302413